The Police Identity Crisis

This book provides a comprehensive examination of the police role from within a broader philosophical context. Contending that the police are in the midst of an identity crisis that exacerbates unjustified law enforcement tactics, Luke William Hunt examines various major conceptions of the police—those seeing them as heroes, warriors, and guardians. The book looks at the police role considering the overarching societal goal of justice and seeks to present a synthetic theory that draws upon history, law, society, psychology, and philosophy.

Each major conception of the police role is examined in light of how it affects the pursuit of justice, and how it may be contrary to seeking justice holistically and collectively. The book sets forth a conception of the police role that is consistent with the basic values of a constitutional democracy in the liberal tradition. Hunt's intent is that clarifying the police role will likewise elucidate any constraints upon policing strategies, including algorithmic strategies such as predictive policing.

This book is essential reading for thoughtful policing and legal scholars as well as those interested in political philosophy, political theory, psychology, and related areas. Now more than ever, the nature of the police role is a philosophical topic that is relevant not just to police officials and social scientists, but to everyone.

Luke William Hunt is a member of the faculty at the University of Alabama, where his work lies at the intersection of philosophy of law, political philosophy, and criminal justice. He is the author of *The Retrieval of Liberalism in Policing* (Oxford, 2019). Prior to entering academia, he worked as an FBI Special Agent.

Innovations in Policing

This series explores innovations in the field of policing and offers the latest insight into the field through research, theoretical applications, case studies, and evaluations. Famous innovations developed over the course of the late twentieth century and into the turn of the twenty-first include approaches such as community policing, "broken windows" policing, problem-oriented policing, "pulling levers" policing, third-party policing, hot spots policing, CompStat, and evidence-based policing. Some of these approaches have been successful, and some have not, while new innovations continue to arise. Improving police performance through innovation is often not straightforward. Police departments are highly resistant to change, but through such research we expect to find further refinement of our knowledge of "what works" in policing, under what circumstances particular strategies may work, and why these strategies are effective in improving police performance.

United Nations International Police Officers in Peacekeeping Missions
A Phenomenological Exploration of Complex Acculturation
Michael R. Sanchez

Ends and Means in Policing
John Kleinig

Stress Inside Police Departments
How the Organization Creates Stress and Performance Problems in Police Officers
Jon M. Shane

Organizational Change in an Urban Police Department
Innovating to Reform
Brenda J. Bond-Fortier

The Case for Youth Police Initiative
Interdependent Fates & the Power of Peace
Nina Rose Fischer

The Police Identity Crisis
Hero, Warrior, Guardian, Algorithm
Luke William Hunt

The Police Identity Crisis

Hero, Warrior, Guardian, Algorithm

Luke William Hunt

NEW YORK AND LONDON

First published 2021
by Routledge
52 Vanderbilt Avenue, New York, NY 10017

and by Routledge
2 Park Square, Milton Park, Abingdon, Oxon OX14 4RN

Routledge is an imprint of the Taylor & Francis Group, an informa business

© 2021 Luke William Hunt

The right of Luke William Hunt to be identified as author of this work has been asserted by him in accordance with sections 77 and 78 of the Copyright, Designs and Patents Act 1988.

All rights reserved. No part of this book may be reprinted or reproduced or utilised in any form or by any electronic, mechanical, or other means, now known or hereafter invented, including photocopying and recording, or in any information storage or retrieval system, without permission in writing from the publishers.

Trademark notice: Product or corporate names may be trademarks or registered trademarks, and are used only for identification and explanation without intent to infringe.

Library of Congress Cataloging-in-Publication Data
Names: Hunt, Luke William, author.
Title: The police identity crisis : hero, warrior, guardian, algorithm / Luke William Hunt.
Description: 1 Edition. | New York : Routledge, 2021. | Series: Innovations in policing | Includes bibliographical references and index.
Identifiers: LCCN 2020053782 (print) | LCCN 2020053783 (ebook) | ISBN 9780367700249 (hardback) | ISBN 9781003145455 (ebook)
Subjects: LCSH: Police. | Criminal justice, Administration of. | Political science–Philosophy.
Classification: LCC HV7921 .H86 2021 (print) | LCC HV7921 (ebook) | DDC 353.3/6–dc23
LC record available at https://lccn.loc.gov/2020053782
LC ebook record available at https://lccn.loc.gov/2020053783

ISBN: 978-0-367-70024-9 (hbk)
ISBN: 978-0-367-70282-3 (pbk)
ISBN: 978-1-003-14545-5 (ebk)

Typeset in Bembo
by Taylor & Francis Books

For Henry and Oliver

Contents

Preface ix

Introduction: A Multifaceted Theory of the Police 1

1 Heroes 16

    Death and Duty 16
    A Police Case Study 19
    A Brief History of Philosophy and Psychology 25
    Old and New Heroism 32
    Conclusion: Epistemic Entitlement 39

2 Warriors 47

    War and Police 47
    Consequential Policing 50
    Police Militarization 54
    The Warrior Ideal 57
    Objections and Positional Requirements 65
    Conclusion: Fear and Force 70

3 Guardians 78

    Whom and What to Guard? 78
    Plato's Guardians 82
    The Guardian Category Mistake 89
    Police Archetypes and Individuation 94
    Conclusion: Democratic Policing and its Limits 97

4   Algorithms and Justice   107
    The Conflation of Fact and Value 107
    Policing by Prediction 110
    Prediction Problems 117
    Justice through Human Rights 121
    Legitimacy and Security of Person through Public Reason 126
    *Conclusion: Public Reason through (Procedurally Just)
    Community Policing 132*

Epilogue: Reorienting the Police Identity   149
    *Defunding the Police, Abolishing the Police, and Other Political
    Reforms 150*
    Recruitment, Training, and Values 154
    Seeking Justice Collectively 158

    Index   168

Preface

This is not the book I set out to write. I had planned to begin a new project on a broader topic after my first book, *The Retrieval of Liberalism in Policing*, was published in late 2018. But the different threads I had in mind somehow converged into the present book. My return to the topic of policing was in part because policing continued to be such a pressing issue in public life. I also returned to the topic because—having spent several years of my life as an FBI Special Agent—I felt obligated to write something else about law enforcement. This was not because I believed I had some sort of privileged perspective. It is rather my belief that the voices of others are more important than the voices of law enforcement at this moment in history. Nor did I write about policing because I believed it would affect the social ethos (few, if any, academic books do that). I returned to the topic simply because I hoped to make a modest contribution to an ongoing conversation.

I began writing the first lines of what would become chapter 4 in January 2019, continuing to work on the manuscript through the end of 2020 with a publication date in 2021. The writing was done in both Blacksburg, Virginia and—after accepting a faculty position at the University of Alabama—in Tuscaloosa, Alabama. A fair amount of the work occurred during a pandemic (as well as a surreal presidential campaign and election in which policing was a significant issue). As someone who enjoys trail running, the pandemic provided even more reasons to spend time outdoors. Accordingly, this book benefited from many hours exploring the natural areas near my new home—especially the isolated forest service roads in the Oakmulgee District of the Talladega National Forest. The day I began sketching this preface—August 29, 2020—I saw a wild hog for the first time (along with a hawk and three turkeys) while running in Oakmulgee.

An early draft of chapter 4 was presented at a criminal law and legal theory workshop at the University of Toronto Faculty of Law in June 2019. I appreciate Vincent Chaio's invitation to participate, as well as his thoughtful comments on my work. An early draft of chapter 4 was also presented at the annual meeting of the Southern Criminal Justice

Association in Nashville, Tennessee, in September 2019, and at the University of Alabama Department of Philosophy in January 2020. I especially appreciate the comments and kindness from my new colleagues in Tuscaloosa. I am of course indebted to the many editors, anonymous reviewers, and other scholars with whom I engaged during this book's formation—including Ellen Boyne, Jack Call, Brian Clack, Raff Donelson, Barry Lam, Jake Monaghan, Stephen Owen, Daniel Quinlan, and Kate Taylor, among others. They have—each in different ways—improved the book tremendously.

This book is about identities, and it thus seems fitting to give special thanks to my parents, brother, and grandparents for the role they played in shaping my own identity. I do not mean simply instilling a particular set of ideas and values—we all go our own way eventually—but rather instilling a sense of unconditional love and support. If anything I do shapes my own children—Henry and Oliver, to whom this book is dedicated—I hope it is likewise giving them the knowledge that they are loved unconditionally. To my wife, Melissa, I owe more than I could possibly put into words. I am so very fortunate that we were assigned to share a mailbox at Governor's School on the Hendrix College campus in the summer of 1996.

L.W.H. Tuscaloosa, Alabama, November 2020

Author photograph

Introduction
A Multifaceted Theory of the Police

Looking back now—as an academic philosopher—it is strange to think of myself sitting in a shooting range classroom at the FBI Academy on Marine Corp Base (MCB), Quantico. It was my first week of New Agent Training, and I was sitting with my fellow New Agent Trainees in an early firearms session. Situated within thousands of mostly wooded acres—which are punctuated by random explosions and marine fire—MCB Quantico is both serene and eerie. The walls of the FBI Academy itself feel deeply oppressive. A relic of 1970s brutalist architecture, the stark academy buildings are linked together by a series of enclosed passageways that do not require one to set foot outdoors. This gives the distinct impression of scuttling back-and-forth in a hamster cage, waiting to escape to a wooded trail at the end of the day—or perhaps off base to a chain restaurant on the weekend. The point is that my four months of training at the FBI Academy was a thoroughly insular experience. At the same time, this insularity created a rich and rewarding experience, strengthening bonds between trainees who were pursuing a decidedly exclusive career path together. One of my fondest memories was spending my evenings with my suite-mates watching *Band of Brothers*, the miniseries produced by Steven Spielberg and Tom Hanks, based on Stephen Ambrose's World War II book. Similar sentiments of exclusivity and bonding could be expressed about the other law enforcement academies—local, state, and federal—around the world.

In a sense, the juxtaposition between philosophy and firearms—between Quantico classroom and college classroom—is not so stark. We were discussing life and death in that first firearms session—a topic that is central to many areas of philosophy. The primary difference is that there are few actual discussions at a law enforcement academy. Police culture is quasi-military in nature and police training is typically a one-way affair: Trainees are told what to do and think, and, importantly, *who they are*. Their self-concept is nudged toward the mythic idea (a story we tell ourselves about how the world works) of a hero on a warrior's path—sheepdogs guarding sheep in an eternal battle against wolves lurking within society. It is admittedly difficult to pin down the various facets of such a nebulous account of the police role. And it is even more difficult—given the complexity of policing—to assess whether there is anything justified about the police mythos. That is the task of this book.

The thesis of the book: The many competing conceptions of the police role—heroes, warriors, guardians, and beyond—have given rise to a police identity crisis. The metaphor is remarkably apt with respect to contemporary police culture. "Identity crisis" is a term from within the history of psychology referring to a theory of psychosocial development: the progression of life stages, relationships, and crises. Roughly, an identity crisis is a life stage in which a person seeks to discover who they are and their role in society; it is thus a time of potential role confusion in which the person is unsure of their self-concept. The idea is that if one can resolve adolescent identity crises positively, then one may have a successful adulthood and later life.[1] This book argues that the police are struggling with an analogous form of role confusion. There is a debate within society and police culture about the very nature of the police role and how police should conceive of themselves.

The traditional method—within academia, at least—for analyzing problems is to take a narrow approach from within a single discipline. We are thus fortunate to have many insightful books and articles on policing from within philosophy, law, criminology, history, psychology, and other disciplines. These sorts of narrow, fine-grained analyses are vital for understanding the details of a problem. Accordingly, I employ a similar attention to detail where appropriate. However, this book will often take a novel departure from the traditional method. I suggest that a wide-ranging analysis encourages a more complete understanding of the problem of policing. By drawing upon a variety of disciplines—including those noted above—this book seeks to illuminate the police identity crisis by identifying larger patterns that become manifest within the human sciences. The book's methodology thus gives rise to a *synthetic* theory about the police identity crisis: a synthesis drawing upon patterns observed from a broad array of disciplines. As the book moves towards its conclusion, this synthetic approach is complemented by an *analytic* inquiry into the various conceptions of the police role. In other words, given assumptions about the meanings of the basic legal, political, and philosophical tenets of liberal societies, the book examines the extent to which various conceptions of the police role are and are not justified.

The role of the police has become one of the most hotly debated, contentious issues facing society, and many of the contemporary conversations have implicit underpinnings from a variety of disciplines. The idea here is to make these underpinnings explicit, drawing out the different lenses through which law enforcement may be understood—each with its own implications. Although this approach will inevitably fail to please everyone, it is a genuine (and modest) effort to join a conversation with multiple scholarly and lay audiences. And while conceiving of the police as heroes, warriors, and guardians is not a new phenomenon, the book's multifaceted explanation—combining several ideas and relating them to the problems western societies now face—is new. It is plausible to think this approach is justified given policing's inherently complex and multifaceted nature—a nature that I hope will benefit from having many "views of the cathedral," so to speak.

The scope of the book: Despite the book's wide-ranging approach, it is of course impossible to do everything. There are deeply important accounts of the police role from within a variety of disciplines. Within philosophy, some have written insightfully about a peacekeeping model of the police, while others have offered normative teleological theories evaluating the police based upon the extent to which they realize collective ends and produce collective goods given collective moral responsibility.[2] I myself wrote a book examining the extent to which contemporary law enforcement practices are consistent with the basic tenets of liberalism—a book steeped in social contract theory, reciprocal rights and duties, and the entrustment of police to provide security.[3] From within the field of law, there is a rather extensive legal literature about various dimensions of police legitimacy and what constitutional democracy requires of the police.[4] The field of psychology has produced illuminating work on procedural justice and other areas vitally important to policing,[5] while sociological work such as Sarah Brayne's *Predict and Surveil* provides detailed, on-the-ground descriptions of the police's use of big data.[6]

There are many who have made tremendous contributions to the scholarly conversation about the role of the police in a constitutional democracy, but it is beyond the scope of this book to give everyone the time and attention they deserve. I hope readers will further explore the growing literature on policing, a portion of which I have tried to acknowledge in both the text and the notes. This book reaches farther afield given the contention that the problems of policing are not limited to the administration of justice and given that the questions philosophers ask are not limited to academic theorizing. Regarding this last point, I will occasionally make general observations regarding the work of an FBI Special Agent (which includes working with local, state, and other federal law enforcement officers) to make points about the police. It should of course be noted that there are many differences between, say, an FBI agent working a white-collar crime investigation and a sheriff's deputy making a roadside stop. To be sure, the functions of federal agents are not exactly replicated by those of street-level bureaucrats such as police officers. In the coming pages, I suggest that the police are not typically known for deliberation, but rather looked upon as heroes who make decisive, split-second decisions under fire. Accordingly, one might contrast this with an FBI agent who spends large amounts of time behind a desk, connecting the dots in a complex white-collar crime or national security investigation. Although an FBI agent's job is undoubtedly different from the job of a uniformed officer, there are fundamental, overlapping features of both jobs. This book focuses upon the concrete commonalities among all law enforcement officers.

A related point is that the book focuses upon policing in the United States. This is in part due to the proliferation of cases in the United States that have received international attention. That said, there are moral, political, and jurisprudential resonances among different states and cultures (such as human dignity, human rights, and the rule of law) that connect different manifestations of policing in a variety of ways. So while much of the context is American, the concept of policing and what the police should do are questions that virtually all societies must ask. The hope is that these connections make the book's framework applicable across the varieties of policing that are found around the globe. Consider, for instance, the cooperation and joint training between American law enforcement agencies and foreign military partners such as the Israel Defense Forces (IDF), leading Angela Davis to connect issues in American policing with ongoing political and human rights issues in Israel.[7] Her work highlight directs connections between U.S. law enforcement officers—from sheriffs to FBI agents—and tactics employed by foreign defense forces. In other cases, the connections to the U.S. may be even more surprising, as William Finnegan's reporting in *The New Yorker* notes:

> According to Paul Hirschfield, a Rutgers sociologist who has written about international law-enforcement practice, the difference [between the U.S. and other developed nations] is partly in the basic work environment. "American police encounter conditions that are more like Latin America than northern Europe.... These vast inequalities, the history of enslavement and conquest, a weak social safety net. The decentralization. Police are more likely to encounter civilians with firearms here. We don't have the levels of police corruption they do in Mexico, but we are not like other developed countries. The legal threshold for the use of force is lower." Another difference is training. In some Western European countries, police academies are as selective as a good American college.[8]

To be sure, international connections (and disconnections) abound. To take just one more international example, the "Toronto Police Force" replaced the word "Force" with the word "Service" to better reflect its approach to policing.[9] That may sound trivial, but it helps illuminate how the themes in this book resonate broadly in the world of policing.

The use of terminology in the book: This book draws upon a variety of academic disciplines, and I have thus tried to make it accessible to a variety of audiences by avoiding unnecessary jargon. Still, it is sometimes necessary to use disciplinary terms given the book's multidisciplinary approach. For example, the terms "individuation" and "archetype" are terms from within the field of psychology.[10] In the context of this book, by individuation I mean the way the police are identified through a persona and archetype, distinguished from the rest of the community. One might characterize individuation as the course by which the police archetype develops in society. From a more traditional psychological perspective, this process is said to include both conscious experience and unconscious processes relating to life and death—issues that are uniquely relevant to a profession such as policing. As we will see, the police "warrior" concept creates a sort of archetype that lends itself to an exclusive brotherhood: a band of brothers tied together by the momentous responsibility and heroism that is inherent in their role. This emphasis upon one's exclusive membership—one's sharing in the archetype's mythos and ethos—contributes to unique moral codes such as protecting members of the brotherhood at all costs. On this latter point, we will consider the so-called "blue wall of silence," which encourages police not to report on (or not to tell the truth about) a colleague's misconduct.

The broader idea is the way that police culture has channeled fear and existential angst, implying that eternal heroism (often manifested through warrior and guardian personas) can account for fear and serve as a central basis for the conception of the police role. In short, here is the analogy that is in play: In the same way a teenager may have an identity crisis in high school—jock, nerd, prep, and so on, the police are in the midst of their own identity crisis—hero, warrior, guardian, and so on. But given the police role and responsibility in society, it is a crisis with much higher stakes.

I want to be clear at the outset that my references to the psychoanalytical tradition are informal and intended to be illustrative through analogy. I will not suggest that police reform should include officers exploring their unconscious feelings toward their parents. Nevertheless, the psychoanalytic tradition can help illuminate the current state of policing, even if by analogy. As we will see, warrior and guardian policing promotes a sort of artificial archetype and individuation, drawing upon the human experience of life and death viewed through the lens of cultural heroism. The problem is that this sort of idealization is not an appropriate conception of the police role inasmuch as our idealizations in political philosophy, policy, and police culture should emphasize the ideal of justice (and ways to pursue that ideal) rather than the ideally virtuous police persona. If this is the case, then we need to shift to a different model for conceiving of the police—one steeped in collectivity. By *collectivity* I am thinking generally of the tension between individuality and the collective arrangements of society and how there might be an analogous individual-collective tension in the context of policing.[11] We thus consider the police identity as an individual warrior or guardian on the hero's path, versus the police identity as a component of a collective pursuit of justice.

The book certainly will not try to reframe (old) strategies—such as community policing—as new solutions, but rather show how individual-collective tension has sabotaged these strategies from the outset. With this in mind, the book makes the novel claim that *public reason* (the idea that government principles should be justifiable to all those to whom the principles are meant to apply) can serve as a unifying rationale and moral foundation for a justified police role that includes established strategies such as community and procedural justice policing.

The assumptions in the book: Here are two assumptions about the police role that seem reasonable: (1) Given public entrustment, the police have a duty to seek justice by promoting security within society; and (2) given other principles and values in society, promoting security is but one facet of justice that the police have a duty to seek. One of the goals of this book is to describe how the police's identity crisis has contributed to the police running afoul of the second point. In other words, in the struggle to embrace various identities and roles, the police have moved away from more holistic conceptions of justice—conceptions that focus upon legitimacy, the rule of law, human dignity, and other legal and human rights. I assume that these values are central to any conception of justice in liberal societies: societies that stipulate one's inherent, equal status and moral worth given one's personhood, which is prioritized in collective arrangements that are based upon reciprocity. Accordingly, the book's methodology for sketching a more just conception of the police role is constrained by four related guidelines. Although these guidelines draw upon John Rawls's *transitional nonideal theory* (in other words, constraints requiring us to address actual injustices in the world by pursuing policies that seek transition to an ideal of justice), they are methodological only. We need not dwell upon the voluminous literature regarding Rawls's substantive commitments of justice.[12] For purposes of this book, my assumptions regarding any substantive commitments of justice—such as a commitment to legitimacy, the rule of law, and human dignity—are sufficiently general and (relatively) uncontroversial. I invoke transitional nonideal theory simply as a background assumption regarding a set of rough guidelines for any pursuit of a more holistic ideal of justice.

For example, in seeking to address any injustice in policing, our policies should, first, simply be *politically possible* given a commitment to reasonable pluralism that allows for an overlapping consensus of views within a diverse society.[13] Consider the diversity within most any city—from ethnicity, religion, and politics, to mental health, gender, and sexual orientation. Given this vast diversity, how do community members and government agents maintain an appropriate and justified communal relationship with each other? One guiding light will be the idea that communities should be regulated by laws, policies, and regulations that can be justified to each member—despite the diversity of perspectives. Second, our policies must be *effective*: they must actually help resolve our problems.[14] For instance, what tactics and rules should the police follow regarding reducing crime and promoting utility in society? Well, it seems obvious that we should promote rules and tactics that are effective at reducing crime. Accordingly, these first two guidelines regarding police reform—political possibility and efficacy—tend to involve social and historical examinations of actual doctrine and practice. This is an area in which evidence-based research in criminology and other social sciences (such as that described in chapter 4) is especially helpful. On the other hand, if effectively increasing security involves, say, pursuing tactics that denigrate police legitimacy, we must consider difficult moral questions regarding the extent to which security and legitimacy should be balanced in society.

This leads to the next two guidelines in the book's methodology, namely: Our policing policies must, third, be *morally permissible* and, fourth, *prioritize grievances based upon severity*.[15] To be sure, there will be disagreement around the edges regarding policing tactics that are and are not morally permissible in liberal societies. Common ground might be reached by beginning with the assumption that the aim of liberal societies is not typically to make people more virtuous or good. Rather, critical standards on which liberal laws and policies are based seek just institutions prohibiting conduct that would harm others. However, one commonality among contemporary conceptions of the police role is that they emphasize idealized personas through individuated heroes, warriors, and guardians. Rather than focusing upon this sort of individualized archetype, the approach herein reorients the police role to collective political values. This means that the target is the ideal of justice—manifested in laws, regulations, and policies—not idealizations of persons and police. The core legal and philosophical tenets of liberal societies and institutions are not based upon the pursuit of an ideally virtuous persona.

But if questions of moral permissibility are based upon political principles, how do we prioritize competing moral claims—say, competing claims between security and equality? This book takes the approach that priority is to be given to grievous (over less grievous) injustices in terms of a lexical ordering (to put it in Rawlsian terms) of political principles. Given that the foundation of liberal societies is based upon one's equal status, moral worth, and dignity, the priority rule is personhood.[16] To take a simple example, suppose the police are pursuing the (morally permissible) value of security by trying to stop property crime in a community. Although a justified value, their strategies for preventing property crime would preclude any tactics that are an affront to one's personhood—given that one's equal status, moral worth, and dignity are prioritized over reducing automobile theft. This is a simplistic point to be sure, but the hope is that it will be filled in over the course of the book.

The account of racism in the book: It should go without saying that any liberal ideal of justice is aspirational—a target for which to aim. I certainly do not mean to suggest that there was some (actual) golden age of policing when the police pursued justice holistically. Consider, say, the police's roots in such things as slave patrols and strikebreaking.[17] But the horrific history of policing does not mean that we should not seek to retrieve the aspirational ideals of liberalism.[18] My approach is thus an appeal to the balance between nonideal and ideal theory in political philosophy. Until we identify and clarify an ideal of just policing (how things should be), we lack an objective, or aim, by reference to which our practical debates about the world (how things are) can be answered. Admittedly, the situation can seem hopeless. Oppressed people have struggled to accomplish collective security for generations, and we need only consider the contemporary state of affairs to see how far we are from justice.

Louisville police officers used a battering ram to enter and execute a search warrant in Breonna Taylor's—a 26-year-old emergency room technician—apartment on March 13, 2020. The police were seeking evidence in a drug investigation and believed that Jamarcus Glover (Taylor's ex-boyfriend) used Taylor's apartment to receive packages. Taylor's boyfriend, Kenneth Walker, was with Taylor when the two heard loud banging at the apartment's front door. The police claimed that they announced themselves, but Walker indicated that he did not hear any such announcement. Fearing that someone was breaking into the apartment, Walker fired his gun and struck one of the police officers in the leg. The police responded by blindly firing several shots into the apartment, shooting Taylor five times and killing her. The police called an ambulance to help the injured officer, though Taylor initially received no medical attention. Glover was subsequently arrested for possession of drugs and stated that Taylor was not involved in drug distribution. Taylor's family said Taylor "had big dreams and planned a lifelong career in health care after serving as an E.M.T."[19]

George Floyd was killed by a police officer in Minneapolis, Minnesota, two months later, on May 25, 2020. The officer knelt on Floyd's neck for eight minutes and forty-five seconds while Floyd—who was handcuffed—exclaimed that he could not breathe. When Floyd became unresponsive, the officer continued to use his knee to pin Floyd's neck to the asphalt street. Protests were held across the U.S.—and around the globe—against police brutality of Black suspects following Floyd's death. These protests coincided with increased calls to "defund" or "abolish" the police, topics to which I turn in the book's epilogue. On August 23, 2020—three months after Floyd's death—the police responded to a woman's call regarding a domestic dispute Kenosha, Wisconsin. When they arrived at the woman's home, the police attempted to subdue and arrest Jacob Blake with a Taser stun gun. Video shows Blake walking around to the driver's side of his vehicle, opening the door, and leaning forward. An officer grabs Blakes's shirt from behind and shoots Blake seven times in the back. Three of Blake's children —aged 3, 5, and 8—were in the vehicle and witnessed their father being shot, which resulted in Blake being paralyzed from the waist down. Blake does not appear to have a weapon in the video, but a knife was found on the floorboard of the car into which he was leaning.[20]

By any measure, these horrific incidents should be remarkable in a liberal society such as the United States. But even at this late stage, in the twenty-first century, police brutality continues with alarming frequency. Indeed, the officer who killed Floyd acted with calm resolve in broad daylight, seemingly unconcerned that his actions were being filmed by citizens who pleaded for him to let Floyd breathe. The incidents are not remarkable because the police sought to make arrests, or even that they used force. For instance, in Blake's case, police were called to the scene and Blake resisted; it was also reported that Blake had an outstanding arrest warrant for domestic abuse-related charges.[21] What makes these incidents remarkable is that they are part of a long series of encounters in which police use what seems to be indiscriminate force against African Americans. Consider, on the other hand, the white gunman (Kyle Rittenhouse) who carried an "assault-style" rifle down the street—past police, who did not even stop him—during the protests following Blake's shooting. Rittenhouse walked past the police unabated, leaving a scene at which he killed two people and injured another.[22] How do we make sense of this when, say, Philando Castile (a Black man) was shot and killed by a police officer in his car (with his girlfriend and girlfriend's 4-year-old daughter looking on) after voluntarily informing the officer that he was (lawfully) in possession of a firearm?

Although these cases seem to suggest that the police exceeded their legal authority, constitutional doctrine is quite permissive when it comes to the police's discretion to use force. Alice Ristroph's legal scholarship makes the important point that—beyond an officer's suspicion—the extent to which people comply with or resist the police plays a significant role in the police's authority to use violence.[23] While that may seem unsurprising and (ostensibly) race-neutral, Ristroph shows how a "duty of compliance" and a "privilege of resistance" are distributed along racial lines.[24] This is especially tragic because the privilege of resistance (for example, declining police encounters, police requests to search, and police demands to answer questions) is a right that the Constitution requires *all* people to assert (by refusing to comply, walking away, remaining silent, and so on).[25] As legal scholar Eric Miller puts it, "Democracy…is a reciprocal process of public participation in government decision-making, rather than a unilateral imposition of the governor's determinations upon the governed."[26] These fundamental concerns have led philosophically-minded scholars such as Ekow Yankah to call for a "philosophical reimaging of the Fourth Amendment" as a way to address "the tense relationship between police and communities of color."[27] With this backdrop in mind, then, I will examine the conception of the police role itself and how it encourages the pursuit of (unjustified) violence in the first place (parallel to broader, societal problems of distributing rights and duties along racial lines).

The more fundamental point is that—in no uncertain terms—racism is a pressing moral, political, and legal problem in policing. Work by Christopher Lebron, Tommie Shelby, and others have provided deep philosophical insight into the backdrop of systemic racism in society. This includes the fundamental clash between democratic principles on the one hand and unwarranted beliefs and attitudes that demean African Americans and their social value on the other hand, as well as broader accounts of the effects that an unjust economic and political system has on the lives of the Black urban poor.[28] I am heartened that there is much good work being conducted on the entrenched, systemic problems of racism in society. But with respect to policing specifically, it should come as no surprise that racism is not the only problem—nor is it obviously the central problem. The law enforcement officers (federal, state, and local) with whom I worked were complex people navigating a difficult job. There are of course many ways racism may become manifest, but the officers I encountered would disavow any hint of explicit prejudice. Of course, some officers are explicitly racist, and, in any event, one may display racism in subtle ways such as relating to some groups with greater fear, hostility, and so on. On the other hand, I *did* work with many law enforcement officers who clearly identified as some sort of Rambo-esque, macho warrior. Indeed, this concept is expressly embraced as part of the police identity by many police trainers inside and outside police academies. Why?

Unlike the secure bubble of academia in which I now find myself, policing can be a dangerous profession in which one is faced with (in the United States, at least) enforcing the law against a public armed to the teeth. That is an external gun policy and gun culture problem, not an internal police culture problem. Moreover, in wealthy, stratified states such as the U.S., the police are asked to focus their law enforcement role on impoverished communities—communities in which we see high levels of violent and property crimes fueled by generations of systematic oppression. The police are mostly powerless to affect the deep, structural policies (economic and political) that create and sustain this stratification, including high-level white-collar crime and government fraud and corruption. Even the FBI—which dedicates many agents to white-collar and government crime—is largely focused upon other "national security" matters. I was an FBI Agent in 2008—during one of the biggest economic scandals in history—and do you know how many top bankers went to jail after the credit crisis that year? One.[29] So we might say that the police's central problem is political given that the focus is typically on one set of social harms and not others. To put it differently, perhaps we have less of a policing problem and more of a class, poverty, and political problem.[30]

I am sympathetic to the idea that focusing upon problems within policing—racism or otherwise—is a distraction from the deeper problems underlying society. However, that idea is not the whole story. While it may be unhelpful to simply exclaim that "all police are racists," it is also unhelpful to simply place all the blame upon capitalist hegemony. True: economic, political, and criminal inequalities are deeply rooted in capitalist relations of production, but that fact does not absolve police culture.[31] In this book I propose a third way to examine problems within policing: An examination of the deeply entrenched conceptions of the police role—police as individual heroes, warriors, and guardians—and the extent to which those conceptions are (in)consistent with the basic legal, political, and philosophical tenets of liberal societies. Given these competing conceptions of the police role, I frame my examination in terms of an identity crisis. The hope is that this approach helps provide a more complete account of what we should talk about when we talk about problems in policing.

The plan for the book: Each of the following four chapters considers a conception of the police and how that conception affects the pursuit of justice. These examinations will be considered from a variety of perspectives: historical, psychological, logical, ethical, and beyond. Chapter 1 examines the history of the police's pursuit of a heroic identity and the extent to which that identity is problematic. One of the central problems is that a heroic ethos obscures the value of pursuing justice holistically and collectively. The chapter begins by describing what might be called the police's existential identity crisis. It is in part the trend toward heroic individuation—and away from collective justice—that lays the groundwork for an unjustified police warrior role. The chapter examines how ideas about manliness (both historically and through a post 9/11 heroic ethos) have something to teach us about policing and governance, particularly with respect to the construction of different mythologies of policing at different times.

Chapter 2 examines the extent to which police responses to societal and crime problems are framed by two related approaches: (1) Utilitarian tactics of crime control and reduction in which the end justifies the (warrior's) means; and (2) officer individuation through a warrior mythos, rather than an emphasis on collectivity. Building upon chapter 1's discussion of policing's focus on heroic battle over evil, chapter 2 introduces the warrior identity. The chapter considers how the warrior ethos embraces the position that enforcing the law and stopping crime is a result that justifies an illiberal and undemocratic means by which the result may be achieved. The upshot of this approach is that warring with a community is justified if it stifles crime and criminals. Police militarization is not a new phenomenon, but the combination of militarization and warriorization has raised new practical and philosophical problems within policing with which the chapter contends.

Chapter 3 examines how police culture has attempted to address the problem of utilitarian police warriors by shifting to a guardian mythos. One of the chapter's tasks is to detangle and clarify the foundational characteristics of the Platonic guardian. Accomplishing this task helps answer questions regarding the extent to which the guardian mythos is in fact a solid foundation on which to build a more holistic, justified conception of the police role. If we assume that a holistic conception of justice entails protecting the rights of all persons in society—including the impoverished and those who have broken the law or who are suspected of breaking the law—then the shift to a police guardian archetype is philosophically confused and exacerbates the police identity crisis. The chapter argues that the ideas stemming from the police guardian conception are neither consistent with a practical understanding nor a philosophical understanding of the guardian concept. The result is a police identity that is idiosyncratic, inapt, and continues to focus upon individual archetypes in the pursuit of justice. Both the warrior mythos and the guardian mythos, then, breed a culture in which crime reduction is privileged over other fundamental values—such as legitimacy, security of person within the community, and human dignity. The upshot is that Plato's guardians—though not a perfect fit with today's police role—make an important contribution to modern thought regarding policing and justice.

Chapter 4 begins by examining how policing's emphasis on heroic warriors and guardians has converged with technocratic strategies driven by algorithms. Sophisticated tactics—such as predictive policing and other advanced technology—might be justified (and effective) when employed within the constraints of a justified police role. However, such tactics exacerbate the problems within policing given the identity crisis examined in prior chapters. Chapter 4 links the identity crisis to technology, suggesting that the solution to the crisis is not that the police should have *no* identity; a conception of the police centered on the pursuit of justice is a good thing, mindlessness in the face of technology is not. In a way, then, chapter 4 shows how technology can dehumanize the police—not just the community—to the extent that it belittles their skills and strips them of agency in the collective pursuit for justice. It is thus a false dilemma to suggest that policing must *either* be subsumed by technocratic judgments encoded in obscure algorithms *or* be based upon a police ethic steeped in the wise discretion—as it were—of hero, warrior, and guardian policing. Accordingly, the second goal of chapter 4 is to set forth a third option: a conception of the police role that is consistent with the basic values of a constitutional democracy in the liberal tradition. The hope is that clarifying the police role will clarify the constraints upon police tactics—even if there is good evidence that various tactics are effective law enforcement strategies.

The book's epilogue begins by considering the calls to "defund" the police following George Floyd's death, along with other political and legal issues that are external to policing. After a survey of these proposals, the epilogue summarizes practical steps that might help reorient policing away from individual heroes, warriors, and guardians, and toward a collective pursuit of justice. In an ideal world, we might reach a broad consensus that crime and the need for police may be reduced by addressing the deep structural inequalities (social and economic) within society. However, the epilogue concludes that—in the meantime—it is reasonable to take steps toward police reforms that are politically possible, effective, and morally permissible in terms of the broad commitments (such as legitimacy, the rule of law, and human dignity) of liberal societies. The basic tenets of justice in liberal societies are inclusive, egalitarian, and interconnected, meaning that police–community strife will not be resolved by simply focusing upon narrow legal standards and reasonableness inquiries regarding the conduct of individual police officers. The central point of the book is not that policing should be understood as an abstract academic problem, but that street-level law enforcement is deeply connected to the problems about which philosophers, legal theorists, psychologists, historians, and others have long thought.

Notes

1 The term "identity crisis" is said to have been coined by famed psychologist Erik Erikson, who is known for his theory of psychosocial development. See, e.g., ERIK H. ERIKSON, IDENTITY AND THE LIFE CYCLE (1980) (1959), among Erikson's many other volumes and papers.
2 See, e.g., JOHN KLEINIG, THE ETHICS OF POLICING (1996); JOHN KLEINIG, ENDS AND MEANS IN POLICING (2019); and SEUMAS MILLER, THE MORAL FOUNDATIONS OF SOCIAL INSTITUTIONS (2010).
3 LUKE WILLIAM HUNT, THE RETRIEVAL OF LIBERALISM IN POLICING (2019).
4 See, e.g., BARRY FRIEDMAN, UNWARRANTED: POLICING WITHOUT PERMISSION (2017); ANDREW FERGUSON, THE RISE OF BIG DATA POLICING: SURVEILLANCE, RACE, AND THE FUTURE OF LAW (2017); Sandra G. Mayson, Bias In, Bias Out, 128 YALE LAW JOURNAL 2218 (2018); TAMARA RICE LAVE & ERIC J. MILLER (EDS.), THE CAMBRIDGE HANDBOOK OF POLICING IN THE UNITED STATES (2019); Eric Miller, Encountering Resistance: Non-Compliance, Non-Cooperation, and Procedural Justice, UNIVERSITY OF CHICAGO LEGAL FORUM (Article 8, 2016); Eric Miller, Challenging Police Discretion, 58.2 HOWARD L. REV. 521 (2015); Alice Ristroph, The Constitution of Police Violence, 64 UCLA LAW REVIEW 1182 (2017); DAVID SKLANSKY, DEMOCRACY AND THE POLICE (2007); Ekow N. Yankah, Pretext and Justification: Republicanism, Policing, and Race, 40.4 CARDOZO LAW REVIEW 1543 (2019).
5 See, for example, Tom Tyler's work on the way justice (especially regarding procedures that shape legitimacy) shapes people's relationships within societies, including WHY PEOPLE COOPERATE (2011); LEGITIMACY AND CRIMINAL JUSTICE (2007); WHY PEOPLE OBEY THE LAW (2006); TRUST IN THE LAW (2002); and COOPERATION IN GROUPS (2000). See also Bernard Harcourt's work on the way that actuarial methods are used to determine whom law enforcement officials target and punish. BERNARD HARCOURT, AGAINST PREDICTION: PROFILING, POLICING, AND PUNISHING IN AN ACTUARIAL AGE (2006).

6 SARAH BRAYNE, PREDICT AND SURVEIL – DATA, DISCRETION, AND THE FUTURE OF POLICING (2021).
7 See ANGELA DAVIS, FREEDOM IS A CONSTANT STRUGGLE: FERGUSON, PALESTINE, AND THE FOUNDATIONS OF A MOVEMENT (2016). See also Amnesty International, *With Whom are Many U.S. Police Departments Training? Israel* (Aug. 25, 2016).
8 William Finnegan, *How Police Unions Fight Reform*, THE NEW YORKER (July 27, 2020).
9 See Toronto Police Service, http://www.torontopolice.on.ca/careers/history.php#:~:text=The%20word%20%E2%80%9CForce%E2%80%9D%20was%20eventually,City%20of%20Toronto%20in%201998
10 See, e.g., the work of Carl Jung.
11 More specifically, I am thinking of the theme of tension underlying Freud's classic text of Western culture, CIVILIZATION AND ITS DISCONTENTS (1930). That book has many (well-documented) flaws—and it is not necessary to discuss it in detail—but I submit that there is an analogous individual-collective tension in the context of policing.
12 See HUNT, *supra* note 3, at chapter 2, discussing this account of John Rawls's transitional nonideal theory.
13 *See* JOHN RAWLS, THE LAW OF PEOPLES 89 (1999).
14 *Id.*
15 *Id.*; JOHN RAWLS, A THEORY OF JUSTICE 267 (1971) (1999).
16 See HUNT, *supra* note 3, at chapter 3 (defending the priority of liberal personhood).
17 For an essay discussing these two points of history, see Alex Gourevitch, *Why Are the Police Like This?* JACOBIN (June 12, 2020).
18 *See* HUNT, *supra* note 3 (examining the extent to which contemporary law enforcement practices are inconsistent with the basic tenets of the liberal tradition in legal and political philosophy).
19 Richard A. Oppel Jr. & Derrick Bryson Taylor, *Here's What You Need to Know About Breonna Taylor's Death*, N.Y. TIMES (Sept. 1, 2020). A Louisville grand jury failed to indict any of the officers involved in the no-knock search that led to Taylor's death. This may seem surprising, but it is important to note that a judge authorized the execution of the search warrant at the apartment because of Taylor's former boyfriend, a suspected drug dealer. When the police entered the apartment, Taylor's current boyfriend fired on the police (not knowing they were police) and wounding one officer; the police returned fire that resulted in Taylor's death. These facts may not favor legal culpability under existing laws, though Louisville subsequently banned no-knock searches (which clearly played a role in this tragedy). Alisha Haridasani Gupta & Christine Hauser, *New Breonna Taylor Law Will Ban No-Knock Warrants in Louisville, Ky.*, N.Y. TIMES (June 12, 2020).
20 Brendan McDermid & Stephen Maturen, *Wisconsin investigators say knife found at scene of police shooting of Jacob Blake*, REUTERS (Aug. 26, 2020).
21 *Id.*
22 *Id.* Although Rittenhouse put himself in the fraught situation—risking escalation by carrying a rifle and reportedly acting as part of a militia—he was being pursued by protesters and was attacked before firing his weapon. There is thus speculation that he may be acquitted under the governing self-defense law. *See* Eric Zorn, *Here's why Kyle Rittenhouse, the teen shooting suspect in Kenosha killings, is likely to get off*, CHICAGO TRIBUNE (Sept. 3, 2020).
23 Alice Ristroph, *The Constitution of Police Violence*, 64 UCLA L. REV. 1182 (2017).
24 *See id.* at 1216, 1228, 1230.

25 Eric Miller, *Encountering Resistance: Non-Compliance, Non-Cooperation, and Procedural Justice*, UNIVERSITY OF CHICAGO LEGAL FORUM 296 (Article 8, 2016).
26 *Id.* at 297.
27 Ekow N. Yankah, *Pretext and Justification: Republicanism, Policing, and Race*, 40.4 CARDOZO L. REV. 1543, 1606 (2019).
28 *See* CHRIS LEBRON, THE COLOR OF OUR SHAME: RACE AND JUSTICE IN OUR TIME (2013); and TOMMIE SHELBY, DARK GHETTOS: INJUSTICE, DISSENT, AND REFORM (2016).
29 Jesse Eisinger, *Why Only One Top Banker Went to Jail for the Financial Crisis*, N.Y. TIMES (April 30, 2014).
30 Of course, others argue (wrongly, in my view) that if policing has a problem, it is just a matter of a few bad apples: the occasional bad character who engages in the occasional bad shooting or decides to arrest a six-year-old at school. *See, e.g.*, Allyson Chiu, *Florida officer fired for 'traumatic' arrests of two 6-year-old students at school*, WASH. POST (Sept. 24, 2019).
31 On these points, see Adolph Reed Jr., *How Racial Disparity Does Not Help Make Sense of Patterns of Police Violence*, nonsite.org (Sept. 16, 2016), https://nonsite.org/editorial/how-racial-disparity-does-not-help-make-sense-of-patterns-of-police-violence

Chapter 1

Heroes

Death and Duty

One of my first assignments as a new FBI Special Agent was to guard a dead body at a crime scene in the mountains. Earlier that day, my office received a call that a woman's body was found in a national park near the Appalachian Trail. Several agents and I arrived at the scene late that evening, but the evidence response team was unable to access and process the scene in the dark. Someone needed to guard the body until morning. I was given this overnight duty as the junior agent in my office. I recall a senior agent—as he left the scene—saying: "There are bears in the area—don't forget about the shotgun in the back of the truck." Alone in the mountains with a dead body, I set to reading the book I had left in my truck: Ernest Becker's *The Denial of Death*.

Becker's famous book draws heavily upon nineteenth- and twentieth-century philosophy and psychology, arguing that people attempt to transcend mortality through heroism. The basic idea is that we seek to overcome mortal constraints symbolically through eternal heroism. As society and culture evolve, people are forced to seek new illusions that permit them to feel heroic. Although I am skeptical of many of the book's sweeping conclusions, one particular excerpt has stuck with me since that reading in the woods: The idea that understanding one's "urge to heroism" is about understanding one's narcissism. It is the self-absorbed sense of immortal heroism that "keeps men marching into point-blank fire in wars: at heart one doesn't feel that *he* will die, he only feels sorry for the man next to him."[1] In a sense, this philosophical and psychological assessment applies to the police in an uncanny way. It would not be glib to say that the police are in the midst of an existential crisis analogous to the stereotypical crises of teenagers and the middle-aged. This metaphorical identity crisis illuminates the police's confused hero trope, which draws upon antiquated notions of masculinity.

The pursuit of a heroic identity and ethos is problematic on a number of levels. The most obvious problem is that it exacerbates the unjustified conception of police warriors examined in the next chapter. The pursuit of the heroic identity and ethos also obscures the police's role of pursuing justice holistically and collectively. A reconception of the police role is the subject of the last chapter of this book. But to get there we must first examine some of the bases of the identity crisis, including the police's pursuit of a heroic ethos that creates tension between collectivity and individuation. It is in part the trend toward heroic individuation (and away from collective justice) that lays the groundwork for some of the policing problems we see today.

The story behind this trend has roots in history, philosophy, and psychology, all of which illuminate the pursuit of "manly" heroic values in policing. The approach of this chapter is thus more discursive than finegrained. The hope is that a wide-ranging analysis encourages larger patterns to become manifest across various disciplines, giving rise to the synthetic account of the police described in the book's introduction. Concrete case studies help bring this bird's eye approach into perspective. They include the example of nineteenth-century policing through Theodore Roosevelt's tenure as New York City Police Commissioner. Roosevelt's varied career in public service represents the dichotomy of collectivity and heroic individuation.[2] This history helps illuminate how the latter perspective—heroic individuation—crystalized into a prominent theory of "manliness" on which contemporary conceptions of the police are based.[3] Despite varying levels of commitment to community policing and police "guardian" principles over the years, the police have often turned away from progressive reform toward a militaristic, cowboy role.

I experienced some of this during FBI New Agent Training at Quantico, where I was encouraged to think like a hero. In addition to the infamous "sheepdog lecture" (described later), I recall hearing statements such as: "You are the heroes—the ones who run toward the gunshots." And that is of course true in one sense: Law enforcement officers *are* supposed to respond to crimes and accept the risk of harm. But this platitude raises a deeper conceptional question: Is law enforcement inherently based upon a heroic identity and ethos, or is it rather based upon a professional duty to pursue community justice given specialized training, tactics, and equipment? I am not suggesting that the FBI or the police would disagree with the latter conception, but I submit that the former conception is the one that gets the most play. This may not sound like a big deal. As long as the police understand that they are not *really* superheroes or cowboys, then what's wrong with a bit of chest-thumping pep talk about heroism?

The first problem is that hero training goes well beyond an innocent pep talk: Police are quite literally trained to be warriors who rely upon aggressive reflex. The second problem is that policing is inherently situational: The heroic identity and ethos discussed in this chapter are at odds with many law enforcement situations that officers face. The FBI Academy at

Quantico has a mock city called "Hogan's Alley," in which trainees engage in mock operations such as executing searches and arrests. During my training at Quantico, I recall being placed in a scenario in which a "bad guy" had the jump on me and my partner. Although the bad guy had the tactical advantage, I took an aggressive, forceful action to confront the threat. If the same scenario had occurred in the real world, I would have been described as a hero had my action worked. However, it didn't work at Hogan's Alley and it wouldn't have worked in the real world. My "heroic" action could have gotten me and others killed because it was misguided and tactically unsound. The relevant evaluative standard was not about heroism or lack thereof.

But police officers are rarely recognized for calm, rational, deliberation—or for taking precautions that protect suspected criminals from harm. They are rather praised for the unusual acts of individual heroism against threats. There are many examples. Consider Detective Conor O'Donnell's actions during the 2017 mass shooting on the Las Vegas strip. It was the deadliest mass shooting in modern American history (58 deaths), and during the shooting Detective Connor "pulled multiple victims from the street to a makeshift triage center." Upon being awarded a service ribbon, his department stated: "Detective O'Donnell's multiple acts of heroism amidst a barrage of gunfire, with no regard for his own personal safety, demonstrated exceptional courage and concern for public safety, and a superior level of professionalism, all in the highest traditions ...."[4] We acknowledge (and glorify) those who meet and go beyond their duty, and it becomes the stuff of legend.

On the other hand, following the same shooting, Officer Cordell Hendrex was treated as a coward and fired when "body camera footage ... showed Hendrex hesitating ... one floor beneath the killer, holding his position for nearly five minutes as rounds continually sprayed into the crowd ... below."[5] The police union president disagreed with the decision to terminate Hendrex,[6] But perhaps Hendrex should have acted differently. Likewise, there is little doubt that Scot Peterson (ridiculed as the "Coward of Broward") could have acted differently during the mass shooting in which a gunman killed 17 students, teachers, and staff members, at a high school in Parkland, Florida on February 14, 2018; Peterson was charged with seven counts of felony neglect of a child for not doing more to protect students, among other violations, with a potential maximum prison sentence of almost 100 years.[7] These officers' hesitation may have been based in part upon fear (which can result in both under and overaggressive responses) rather than training emphasizing calm, rational, deliberation. But any failures are more accurately characterized as failures of professional protocol—not cowardly failures of the heroic ethos—especially given unique protocols for responding to active shooters.

Evaluative terms such as "heroic" and "cowardly" are often separated by a fine, flexible line in policing. Minnesota police officer Jeronimo Yanez took quick, decisive, and aggressive action when he shot and killed motorist Philando Castile seconds after being informed that Castile possessed a handgun (discussed in the next chapter). Yanez—who had attended police "warrior" training—was charged criminally (and ultimately acquitted) for the highly questionable shooting, stating at trial: "I was scared to death …I thought I was going to die."[8] The larger point is that the construction of the police identity has high stakes. The police are not mythic heroes who should be judged by daring feats, risks, and bravery. They are government agents whose role is to seek justice in their communities. This can mean responding to an active shooter, assisting a stranded motorist on the highway, or protecting the rights of a criminal who is being arrested. But if that's the case, why do the police so often embrace a cowboy model of heroism? To answer this question, we turn to the early days of modern policing and how policing has evolved since then.

A Police Case Study

William Bratton posted nine policing principles on his blog when he was New York City Police Commissioner the second time (2014–2016), stating: "I carry these with me everywhere. My Bible."[9] The nine principles are said to have been enunciated by Sir Robert Peel, a British statesman who served twice as Prime Minister in the middle of the nineteenth century.[10] It seems that the principles were actually created by the first Commissioners of Police of the Metropolis (Charles Rowan and Richard Mayne); in any case, they were set out in the "General Instructions" issued to new police officers in 1829.[11] Bratton's version of the list reads as follows:

> PRINCIPLE 1 "The basic mission for which the police exist is to prevent crime and disorder."
> PRINCIPLE 2 "The ability of the police to perform their duties is dependent upon public approval of police actions."
> PRINCIPLE 3 "Police must secure the willing cooperation of the public in voluntary observance of the law to be able to secure and maintain the respect of the public."
> PRINCIPLE 4 "The degree of cooperation of the public that can be secured diminishes proportionately to the necessity of the use of physical force."
> PRINCIPLE 5 "Police seek and preserve public favor not by catering to the public opinion but by constantly demonstrating absolute impartial service to the law."
> PRINCIPLE 6 "Police use physical force to the extent necessary to secure observance of the law or to restore order only when the exercise of persuasion, advice and warning is found to be insufficient."

PRINCIPLE 7 "Police, at all times, should maintain a relationship with the public that gives reality to the historic tradition that the police are the public and the public are the police; the police being only members of the public who are paid to give full-time attention to duties which are incumbent on every citizen in the interests of community welfare and existence."

PRINCIPLE 8 "Police should always direct their action strictly towards their functions and never appear to usurp the powers of the judiciary."

PRINCIPLE 9 "The test of police efficiency is the absence of crime and disorder, not the visible evidence of police action in dealing with it."[12]

It is ironic that Bratton thought of these principles as his Bible. This is in part because he was one of the forerunners of predictive policing, which I argue (in chapter 4) is often implemented in a way that is contrary to community and Peelian policing principles. It is also interesting to note that the above list seems to exclude a few parts of the Peelian principles. For example, principle 1 reads as follows: "The basic mission for which the police exist is to prevent crime and disorder." However, the British Home Office lists the principle as follows: "To prevent crime and disorder, as an alternative to their repression by military force and severity of legal punishment." This is a small omission with a disproportionately large impact on the principle's meaning. The Peelian principles form the basis of what is known as "policing by consent," which is based upon the "common consent of the public" rather than the fear-inducing power of the state.[13] The reference to military force and severe legal punishment is thus crucial to the principle's sentiment.

The embrace of the Peelian principles foreshadows the philosophical, political, and psychological evolution of policing that followed the creation of the London Metropolitan Police in 1829. We will return to these issues in later chapters, discussing just how far contemporary policing has moved from community and Peelian principles. But I first turn to a slice of nineteenth-century policing history in the United States: The progressive reform that Theodore Roosevelt introduced when he was named President of the Board of Commissioners for the New York City Police Department in 1895.

Roosevelt's police reform is situated within the broader progressive era that swept across the United States at the end of the nineteenth century. The progressive movement was focused upon addressing a number of emerging problems stemming from industrialization and urbanization, including class conflict and political corruption.[14] Roosevelt's tenure as New York's police commissioner undoubtedly addressed many of these problems. As we will see, he introduced a number of measures that helped establish "police professionalization" (or a "professional model" of policing) in New York, efforts that were in many ways based upon the policing standards associated with Robert Peel. On the other hand, we will also see how Roosevelt's notorious obsession with manhood and physical courage helped establish a conception of police as heroic individuals. Ironically, then, Roosevelt's nineteenth-century police reform made productive strides against the crisis of police corruption and incompetence, while at the same time helping to solidify an emerging conception of militant police warriors.

Roosevelt served as New York's police commissioner from 1895 to 1897, the period immediately following an investigation into the corrupt practices of the New York Police Department in 1894. The investigation was conducted by what came to be known as the Lexow Committee, a New York State Senate Special Committee that helped bring to light "[t]he vast influence of political patronage [that] was particularly strong in the Police Department."[15] The investigation of the police went far beyond political corruption, documenting widespread brutality, fraud, and other crimes. Victims of brutality testified before the committee, unrecognizable from blood and bruises: One immigrant testified that "he had been safer in the hands of the czarist Cossacks than in the custody of the New York Police," while another immigrant testified that "upon refusing to pay a patrolman a $50 extortion fee, she was arrested as a prostitute and her children sent to an asylum."[16] Upon taking the reins as police commissioner, Roosevelt sought to reform these and other abuses by focusing upon "the gospel of morality" and "the gospel of efficiency."[17]

Another way of describing Roosevelt's "gospels" is a philosophy of policing based upon professionalism: "the emphasis on expertise, the distrust of politics, the use of administrative structures and the values of efficiency ...."[18] It is here that we can begin to see the mixed legacy of Roosevelt's reform efforts. To be sure, the professional model of policing brought many improvements, including more efficient control and organization, heighted recruitment and training standards, improved discipline and technology, and a more narrowly defined police role.[19] However, Roosevelt's professional model included two central problems: First, it overly relied upon a "military analogy" as a way "of improving the image and of facilitating the professional identity of the police."[20] Second, the military identity was exacerbated by Roosevelt's enforcement of morality through legalistic policing, which James Q. Wilson described as enforcing the law "as if there were a single standard of community conduct—that which the law prescribes."[21] Of course, this sort of policing seems like a vast improvement over politically corrupt and biased policing with which Roosevelt was concerned, but it also raises a new set of concerns. For example, consider how some states have concluded that recreational marijuana use is morally questionable and thus legally prohibited. But all things considered, it is questionable whether seeking to arrest everyone who violates laws against such acts is the best way for the police to pursue justice.

In the same way, it is questionable whether it would be justified for the police to arrest everyone who breaks laws against jaywalking given a broader conception of justice. The point is that professional discretion is a necessary tool that can be used by the police for good or ill.[22]

The military identity—coupled with legalistic policing—is remarkably similar to the contemporary police warrior–guardian identity discussed in the next two chapters. This identity emphasizes law enforcement at the expense of other values that are central to the police's pursuit of justice. Consider how Roosevelt embraced a professional model—which evolved from Robert Peel's policing principles—emphasizing a militarist identity. As scholars on this period have noted, nineteenth-century police reformers embraced the military identity for the sake of administrative efficacy:

> Such an approach to law enforcement was seen as a means of promoting efficiency, order, and discipline. The armed forces were rigidly authoritarian and strictly hierarchical, a suitable example for the ideal police department the progressives were attempting to mold.[23]

Naturally, efficiency is viewed as a desirable goal for government agencies, and so it makes sense to embrace a policing model that seems to promote that value. However, the professional model—especially its military facet—includes attributes beyond the value of efficiency, namely: a heroic battle against the enemy. The problem is that these attributes may be distorted in a way that conflicts with the broader (non-militaristic) goals and values that form a holistic ideal of justice in liberal societies.[24]

Many of these militaristic distortions of the professional model are unsurprising because they seem commonplace today. Roosevelt himself described the police as "warring against crime" and in "resolute warfare against every type of criminal."[25] Given the more recent "war on drugs," "war on terrorism," and so on, we have become numb to this sort of talk about the police role and identity. But Roosevelt's special emphasis on the heroic ethos deserves particular attention. For it is this early emphasis on the heroic ethos that helps establish the police identity as one of personal bravery—rather than the collective pursuit for justice. Roosevelt's New York Police Department became fixated on awarding medals and other military awards for feats of gallantry.[26] He believed that police should be evaluated as soldiers on a battlefield who were expected to display acts of bravery. Just as "the best soldiers are those who win promotion by some feat of gallantry on the field of battle,"[27] police officers were expected to embody a heroic ethos in order to advance their careers:

> In making promotions we took into account not only the man's general record, his faithfulness, industry and vigilance, but also his personal prowess as shown in any special feat of daring, whether in the arresting

of criminals or in the saving of life—for the police service is military in character, and we wish to encourage the military virtues.[28]

In no uncertain terms, then, the "progressive" police reform of the nineteenth century promoted a police identity based upon the militaristic heroism of individual officers.

It is remarkable how little has changed since then. Indeed, the International Association of Chiefs of Police (IACP) selects a "Police Officer of the Year" award each year, which "recognizes outstanding achievement in law enforcement and honors heroes."[29] Naturally, these individual officers are viewed as exemplars of the policing profession given that they are deemed "police officer of the year." A great many of the award recipients were honored based upon heroic actions taken while in combat situations. For instance, while at Quantico for FBI New Agent Training, my fellow trainees and I were told about the 1986 recipient, Special Agent Edmundo Mireles. The IACP website sets the scene by describing "bullets flying" after a bank and armored car robbery in Miami:

> After killing two FBI agents and wounding five agents, the suspects tried to flee in the fallen officer's car. With a shattered left arm and a wound to the head, Mireles kept firing and was able to kill both suspects before they escaped.[30]

In 2019, one of the award finalists was selected for saving a hostage by shooting a knife-wielding suspect in the head:

> [The suspect] was now swinging the knife more aggressively toward his hostage. Fearing the hostage was about to be stabbed, [the] [o]fficer ... fired one shot from his rifle from about 15 feet away, striking the suspect in the head. He fell to the ground, leaving the hostage uninjured.[31]

To be sure, these harrowing acts of courage under fire can be commendable and an inspiration to others. It is nevertheless reasonable to raise the question of this chapter: Should such acts of heroism serve as a basis for our conception of the police role?

Of course, promoting bravery and a heroic ethos are not the only ways the police role is promoted—not now, and not historically under prominent commissioners such as Roosevelt. In his book on Roosevelt's tenure as police commissioner, Jay Stuart Berman notes the following professionalization efforts in addition to militarization: (1) Strong centralized executive control; (2) recruitment of qualified personnel; (3) training; (4) strict discipline; (5) application of technology; (6) defined and limited police functions.[32] Consider the issue of recruitment. As with policing today, the recruitment of qualified, professional officers has been a problem since the advent of modern policing. Sir Robert Peel considered the success of the London Metropolitan Police to hinge upon selecting the very best candidates for the job.[33] But this raises the fundamental question with which this book contends: What is the justified conception and role of the police in liberal societies? Are we looking for heroes, warriors, or something else altogether?

On this question, reformers in Roosevelt's era believed that police professionalization meant limiting the police role to one central task: crime control.[34] Coupled with Roosevelt's emphasis on military heroism, it is not difficult to see how a cowboy–crimefighter identity became the de facto professional identity of the police. Indeed, Roosevelt shared the belief that "the one all-important element in good citizenship is obedience to the law and nothing is more needed than the resolute enforcement of the law."[35] The police role was thus viewed as a strict crime-fighting and law enforcement role. There was little concern with how such a narrowly conceived police identity and strategy might fit into broader conceptions of societal justice. As Berman notes, Roosevelt's rationale was that taking a strict, legalistic approach to law enforcement would result in "divorcing the police from politics."[36] Unfortunately, this is wishful thinking.

We now know that an overly legalistic approach to law enforcement—resulting in the arrest and incarceration of large numbers of people for relatively minor offenses—is not apolitical. It is precisely this sort of narrowly construed policing strategy that contributed to mass incarnation in the late twentieth century and beyond. For example, strict enforcement strategies regarding crimes such as simple possession of narcotics (which have included mandatory minimum prison sentences) have resulted in egregious racial and ethnic disparities in the contemporary criminal justice system. The police do not have infinite resources, and the decision to focus upon strictly enforcing some crimes rather than others can involve political calculation. We of course see this in media campaigns declaring "war" on drugs (and terrorism), while remaining relatively lax when it comes to white-collar, corporate, and government crimes.

Part of the problem with Roosevelt's legalistic police role is a failure to recognize the necessity of professional discretion: "An officer to whom is confided the carrying out of laws has no such discretion."[37] Again, it is simply impossible (and contrary to the goals of justice) to enforce every violation of narcotics laws, or every act of speeding and jaywalking, and so on. Finite resources mean that the police must exercise limited, professional discretion in a way that is consistent with the rule of law specifically and justice generally. Of course, the difficulty is identifying the just limits of discretion—a topic I have addressed elsewhere—but there are reasonable rules of thumb that are consistent with the rule of law.[38] For example, it is easy to make arrests in open-air drug markets that result in significant prison terms. However, it is questionable whether strictly enforcing narcotics possession laws (and filling prisons with people convicted of simple possession of narcotics) is justified. A strong case can be made that the police's limited resources should be focused upon enforcing laws that prohibit the trafficking of narcotics, or focused upon economic crimes that perpetuate socioeconomic disparity within communities. This is not a controversial claim, but rather a simple manifestation of the role of discretion that is consistent with rule of law principles in the pursuit of justice. The point is that a legalistic, formal approach to law enforcement is not necessarily the most practicable, effective, or morally justified approach to justice. This is especially the case when police are construed as heroic crime fighters on a soldier's (or warrior's) path.

Roosevelt's tenure as New York Police Commissioner was a mixed bag. Efforts to remove the police from politics and improve recruitment and training were in many ways transformational. His emphasis on the appropriate application of technology in policing was also prescient, though (in chapter 4) we will see how contemporary policing strategies have been blinded by the allure of technology. One of the more significant legacies of this era is the military analogy and the emphasis on a police's officer's bravery and heroism. These efforts help entrench the view that the police identity is one of personal heroism. The broader point is that the early history of police reform and professionalization—both its hits and its misses—continue to be relevant today. It is fitting to conclude this section by noting how Roosevelt advocated for police recruits being tested on whether they have a basic grasp of history and government:

> [Q]uestions of a simple kind in American history and government were especially appropriate to the Police Force, because the men who ... represent to the average citizen, the power of American law, ought to have that simple knowledge of the country's history and government.[39]

To be sure, institutional power is constrained morally by a polity's ideals and values. It is in this spirit that we turn to more philosophical questions about the police identity.

A Brief History of Philosophy and Psychology

Roosevelt is one of the most well-known U.S. presidents for a variety of reasons, but his tenure as New York Police Commissioner is not one of those reasons. He is rather associated with virility—the manly cowboy charging a hill on horseback in the Spanish–American War in 1898. It is this facet of the Roosevelt persona (even if based upon a simplistic cartoon) that helps explain his emphasis on heroism in policing.[40] The Rooseveltian persona is also a case study in some of the prominent psychological and philosophical theories of the era.

Roosevelt's heroic, masculinized persona was not apparent during the first years of his political career. On the contrary, his manhood was routinely questioned during his time as a young, newly elected New York assemblyman in 1882. Gail Bederman describes how "[d]aily newspapers lampooned Roosevelt as the quintessence of effeminacy" (e.g., "Jane-Dandy," Punkin-Lily").[41] He addressed this problem in short order—refashioning himself as a heroic frontiersman and the epitome of late nineteenth-century masculinity.[42] This began in part on his first trip to South Dakota's Badlands, where Roosevelt resolved to purchase a cattle ranch in 1883—and from where he sent dispatches back east of his cowboy adventures "galloping over the plains, day in and day out, clad in buckskin shirt and leather chaparajos, with big sombrero on my head."[43] He published a series of books on hunting and ranch life during this time, portraying himself as a heroic rancher who must "possess qualities of personal bravery, hardihood, and self-reliance ...."[44] This allowed him to run for New York City Mayor as "Cowboy of the Dakotas" in 1886.[45] Similar themes continued in books such as *The Winning of the West* (1889), a history of the late eighteenth-century American frontier that focused on a particular notion of manhood: "The west would never have been settled save for the fierce courage and the eager desire to brave danger so characteristic of the stalwart backwoodsmen."[46]

It was the outbreak of the Spanish–American war in 1898 that allowed Roosevelt to cement his cowboy persona: Colonel Roosevelt, the heroic "Rough Rider." Roosevelt was assistant secretary of the navy in the leadup to the war, resigning that post to form a regiment of soldiers (the Rough Riders) who embodied the heroic identity that Roosevelt had long pursued.[47] He welcomed attention from journalists, and his Rough Riders' masculine heroics became legendary—especially the famous battle of San Juan Hill (Kettle Hill) in which Roosevelt led the Rough Riders in a horseback charge. With this heroic persona firmly in place, Roosevelt's political career took off after he returned from the war.[48]

Of course, if one abstracts away from the atrocities of war generally—and of the Spanish–American war specifically—it is possible to appreciate the bravery and heroism of Roosevelt and the other Rough Riders. In the simplest formulation, one might say that war is a unique opportunity for eternal self-sacrifice—an opportunity to die defending one's country from an external, existential threat. Given these stakes, unabashed heroism can seem appropriate in wartime soldiering—even if not strictly speaking required—assuming the soldier's actions are consistent with competing moral, political, and legal norms. In Roosevelt's case, one might think that his obsession with manliness and toughness was simply a defense and compensatory response to having been a sick and fragile child (along with the effeminate characterizations noted above). On the other hand, Roosevelt's heroic ethos (manifest in both war and policing) illuminates a broader existential response to individual mortality. Roosevelt puts the point quite clearly in his autobiography: The man who lives the strenuous life views his life "as a pawn to be promptly hazarded whenever the hazard is warranted by the larger interests of the great game in which we are all engaged."[49] Whether the heroic identity and the pursuit of eternal heroism is appropriate in the theater of war, I do not know. What is of pressing concern here is the justification of a heroic, manly identity as the foundation of an ever-evolving police identity. To examine this phenomenon, it helps to consider some of the nineteenth century's philosophical and psychological movements—movements that serve as an illuminating backdrop to the heroic exploits of the era.

The scientific backdrop for these philosophical and psychological movements was in many ways Darwinism. Charles Darwin's *On the Origin of Species* (1859)—and the theory of evolution generally—disrupted assumptions about humanity's central, unique place in the world.[50] The theory was viewed by some as a devastating blow to the meaning and structure of the world. That view has not changed in our time, especially considering events such as the "Scopes Monkey Trial" (*The State of Tennessee v. John Thomas Scopes*)—or the fact that a twenty-first-century U.S. Vice President (Mike Pence) does not accept evolution.[51] Following Darwin was Nietzsche's *The Gay Science* (1882) and *Thus Spoke Zarathustra* (1883), which included the famous pronouncement, "God is dead." Although it is impossible to capture the richness of this pronouncement—and Nietzsche's work generally—in a few sentences, it is fair to say his work denied much of the foundation upon which Western (Christian) civilization had long rested.[52] More generally, his work acknowledged the rigor of science, while at the same time acknowledging that our limited cognitive powers have led to deep delusions (notably, in his view, the delusions of the Christian afterlife). In America, the nineteenth-century merger between scientific and philosophical thought culminated in the work of psychologist and philosopher William James. We call the philosophical method developed by James (and others) in this era *pragmatism*. Pragmatism sought to evaluate the truth of ideas—including theological ideas—in terms of the concrete value (or "cash value") those ideas have in life.[53] The broader goal was to combine empiricist commitments to experience and fact with transcendental commitments to religious propositions. James thus presented a method for evaluating conflicts between scientific and religious ideas—one that tempered (not negated) religious worldviews with epistemic standards based upon facts and practical consequences.

This sketch of the nineteenth-century scientific backdrop suggests a paradigm shift regarding humanity's presumed centrality in the world—a shift that illuminates the philosophical and psychological trajectory of the era in which Roosevelt and other societal reformers worked. We have seen how Roosevelt attempted to alter his perceived effeminacy by embracing a certain conception of heroic masculinity. Likewise, through his own words, we see how he attempted to alter his mortality by pursuing "the larger interests of the great game in which we are all engaged." Interestingly, this attempt by Roosevelt to construct a heroic persona is remarkably consistent with the psychological assessment of humankind by Danish philosopher Søren Kierkegaard.

Kierkegaard died at the age of forty-two in 1855, just three years before Roosevelt's birth. He left behind what became one of the classic works on anxiety, which was first translated as *The Concept of Dread*.[54] A prominent theme in Kierkegaard's work is the idea that one must recognize and accept one's mortality, rather than proceed through life deluded:

> When such a person knows more thoroughly than a child knows the alphabet ... that terror, perdition, annihilation, dwell next door to every man, and has learned the profitable lesson that every dread which alarms may the next instant become a fact, he will then interpret reality differently ....[55]

By facing this existential dread and awaking from the deluded dream in which most people live, one is able to see one's self in relation to something greater (faith in God, in Kierkegaard's case). The idea is that illumination permits one to discard mortal aims in favor of transcendental aims.

On that overnight FBI assignment in the mountains—reading Ernest Becker's *The Denial of Death* at a murder crime scene—I noted in the book's margins how Becker related Kierkegaard's work to heroism and contemporary culture:

> Man breaks through the bounds of merely cultural heroism; he destroys the character lie that had him perform as a hero in the everyday social scheme of things; and by doing so he opens himself up to infinity, to the possibility of cosmic heroism, to the very service of God. His life thereby acquires ultimate value in place of merely social and cultural, historical value.[56]

But reading it now—in light of contemporary psychology—it sounds almost hackneyed, veering toward an existentialist trope. In any event, how exactly would such a philosophical–psychological theory relate to Roosevelt? Beyond the historical records, it is of course impossible to say what was in Roosevelt's mind. When Roosevelt described hazarding life for the "the larger interests of the great game," it is possible that he meant shedding the finite heroism of everyday life in favor of cosmic heroism. It is also possible that he was rather thinking of hazarding one's life for an earthlier form of heroism—in service to one's country, for example. And it is possible that it was some combination of heroism that Roosevelt had in mind. The only thing that is relatively clear is that he was centrally focused on heroic individuation—the pursuit of a heroic self-concept. Many nineteenth-century philosophers and psychologists suggested that these sorts of heroic pursuits were a response to the knowledge that we will die—in other words, an attempt to understand and perhaps transcend mortality. German philosopher Arthur Schopenhauer famously described death as the "muse of philosophy" (1818),[57] while William James described how our knowledge of death is "the worm at the core" (1902) of the human condition.[58] To be sure, the idea that death is a moving and motivating theme in life is not a new one. Death is historically viewed as the universal concern that often drives one's actions and self-conception—heroic or otherwise.

These lines of thought continued through the emergence of the psychoanalytic tradition of the era. This is especially the case with respect to the idea that human anxiety and conflict must be resolved through heroic rejection of the mundane in favor of the majestic. For example, Austrian psychoanalyst Otto Rank put it this way: the "need for a truly religious ideology ... is inherent in human nature and its fulfillment is basic to any kind of social life."[59] To be sure, this sounds decidedly quaint considering twenty-first-century technology, geopolitics, and a general shift in cultural values. But the psychoanalytic conclusion is not—at least by some commentators' lights—an antiquated, anti-scientific prop for religion. Becker described it as being based upon "the logic of the historical-psychoanalytic understanding of man .... [and] his elaboration of the nature of neurosis."[60] Neurosis means different things to different people, and early psychoanalysts certainly had their own understanding of the condition. What possible relation could neurosis have in the context of the police's heroic ethos?

It is interesting to consider how the psychoanalytic account of neurosis is situated within the classic tradition of distinguishing nonpathological mood states and pathological disease—a tradition going back to Aristotle's *Problemata.*[61] One such account characterized neurosis as suffering from "painful truth," which is a kind of internal conflict.[62] In other words, neurosis was viewed as the result of failing to deceive oneself with illusions about one's existential condition, with Rank writing:

> [T]he suffering of the neurotic comes ... from painful truth .... He suffers, not from all the pathological mechanisms which are psychically necessary for living and wholesome but in the refusal of these mechanisms which is just what robs him of the illusions important for living .... [Such a person] is much nearer to the actual truth psychologically than the others and it is just that from which he suffers.[63]

What Rank is pointing to is the need for adequate defense mechanisms to contend with the human experience. In the context of the police's heroic ethos, then, we might reframe the issue in terms of the protection of the ego against fear of death and annihilation. Becker characterizes the difficulties of grappling with big, existential questions this way:

> [M]en aren't built to be gods, to take in the whole world; they are built like other creatures, to take in the piece of ground in front of their noses. Gods can take in the whole of creation because they alone can make sense of it, know what it is all about and for. But as soon as man lifts his nose from the ground and starts sniffing at eternal problems like life and death, the meaning of a rose or a star cluster—then he is in trouble.[64]

Although this is evocative language—many have felt existential angst while pondering the universe—it seems to paint with too broad a brush. In other words, it relies upon limited perspective to draw universal conclusions. When one considers the diversity of life perspectives—social, economic, gender, ethnic, mental health, and so on—it stands to reason that there are equally diverse ways to approach (and respond to) life, death, and the meaning of a rose. A middleclass, white, male academic probably sees these issues differently than a migrant worker, who probably sees them differently than a school teacher in India, and so on. Nevertheless, there does seem to be a much narrower observation that is apt: *Some* people—*sometimes*—fail to acknowledge their existential reality. And according to some of the rich insights of the psychoanalytic tradition, the internal conflict that results from failing to acknowledge one's existential reality might lead to fragility of the self and the need to bolster our sense of self, say, through a heroic ethos.[65]

As we will see, this is startlingly relevant to the heroic ethos within the narrow domain of policing—an ethos that began to be formalized under Roosevelt's tenure and continues in today's police warrior–guardian culture. One reason for this is simply the fact that the risk of death is part of the job description in policing. Indeed, during my first training sessions at Quantico mentioned earlier, I was given this *reality check* explicitly. It was a profound moment in both my training and my life and it affected me (and others) greatly. The other trainees and I were forced to face the reality that the job may kill us (or require us to kill another). We discussed and trained for situations in which we or others could die. We watched videos of actual officers dying on the job—videos in which we saw and heard screaming and pleas for help as life drained from the body. In a sense, this is as it should be. Many people choose careers in law enforcement without considering these issues, and it is vitally important that people acknowledge the reality of the job before they're on the job.

But here's the rub: There are a great many ways to acknowledge one's existential reality and respond to that reality—whether in life generally or police specifically. One's response to this reality is maladaptive and unhealthy when the response excessively or disproportionally affects one's life or the lives of others—such as when one finds salvation only in a narrowly defined activity or relationship. This occurs in policing to the extent that law enforcement officers are taught to respond to their existential reality as heroes in an eternal battle of good versus evil. As Rank puts it: "The neurotic type ... is bound up in a kind of magic unity with the wholeness of life around him much more than the adjusted type who can be satisfied with the role of a part within the whole."[66] The police hero ethos is a collective ideology that—somewhat paradoxically—emphasizes and rewards heroic individuation rather than collective justice. We see this explicitly in the advent of progressive policing under Roosevelt, who reinforced individual heroics through the pageantry of awarding medals and other military rewards for feats of gallantry. Heroism was also a practical matter for the police officer, given that it was the criteria by which one's career was advanced. By considering how the response to the existential reality of policing is this sort of heroic individuation—rather than collectivity—we can begin to see connections to contemporary conceptions of the police that are based upon warriors and guardians. In a sense, heroism has become a defense against death that serves as the basis of the police conception.

On the surface, this can be seen through the popular sheepdog metaphor in police culture, as well as how the metaphor plays out in training and practice. Police are heroic sheepdogs on a warrior's path to protect the sheep from wolves. This stark dichotomy between sheep and wolves, good and evil, is a superficial attempt to frame the mortal risk that comes with being a law enforcement officer. The police role becomes inexplicably intertwined with the wholeness of life through an eternal struggle against the real and perceived threat of wolves.[67] But who are the wolves? They are not like most of us (sheep), meaning that they are a different type of person altogether—what we might call *other*. The idea of the *other* becomes manifest through "us versus them" rhetoric in policing. To be sure, the generic "other" or "them" is in part different (from "us") because it is associated with criminal behavior.[68] But it is not just any kind of criminal behavior. When law enforcement officers are given their heroic mission to fight wolves, government and corporate executives don't typically come to mind. This is in spite of the fact that a single white-collar criminal might affect communities as much as a single violent criminal. Those in the wolf category are thus dehumanized based upon particular crimes—those perceived as inherently violent—that affect particular communities. On the other hand, white-collar and other criminals are more likely to be overlooked given the sheep–wolf dichotomy, even though white-collar and corporate crime can exacerbate socio-economic disparities that contribute to a cycle of violence. White-collar criminals work, act, and look like most sheep: We do not fear them because they are familiar to us. This dichotomy allows the police to focus their heroic mission on subjugating particular groups of criminals, which perpetuates the status quo of control and power over some groups rather than others.

The larger point is that nineteenth-century philosophy and psychology have something to say about the connections between historical and contemporary conceptions of the police role. We have seen how conceptions of the police role have been focused disproportionately upon heroic individuation rather than collectivity. This pursuit of a heroic self-concept has long guided efforts in police reform—from the NYPD under Roosevelt's tutelage, to contemporary departments in which trainees are taught to be warriors on a hero's path. What remains is a deeper exploration of this heroic ethos—its norms and values—and how that ethos is relevant (if at all) to the actual job of policing. One of the surprising discoveries from such an exploration is the way the heroic ethos is conflated with particular notions of "manliness." Such narrow conceptions of heroism result in a central problem: They are inconsistent with the fundamental moral, political, and legal tenets of liberal societies, obscuring broader conceptions of heroism within society.

Old and New Heroism

There are many ways to think of heroism, but one conception stands out in the context of policing: the *manly* hero. So far, this claim has been supported with circumstantial evidence: Nineteenth-century history, philosophy, and psychology allow one to make plausible inferences about the way the police role evolved from a narrow conception of heroism. We may now consider the extent to which there is a direct connection between that conception of heroism and *manliness*. This is an important exercise for a straightforward reason: If the police role is conceived in terms of heroism—and the predominant heroic ethos is based upon notions of manliness—then we ought to evaluate the idea of *manly heroism* and the extent to which it is justified in the context of policing.

The idea of manliness is likely to conjure all sorts of caricatures and stereotypes—from Rambo and Roosevelt to Hemingway and Harrison Ford. In the policing context, I am reminded of a popular training program that popularized the sheepdog warrior metaphor mentioned earlier—and the way the police trainer closes his training with a literal chest thump, imploring officers to "look over the city and let ... [their] cape blow in the wind."[69] But we should begin with an open mind, considering whether ideas of manliness are based upon principles and values that are necessary components of policing. There are several places one could begin when examining manliness, especially considering that entire academic centers have been devoted to "the study of men and masculinities."[70] I begin with a prominent account by Harvey Mansfield, a Harvard Professor of Government who wrote the unambiguously titled book, *Manliness*.[71]

Mansfield's goal is to provide a "modest defense" of manliness, which begins by invoking the terrorist attacks of September 11, 2001:

> Americans were sharply reminded that it is sometimes necessary to fight, and that in the business of government, fighting comes before caring. Women were reminded that men can come in handy. The heroes of the day were (apparently) exclusively male—as were the villains. Does this mean that the gender-neutral society is valid only in peacetime?[72]

This is a good place to begin because it is easy to extend Mansfield's line of thinking to current thinking about the police. In fact, the sentiment is remarkably similar to the way current and former law enforcement officers (myself included) have been taught to view their societal role: Wolves (criminals) are lurking in communities and we need heroic sheepdogs (police on the warrior's path) to defend the sheep (everyone who is not a heroic warrior) by fighting the wolves. In other words, Mansfield—and those who conceive of the police as a sheepdog warrior—seem to view heroism as involving qualities that are associated with stereotypical manliness, namely: violence and fighting, especially in the context of "good vs. evil."

Mansfield is of course aware of broader stereotypes about manliness and thus seeks to identify and define the good parts of manliness—the qualities we like in the 9/11 heroes, for instance. The initial, defining components of manliness are said to be *confidence* and *command*.[73] With respect to the former: "The confidence of a man gives him independence of others. He is not always asking for help or directions or instructions."[74] And with respect to command:

> The manly man is good at getting things done, and one reason is that he is good at *ordering* people to get them done .... Manly men take authority for granted—the need for authority in general and their own particular authority.[75]

As for this initial definition, then, Mansfield concludes that "[m]anliness can have something heroic about it," which can be both good and bad.[76] This initial assessment is problematic within the context of policing. Many people might think that confidence and command are admirable values, but in the abstract they obscure the role of competing values that are especially important to policing.

Consider the conception of confidence as "independence of others." Confidence and independence of course have value in personal and public life, particularly given that a lack of confidence and too much dependence are at the other end of the spectrum. But it is not controversial to say that liberal societies are *collectives* in which people reciprocate to produce a state of affairs that is morally and prudentially superior than the alternatives. This is especially true in the context of policing. The police are not lone warrior-heroes seeking to rid the collective of evil. Rather, they are fellow members of the collective—a collective in which rights and duties are balanced between all members. To be sure, one of the police's central duties is to maintain peace and security among members of the collective. That duty arises when some members of the collective break the rules and commit crimes. But justice is not meted out independent of the collective. Given their equal status and worth, all members of the community have a stake in achieving a just state of affairs—one that is based upon collective principles such as the rule of law, rather than unrestrained law enforcement discretion. It would of course be odd to think of the police in terms of the heroic warriors of Greek mythology (Achilles in an epic battle to the death, for instance), though Mansfield does draw extensively upon Achilles and other ancient exemplars of heroism in his discussion of manliness. My point is simply that if prominent conceptions of heroism are based upon manliness—and manliness is based upon confident independence from others—then such conceptions of heroism may conflict with the police's role as a member of a liberal political collective.

Similar problems are raised by conceptions of heroism based upon manly *command and authority*. Here again, command and authority are certainly valuable in public life, including because it would be difficult to think of a security force without such values. But an almost exclusive emphasis on command and authority (which seems to be the prevailing emphasis in policing) paints a decidedly inadequate account of the just pursuit of security in the liberal collective. This is chiefly because discussions of authority in liberal collectives are nonstarters outside the context of *legitimacy*—the right to command and be obeyed. Legitimacy is a complex idea that will be addressed more fully in chapter 4. Here the basic point is that the ability to command and impose one's will and authority have no value in a liberal collective when based simply upon the coercive use of force. That does not mean that coercive force is unjust in liberal collectives generally or policing specifically, but it does mean that such force must be based upon legitimate authority in order to be just. Mansfield describes manly authority as "self-assumed," and that the manly man "not only knows what justice requires, but he acts on his knowledge, making and executing the decision that the rest of us trembled even to define."[77] The idea of executing justice based upon *self-assumed* authority—rather than authority grounded in consent from the governed—would be deeply problematic in public life. The upshot is that if some conceptions of heroism are based upon manliness—and manliness is based upon abstract notions of command and authority—then such conceptions of heroism are inconsistent with the police role inasmuch as they overlook values such as legitimacy. As we will see, this is no mere ivory tower concern. Contemporary policing has evolved in a way that prioritizes so-called "law and order" strategies at the expense of strategies that promote legitimacy. Authority and legitimacy are not mutually exclusive values. The problem is that conceptions of heroic manliness in policing greatly emphasize the former over the latter.

One response—to which Mansfield and others have alluded—is that "the sciences on the whole confirm … the common-sense view that the sexes differ: men more aggressive, women more caring."[78] In other words, there are obvious, natural differences between the sexes (size, strength, hormones, organs, and so on) and those natural differences are relevant to our understanding of manliness and how it might be useful in certain contexts. So one might argue that manly heroism is both natural and useful when defending others from violence, or in professions that require the use of force against others—such as policing. But even if one assumes that stereotypical heroism is in some sense consistent with human nature and has utility in some contexts, it does not follow that we *ought* to embrace the stereotypes of manly heroism. If one's "natural" inclination is to seek revenge upon another to protect one's honor—perhaps a duel to the death—it does not follow (obviously) that the inclination is justified. Analogously, if one is naturally large, strong, and assertive, it does not follow that such traits should be wielded in any particular way simply because they are "natural" or have utility. We rather make normative arguments—based upon practical, political, legal, and moral values—about whether and when it is appropriate to invoke the utility of such traits. Superior size, strength, and confident authority—whether male or female—might be useful when physical force is necessary or when, say, a police officer must chase a criminal suspect on foot. However, with respect to the vast majority of police functions (which do not involve law enforcement or the use of force) there is no natural justification for the imposition of one's superior size, strength, and confident authority upon others. In any case, an obvious problem here—discussed in the conclusion of this chapter—is a failure to consider the perspective of officers who happen to be female.

As Mansfield sees it, though, the problem is the way science examines sexual differences in a piecemeal fashion, "seeking quantifiable precision" by focusing upon individual traits (such as those noted above) rather than examining manliness holistically:

> Regarding individuals as wholes, [scientific] studies are so imprecise as to say almost nothing. These studies stand in need of the precision that would gain from biography and history, showing manly individuals in action. What does John Wayne or Theodore Roosevelt show us about

manliness in its completeness? A manly man is nothing if not an individual, one who sets himself apart, who is concerned with honor rather than survival of his individual being. Or, better to say, he finds his survival only in his honor.

This sentiment brings into remarkable focus the problem with the police–hero conception. Mansfield's idea of *manliness in its completeness*—an individual who sets himself apart based upon eternal honor—exemplifies the philosophical and psychological assessment of the heroic ethos discussed in the last section. As Mansfield puts it, manly aggression is based upon an assertion and a cause: "if you risk your life to save your life, your 'life' must be some immaterial cause, some version of Abstract Justice."[79] Within the framework of this sort of heroism, the police role becomes associated with the wholeness of life through an eternal struggle between good and evil. When law enforcement officers are given their heroic mission to fight evil, the police role is dramatized in a way that justifies the subjugation of evil groups within society (or "wolves"). At the same time, this sort of heroic ethos within policing undercuts broader conceptions of societal justice that are based upon collectivity.

What we are seeing is an attempt to tie manliness to a universal heroic ethos that transcends the mundane concerns of mortal life. There is a further attempt to show how this sort of heroism is vitally important in our time. Following a discussion of Achilles from Homer's *Iliad*, Mansfield writes: "In our time there are many who say that heroes lack humanity and few who will admit that humanity needs heroes. But at all times heroes have to assert themselves."[80] This sort of heroic assertion is supposedly tied to honor—and assertion of "the defense of a general or universal principle or cause that is attached to the community."[81] And so we have come full circle, returning to the narrow heroism of the nineteenth century discussed in the philosophy and psychology of that century: nihilism followed by transcendental heroism.

This sort of narrow, manly heroism is rife with problems. In an incisive review of Mansfield's *Manliness*, Martha Nussbaum noted the logical limits of manly heroism:

> Mansfield announces that his own definition of manliness is "confidence in the face of risk." We might have some issues with the proposal. Don't brave people often feel afraid? Aristotle thinks they do, and rightly, for the loss of life is especially painful when one has a good life. And what about risk? Doesn't manliness also come into play in facing the inevitable, such as each person's own death? And what sort of risk? Are we talking about the physical realm or the moral realm? Barry Bonds has a lot of physical confidence while being (apparently) a moral coward. Socrates probably wasn't up to much furniture-moving,

and Seneca is always whining about his stomach problems; but both had the confidence that counts morally, when they stood up to unjust governments and went to their deaths.[82]

Nussbaum's broader point seems to be that manliness is not a single trait, but rather a variety of traits. Likewise, there is no single trait that exemplifies heroism, but rather a variety of heroic traits—an especially important point in the realm of policing. Nussbaum puts it this way:

> Above all, we need to follow Aristotle's lead and distinguish the sort of courage that stands up for a valuable goal from both upper-body strength and punch-'em-out aggression. That sort of courage, which was the only sort that Aristotle thought a true virtue, always good no matter what the circumstance, requires the ability to reflect on what risks are worth running, on what goals are noble and what goals trivial or even base. It is because the Gary Cooper character exemplifies this sort of reflection, and not only because he is unafraid to face a villain, that he is deemed a hero; but one can have that sort of reflection and not have much in the way of physical strength.[83]

In short, the heroic ethos goes well beyond narrow conceptions based upon confidence, command, aggression, and reckless risk-taking. Nussbaum suggests, for instance, that Franklin Delano Roosevelt—not Theodore Roosevelt—is a truer exemplar of Aristotelian courage:

> He stood up for people in situations that were risky in all sorts of ways (the danger of a socialist revolution, the dangers of countless deaths of innocent people, the dangers of Nazi Germany and imperial Japan) .... But how many would have thought him a John Wayne, even then?[84]

She adds that conceptions of Aristotelian courage might draw from Samuel P. Oliner and Pearl M. Olineri's work in *The Altruistic Personality*, which identified "caring attitude" and a sense of "responsibility" as traits highly correlated with those of courageous acts.[85]

Of course, these traits are not necessarily precluded from Mansfield's conception of heroic manliness, but they are clearly overshadowed. For example, as Nussbaum notes, work such as Daniel Boyarin's *Unheroic Conduct* provides a much-needed counterweight to narrow, Western notions of manly heroism.[86] *Unheroic Conduct* begins with a passage from Freud's *The Interpretation of Dreams*.[87] When Freud was a boy, his father described an incident that occurred when Freud's father was himself a young man: A Christian approached him on the street, knocked off his hat, and said "Jew! Get off the pavement!" The young Freud asked his father how he responded to the man, and his father stated quietly: "I went into the roadway and picked up my cap." Freud writes that his father's response "struck me as unheroic conduct on the part of the big, strong man who was holding the little boy by the hand."[88] In other words, Freud was ashamed of his father's conduct because it lacked manly heroism.

It is precisely this view of heroism that Boyarin pushes back against, arguing that the historic, "ideal" Jewish man was studious and non-violent: "The House of Study was … the rabbinic Jewish equivalent of the locker room, barracks, or warship … [even though it was] read as female in the [broader] cultural environment."[89] Boyarin suggests that this understanding of ("unheroic") manliness was present until Jews assimilated into Western society and its conception of manliness as "physical strength, martial activity and aggressiveness."[90] According to Boyarin, then, there are well-established alternative conceptions, including the way "the Talmud imagines an alternative to phallic, aggressive, machismo as a definition of manliness …."[91] Boyarin's work is a stark contrast to the myopic account of heroic manliness suggested by Mansfield, illuminating the way that narrow accounts of manly heroism are question begging (heroes are manly because they act like men). This is significant because such question begging can result in a failure to consider the different ways that one might be heroic. Nussbaum has sketched alternative accounts of courage and heroism. This included the different ways that FDR stood up for people and principles—as well as the caring attitude and responsibility displayed by rescuers of Jews during the Holocaust—not merely the confidence, command, aggression, and risk-taking exemplified by someone such as Theodore Roosevelt. The point is not that these different conceptions are mutually exclusive, but rather that the idea of so-called manly heroism fails to tell the whole story—both in terms of heroism generally, and the heroic ethos in policing specifically.

Does this mean that the police should take their cue from someone such as Mister Rogers—the host of the children's television series, *Mister Rogers' Neighborhood*? Well, yes—but let me explain. Rogers was known for his ability to connect with a wide array of people: "We *make* so many connections here on earth. Look at us—I've just met you, but I'm investing in who you are and who you will be, and I can't help it."[92] This ability to connect with people was so important to Rogers—a pale, skinny, cardigan-wearing old man—because it helped give him *legitimacy*. Tom Junod wrote a well-known profile of Rogers in which he describes Rogers's ability to connect with people as a sort of superpower: "And so in Penn Station, where he was surrounded by men and women and children, he had this *power*, like a comic-book superhero who absorbs the energy of others until he bursts out of his shirt."[93] It is perhaps this sort of "heroic" power that the police need—especially when it comes to fostering legitimacy through community policing. But it is not just legitimacy that relational heroism promotes. Indeed, the ability to connect with others is a vital law enforcement tool, particularly with respect to, say, the police's job of (lawfully) questioning witnesses and criminal subjects and gathering intelligence by developing informants. People are generally much more willing to talk to people they trust, not people who compel, coerce, and force them to talk.[94]

The point is that it is worth considering heroism that extends beyond the stereotypical conceptions described by Mansfield and others. To give one more example, consider how archaic conceptions of heroism might exacerbate problems such as the so-called *blue wall of silence*—the informal code among some police officers not to report on a colleague's misconduct, but instead plead ignorance of another officer's wrongdoing or claim to have not seen anything.[95] Although this code is steeped in a distorted sense of honor, there is of course nothing heroic about protecting wrongdoers. And when misconduct ultimately becomes public, it is exacerbated by the deceit of the coverup—further eroding trust and legitimacy. The beginnings of a new conception of police heroism can be seen in emerging strategies that have been embraced by historically troubled departments in cities such as New Orleans and Baltimore.

The New Orleans Police Department adopted the "EPIC" program (Ethical Policing is Courageous), which focuses upon the idea of active bystandership. The EPIC program helps foster an expectation that officers should step in when a colleague is misbehaving. This might include situations in which an officer assaults a citizen, lies on a report, or plants evidence. In such situations, officers are trained to step in and say, "I got this. Back off." The idea is that other officers will then follow suit and peer pressure encourages bad actors from engaging in bad acts in the first place. A reported example includes a case in which officers handcuffed a man after a fight. A sheriff's deputy walked up and kicked the cuffed man in the face. Rather than look the other way, the arresting officers responded to the deputy by saying, "We don't roll like that anymore." The sheriff's deputy was then arrested. Such an action opposes entrenched police norms and codes, and it requires a fundamental shift in how officers view the police role—particularly the heroic ethos within that role.

Conclusion: Epistemic Entitlement

The American Film Institute (AFI) sponsored a television special in 2003: *100 Years ... 100 Heroes & Villains*.[96] It is interesting to consider the wide variance in the top three positions: Atticus Finch (*To Kill a Mockingbird*, 1962), Indiana Jones (*Raiders of the Lost Ark*, 1981), and James Bond (*Dr. No*, 1963).[97] As an Alabama attorney representing a black man accused of raping a white woman in the 1930s, Finch is typically viewed as a moral hero who stands up for the rights of the oppressed. Conversely, Indiana Jones and James Bond are glorified as swashbuckling men of action who take mindless risks with undaunted courage and sex appeal. Buried some way down this list (#33) is perhaps a less flamboyant character: the police chief Marge Gunderson (*Fargo*, 1996). As one of the few women on the list, Gunderson (portrayed by Frances McDormand), represents a different kind of hero: The calm, reasonable, and pragmatic professional.

In *Fargo*, the pregnant Gunderson navigates a triple homicide investigation with calm competence and professionalism, which is juxtaposed with the often-shoddy police work of others. Mansfield thinks the film says "that rule-bound professionalism is replacing erratic manliness in occupations that were once manly, and that by this means women who are steadier than men, can replace them, or at least do as well. Women don't fly off the handle so easily."[98] The film leads Mansfield to ponder whether professionalism might make it possible to leave heroic manliness behind. But the question is quickly reframed as whether manliness itself can be professionalized—in the sense that manliness can be thought of as a profession that "is teachable and ... produces results."[99] He concludes that manliness is teachable, but only if one is already courageous: "The woman policeman in *Fargo* was a professional who followed the rules and occasionally taught them to her foolish male colleagues, but did she not have a manly spirit in addition?"[100] It is not clear (to me) what that question means. As we have seen, the sort of manliness described by Mansfield presupposes a narrow conception of the heroic ethos that is often conflated with a warrior ethos (Achilles, Theodore Roosevelt, and so on).

Of course, I myself have done something similar because—as a man—I have necessarily written this chapter's critique of manliness from a man's perspective. Accordingly, the critique inevitably has a masculine slant, which might be describe as a metalevel instance of the chapter's underlying worry about masculine-centric conceptions of heroism. This is related to what Kate Manne describes as "epistemic entitlement" in her book, *Entitled*.[101] Manne defines epistemic entitlement as "peremptorily assuming greater authority to speak, on the part of a more privileged speaker."[102] We can associate this with the more informal—and gloriously titled—term known as *mansplaining*:

> [A] man presuming to 'explain' something incorrect(ly) to a more expert female speaker or set of speakers—and in an overly confident, arrogant, or overbearing manner, which often results in his not backing down or admitting to his mistake after it has been authoritatively pointed out to him.[103]

The basic idea is that epistemic entitlement is the foundation of mansplaining. Although I am no doubt guilty of some degree of epistemic entitlement, the hope is that my perspective is in some sense warranted given that I experienced law enforcement's culture of manly heroism. At the same time, it is my belief that the voices of others are more important given the state of policing. We should thus appeal to the many women who have expressed deep concerns about the way that law enforcement success or failure is based upon subjective gender norms. Consider, for example, an interview of ten former FBI special agent trainees that aired on national television in 2019.[104] The women sued the FBI to end the "good old boy" network at the FBI's academy in Quantico, Virginia, which they say fosters a culture of harassment, discrimination, and retaliation against women. One former trainee recounts: "In every area of training where there was a quantitative measure of failure or success, we all met and exceeded expectations. Everyone here is sitting here because the subjective portion of evaluation and training is ripe for abuse." The interviewer then asks the group of women: *Passing or not passing came down to what in the end?* In unison, the ten women answer: "gender."[105]

In closing this chapter, the larger point I want to make is that there are specific actions by the police that we might describe in terms of archaic notions of heroism, as with the officer's actions during the Las Vegas mass shooting described earlier. But the archaic heroic ethos itself is no longer a justified option in contemporary society. To be sure, there continues to be much hardship and conflict in the world, and we often describe people as overcoming obstacles heroically. But the suggestion of a traditional heroic ethos today is myth-making: an artificial narrative that harkens back to what is perceived as the (now lost) bigness of life captured through a sacred tradition. Of course, even the professions that are deemed most heroic— policing, firefighting, soldiering, for example—are not representative of this sort of imagined heroic culture or society. The use of force—and law enforcement generally—is an important part of policing, but it is not the only part (and it is not a significant part for many officers). Even those who are not deeply entrenched within day-to-day police bureaucracy do not engage in weekly gunfights. This is not to say that police officers rarely encounter danger or difficulty—many certainly do. The point is that the police are vital public servants, regardless of whether they are conceptualized as "heroes" who fight violence with valor. They serve the public in many ways, whether responding to an automobile accident, testifying in court, documenting and resolving a domestic dispute, or seizing a person in way that is consistent with the person's rights.

Nevertheless, the idea of an archaic heroic ethos lives in popular culture—through literature, film, and music—and our institutions strain to replicate that idea. So it goes in policing: Police are conceived as heroes based in part upon the idea of a deep societal divide between good and evil, with the police serving as heroic warriors in an existential battle against evil-doers. We have seen eccentric examples of this, as when police trainers suggest that officers drive to a bridge at the end of their shift to "[l]ook over the city and let … [their] cape blow in the wind."[106] It does not seem unfair to say that this sort of conception of the police role is based upon myth-making that draws upon confused stereotypes of an archaic heroic ethos. More to the point, such conceptions are in many ways inconsistent with the police's role of serving the public by seeking all facets of justice, including reciprocal community relationships (not solitary heroism) and guarding the rights of "wolves" (not just "sheep").

Transformational developments in history, philosophy, and psychology help frame the way that archaic notions of the heroic identity evolved in the modern era—which in turn help frame the coinciding rise of modern policing. There were of course many other factors that explain the evolution of the police role. The dramatic changes in society—including cultural, industrial, economic, and technological revolutions—over the last two centuries cannot be overstated. Such changes undoubtedly influenced crime rates in different ways in different places—the United States and beyond. But parallel developments in philosophy and psychology help explain the police's response to such societal changes. And the police's response to contemporary crime problems illustrates the continued evolution of the police identity. This chapter sketched alternative conceptions of the heroic ethos, including those based upon promoting justice holistically and protecting the rights of others. Such conceptions will be important as we move toward a more comprehensive conception of the police role in chapter 4, but we now turn to the entrenched conception of police as (heroic) warriors.

Notes

1 ERNEST BECKER, THE DENIAL OF DEATH 2 (1973).
2 See, e.g., JAY STUART BERMAN, POLICE ADMINISTRATION AND PROGRESSIVE REFORM: THEODORE ROOSEVELT AS POLICE COMMISSIONER OF NEW YORK (1987); and GAIL BEDERMAN, MANLINESS AND CIVILIZATION, Chapter 5, *Theodore Roosevelt: Manhood, Nation, and "Civilization"* (1995), for these competing perspectives.
3 *See* Theodore Roosevelt, *The Manly Virtues and Practical Politics*, THE FORUM (July 1894). ("Another thing that must not be forgotten by the man desirous of doing good political work is the need of the rougher, manlier virtues, and above all the virtue of personal courage, physical as well as moral.").
4 Brian Amaral, *Hero of Las Vegas mass shooting honored at R.I. State Police ceremony*, PROVIDENCE JOURNAL, May 16, 2019.
5 Rachel Crosby, *Police fire officer who waited in hallway during Las Vegas massacre*, LAS VEGAS REVIEW-JOURNAL, July 2, 2019.
6 *Id.*
7 Adeel Hassan, *Scot Peterson Is Released on Bond. Here's How He's Explained His Actions During the Parkland Shooting*, N.Y. TIMES (June 6, 2019).
8 Shaila Dewan & Richard A. Oppel, Jr., *We Expect Police to Be Brave For Us. But What Happens When They're Not?* N.Y. TIMES, June 5, 2019.
9 *Sir Robert Peel's Nine Principles of Policing*, N.Y. TIMES, April 15, 2014.
10 There is doubt that Peel himself compiled a formal list of principles. *See* Susan A. Lentz & Robert H. Chaires, *The Invention of Peel's Principles: A Study of Policing "Textbook" History*, 35.1 JOURNAL OF CRIMINAL JUSTICE 69–79 (2007).

11 UK Home Office, *FOI Release: Definition of policing by consent*, December 10, 2012, https://www.gov.uk/government/publications/policing-by-consent/definition-of-policing-by-consent
12 *Sir Robert Peel's Nine Principles of Policing, supra* note 9.
13 UK Home office, *supra* note 11.
14 *See generally* MICHAEL MCGERR, FIERCE DISCONTENT: THE RISE AND FALL OF THE PROGRESSIVE MOVEMENT IN AMERICA, 1870–1920 (2003).
15 BERMAN, *supra* note 2, at 17; see generally BERMAN, *supra* note 2, at chapter 2, for a history of the Lexow Committee's investigation of the New York Police Department.
16 *Id.* at 29 (citing *New York State Senate, Report and Proceedings*, 31, 41).
17 Roosevelt, *supra* note 3.
18 Wayne K. Hobson, *Professionals, Progressives, and Bureaucratization*, 39 THE HISTORIAN 640 (1977).
19 See BERMAN, *supra* note 2, at 8, for a comprehensive summary of the professional model.
20 *Id.*
21 JAMES Q. WILSON, VARIETIES OF POLICE BEHAVIOR 172 (1973). *See* BERMAN, *supra* note 2, for a discussion of Roosevelt's enforced morality through legalistic policing.
22 See LUKE WILLIAM HUNT, THE RETRIEVAL OF LIBERALISM IN POLICING 47–52 (2019), for an overview of various ways that discretion relates to the police role.
23 BERMAN, *supra* note 2, at 60.
24 See HUNT, *supra* note 22, at chapter 2, for a broad outline of an ideal of justice in the liberal tradition. See also *infra* the Epilogue of this book.
25 THEODORE ROOSEVELT, AMERICAN IDEALS (Administering the New York Police Force) 215–29 (1900).
26 BERMAN, *supra* note 2, at 61.
27 Theodore Roosevelt, *Taking the Police Out of Politics*, 20 COSMOPOLITAN 45 (November 1895).
28 ROOSEVELT, AMERICAN IDEALS, *supra* note 25, at 226.
29 *Police Officer of the Year*, INT'L ASS'N CHIEFS POLICE, https://www.theiacp.org/news/blog-post/meet-the-2019-iacptarget-police-officer-of-the-year-award-finalists
30 *Id.* at https://www.theiacp.org/2019-iacptarget-police-officer-of-the-year
31 *Police Officer of the Year, supra* note 29.
32 *See* BERMAN, *supra* note 2, at chapter 5 (Applied Efficiency: The Professional Model).
33 *See* CHARLES REITH, THE POLICE IDEA 245 (1938).
34 *See* ERIC MONKONNEN, POLICE IN URBAN AMERICA 1860–1920, 147–50 (1981); DAVID JOHNSON, AMERICAN LAW ENFORCEMENT: A HISTORY 69 (1981).
35 ROOSEVELT, AMERICAN IDEALS, *supra* note 25, at 224.
36 BERMAN, *supra* note 2, at 96.
37 Roosevelt, *Taking the Police Out of Politics, supra* note 27, at 51.
38 See HUNT, *supra* note 22, at 47–52, 196–201, examining discretion, the rule of law, and constraints upon deviations from the rule of law.
39 BERMAN, *supra* note 2, at 73 (citing Theodore Roosevelt to F.S. Black, January 8, 1897, Municipal Archives, City of New York, Police Department File).
40 *See, e.g.*, David Gessner, *Trump venerates Teddy Roosevelt, but Roosevelt would have hated Trump*, WASH. POST (Sept. 29, 2020) (describing how Roosevelt was a "complex figure").

41 BEDERMAN, *supra* note 2, at 170.
42 *Id.* at 171.
43 EDMUND MORRIS, THE RISE OF THEODORE ROOSEVELT 222–23, 281 (1979) (quoting interview in *New York Tribune*, July 28, 1884).
44 THEODORE ROOSEVELT, RANCH LIFE AND THE HUNTING TRAIL 7 (New York: Winchester Press, 1969).
45 MORRIS, *supra* note 43, at 349–53.
46 THEODORE ROOSEVELT, THE WINNING OF THE WEST (4 vols.) (1889–96).
47 MORRIS, *supra* note 43, at 614–61.
48 *Id.* at 665.
49 THEODORE ROOSEVELT, AN AUTOBIOGRAPHY, *The Vigor of Life* 52 (1985) (1913).
50 CHARLES DARWIN, ON THE ORIGIN OF SPECIES (1859).
51 *See, e.g.*, Shaena Montanari, *VP-Elect Mike Pence Does Not Accept Evolution: Here's Why That Matters*, FORBES (Nov. 10, 2016). The "Scopes Monkey Trial" was a U.S. legal case (1925) in which a high school teacher (Scopes) was accused of violating Tennessee's Butler Act, which prohibited the teaching of evolution in public schools.
52 *See* FRIEDRICH NIETZSCHE, THE GAY SCIENCE (1882); THUS SPOKE ZARATHUSTRA (1883).
53 *See* WILLIAM JAMES, PRAGMATISM: A NEW NAME FOR SOME OLD WAYS OF THINKING (1907).
54 SØREN KIERKEGAARD, THE CONCEPT OF DREAD (Princeton, trans. Walter Lowrie 1957) (1844).
55 *Id.* at 140.
56 BECKER, *supra* note 1, at 91.
57 ARTHUR SCHOPENHAUER, THE WORLD AS WILL AND IDEA, III, 249 (Routledge, 1964).
58 WILLIAM JAMES, THE VARIETIES OF RELIGIOUS EXPERIENCE (1902).
59 OTTO RANK, BEYOND PSYCHOLOGY 273–74 (Dover books, 1958) (1941); *see, e.g.*, OTTO RANK, ART AND ARTIST (1932).
60 BECKER, *supra* note 1, at 175.
61 Jennifer Radden, *Aristotle: Brilliance and Melancholy*, *in* THE NATURE OF MELANCHOLY: FROM ARISTOTLE TO KRISTEVA (2002).
62 OTTO RANK, WILL THERAPY AND TRUTH AND REALITY 251–52 (Knopf, 1945) (1936).
63 *Id.*
64 BECKER, *supra* note 1, at 178.
65 *See* RANK, WILL THERAPY, *supra* note 62, at 251–52 ("To be able to live one needs illusions … [including] a secure sense of one's active powers …. The more a man can take reality as truth, appearance as essence, the sounder, the better adjusted, the happier will he be ….").
66 *Id.* at 146–47.
67 *See* Eva Jonas, Andy Martens, Daniela Niesta Kayser, Immo Fritsche, Daniel Sullivan, & Jeff Greenberg, *Focus theory of normative conduct and terror-management theory: the interactive impact of mortality salience and norm salience on social judgment*, 95.6 JOURNAL OF PERSONALITY AND SOCIAL PSYCHOLOGY 1239–51 (2008) (suggesting that the effect of "mortality salience" on people's social judgments depends on the salience of norms).
68 *See* Jon Maskaly & Christopher M. Donner, *A Theoretical Integration of Social Learning Theory with Terror Management Theory: Towards an Explanation of Police Shootings of Unarmed Suspects*, 40.2 AMERICAN JOURNAL OF CRIMINAL JUSTICE 205–24 (2015) (discussing the "'us versus them' phenomenon, in which law

enforcement officers are seen as inherently good while the remainder of society is seen as potentially dangerous").

69 See police trainer Dave Grossman in the documentary, DO NOT RESIST (Craig Atkinson, 2016).
70 *See, e.g.*, the Stony Brook University *Center for the Study of Men and Masculinities*.
71 HARVEY C. MANSFIELD, MANLINESS (2006).
72 *Id.* at x, 11.
73 *Id.* at 16.
74 *Id.*
75 *Id.* at 17.
76 *Id.* at 20.
77 *Id.* at 18.
78 *Id.* at 26.
79 *Id.* at 49.
80 *Id.* at 58.
81 *Id.* at 65.
82 Martha Nussbaum, *Man Overboard*, THE NEW REPUBLIC (June 22, 2006). Nussbaum notes that Mansfield's formulation of manliness as "confidence in the face of risk" is contradicted by other formulations that his book proposes.
83 *Id.*
84 *Id.*
85 *Id. The Altruistic Personality* is a study of rescuers of Jews during the Holocaust. SAMUEL P. OLINER & PEARL M. OLINERI, THE ALTRUISTIC PERSONALITY: RESCUERS OF JEWS IN NAZI EUROPE (1988).
86 DANIEL BOYARIN, UNHEROIC CONDUCT (1997).
87 SIGMUND FREUD, THE INTERPRETATION OF DREAMS 197 (1900) (reprint).
88 *Id.*
89 *Id.* at 143–44.
90 *Id.* at 78.
91 *Id.* at 127.
92 Tom Junod, *Can you say ... Hero?* ESQUIRE (Nov. 1998). I am grateful to Phyllis Hunt for sending me this article on December 9, 2019.
93 *Id.*
94 To be clear, then, these sorts of social skills may be wielded by the police deceptively, which I will consider (in the context of "procedural justice") in chapter 4. At a minimum, it is of course vital that police deception is consistent with rule of law principles and one's rights.
95 Tom Jackman, *New Orleans police pioneer new way to stop misconduct, remove 'blue wall of silence'*, WASH. POST (June 24, 2019).
96 *See* AMERICAN FILM INSTITUTE, https://www.afi.com/afis-100-years-100-heroes-villians/
97 *Id.*
98 MANSFIELD, *supra* note 71, at 76.
99 *Id.* at 225.
100 *Id.* Despite the necessity of the "manly spirit" in the policing profession, Mansfield concludes that "our gender-neutral society needs to readopt the distinction between public and private .... In public it should be gender-neutral, in private not. In public it should not permit sex stereotypes to operate; in private it should admit that they are true." *Id.* at 241.
101 KATE MANNE, ENTITLED—HOW MALE PRIVILEGE HURTS WOMEN, chapter 8 (2020).
102 *Id.* at 140.

103 *Id.* at 139.
104 NBC *Today* (May 30, 2019), https://www.today.com/video/former-female-fbi-trainees-open-up-about-gender-discrimination-lawsuit-60554821952
105 *Id.*
106 DO NOT RESIST, *supra* note 69.

Chapter 2

Warriors

War and Police

The government response to protests against police brutality inched closer to what might be described as a martial response during the final months of the Trump administration, including through the use of

> military helicopters and military police to help law enforcement personnel clear a path through unthreatening Black Lives Matter and kindred protesters so that [the President] could walk from the White House across Lafayette Square for a photo op with a Bible at a church [flanked by military officials].[1]

The President proclaimed himself "your president of law and order" just before the event.[2] This might seem like mere theatrics, but the episode occurred in conjunction with the expansion of the U.S. Department of Homeland Security's (DHS) federal intelligence collection and law enforcement power relating to protests against police brutality. The DHS was created as part of a national strategy to secure the United States from terrorism following the September 11 attacks. However, following protests against police violence in 2020, DHS authorized federal agents to engage in domestic surveillance and intelligence collection to protect statues and monuments from damage and vandalism.[3] As legal scholars noted, this was alarming because the authorization

> uses the cover of minor property damage, whether to federal property or otherwise, to justify intelligence gathering against ordinary Americans—most of whom have nothing to do with the underlying property damage, and many of whom are engaged in the most American of activities: peacefully protesting their government.[4]

Nearly two dozen people were arrested by federal agents (but not charged) during demonstrations against police brutality in Portland from July to

August 2020. A typical account of the arrests: "An unmarked van pulled in front of [the arrestee]. Doors slid open. Heavily armed men in camouflage tactical gear surrounded [the arrestee] and took him into custody."[5] These trends suggest a blurring of the lines between military operations, law enforcement operations, and (domestic) intelligence operations.

This sort of line-blurring is especially alarming because the lines demarcate fundamental commitments regarding legal, political, and philosophical principles of governance. In the United States, police power is derived from the Tenth Amendment to the U.S. Constitution, which gives states the rights and powers "not delegated to the United States."[6] Accordingly, states have the power to establish and enforce laws protecting the welfare, safety, and health of the public. There is overlap in the context of federal law enforcement investigations, but the *domestic* use of the military is strictly limited by legislation such as the Posse Comitatus Act of 1878 and the Insurrection Act of 1807.[7] A closely related issue—the subject of this chapter—is the extent to which these boundaries have been circumvented through the warriorization of policing. In other words, the practical distinction between the police and the military has eroded. This phenomenon continues to gain traction given the support of militarization from within policing.

For example, the mayor of Minneapolis banned police "warrior" training after a series of fatal shootings by the police in 2019.[8] This did not go over well with police leaders. The Minneapolis Police Union openly defied the mayor, announcing that it was "partnering with a national police organization to offer free 'warrior-style' training for any officer who wants it."[9] The mayor argued that the popular warrior training was "fear-based" and "violate[s] the values at the very heart of community policing."[10] The police union president defended the training—valued at $55,000.00 per year—stating: "It's not about killing, it's about surviving."[11] The disagreement was not only about the rights and obligations of officers, but the very nature of the police role itself.

This episode illustrates how the warrior mythos has by now become ubiquitous within local, state, and federal law enforcement agencies.[12] What does it mean to say that the police are warriors? Perhaps we should first ask how we got from heroes to warriors. Theodore Roosevelt's tenure as New York's Police Commissioner was a concrete example of the early emphasis on heroism in policing—not to mention a case study in some of the prominent psychological and philosophical theories of the era. The warrior mythos is deeply connected to the idea of transcending mortality through eternal heroism, though the warrior mythos goes much further than that. Recent scholars have cited Roosevelt approvingly in this regard, suggesting that his words serve as the ideal description of the police's warrior path:

> The credit belongs to the man who is actually in the *arena*; whose face is marred by dust and sweat and *blood*; who strives *valiantly*; who errs

and comes short again and again; who knows the great *enthusiasms*, the great *devotions*, and spends himself in a *worthy cause*; who, at the best, knows in the end the triumph of *high achievement* and who, at worst, fails while *daring* greatly, so that *their place* will never be with those cold and timid *souls* who know neither victor or defeat.[13]

The sentiment of this excerpt is not unlike that of one of the *Rocky* films, with its emphasis on heroically (and bloodily) overcoming odds and obstacles in the arena—daringly devoting oneself to a worthy cause that secures one's place in history. Of course, this is all innocent enough in principle, and I recall that this very quote by Roosevelt was on the desk of a senior agent who became a trusted mentor and friend when I was a young FBI Agent. But it is troubling that Roosevelt's words might be viewed as an idealized description of the police role: a hero on the warrior's path. It is one thing to get lost in a work of fiction—or ponder the words of a "manly" president—but it is quite another to send officers into the streets with the understanding that they are individual warriors embarking on a bloody, transcendental, mission of good versus evil.

The advent of the police warrior mythos was a long time coming. It evolved in conjunction with decades of corruption, semi-reform, racism, socioeconomic disparity, and general cultural upheaval—especially the turmoil of the 1960s—leaving police feeling overwhelmed and ill-equipped. The causes of this turmoil are of course deeply complex and go beyond the scope of this book; systematic economic and ethnic bias and inequality are too much to tackle here. However, it is also clear that the warrior mindset was bolstered by decades of "law and order" policies that were "tough on crime" at the expense of other values and strategies such as legitimacy and community policing. After Lyndon B. Johnson's "war" on crime, President Reagan officially declared a "war" on drugs in 1982.[14] To be sure, the "tough on crime" mentality has spanned the political spectrum. Ten years after Reagan's war on drugs, presidential candidate Clinton stated: "I can be nicked a lot, but no one can say I'm soft on crime."[15] President Clinton subsequently supported the war on drugs and a federal "three strikes and you're out" law, with the Justice Policy Institute noting that his "policies resulted in the largest increases in federal and state prison inmates of any president in American history."[16] This was followed by policing's institutional redesign in the context of the "war" on terrorism after September 11, 2001. On that day, I was walking into the University of Tennessee College of Law during my first semester of law school. Everyone was of course glued to the televisions in the law school's common area, and I recall hearing a student say that we should "nuke 'em." It didn't matter who we fought; the student simply wanted a war, and he got one. Along with the military, law enforcement at every level was reoriented to fight another war within our borders.

Where do things stand today? The recent "First Step Act of 2018" is the most significant federal criminal justice reform in decades. Still, it is a modest first step. The law eases the sentences of some inmates in federal prison, but it is unlikely to affect the problem of mass incarceration significantly because it does not address the many inmates incarcerated in state and local facilities. Nor does the law address problems within policing. Indeed, the warrior identity continues to evolve at a troubling speed, facilitating a utilitarian security state by blurring the distinction between police officer and solider. This distinction is deeply important to liberal policing and its constraints upon coercion, violence, and force. One of the central problems, then, is the police's focus upon a warrior identity, rather than the positional moral requirements of law enforcement officers in a liberal polity. As we will see, the police's unique *positional* requirements work in tandem with *general* moral requirements owed to all persons.

To pull together these different threads, the chapter examines how the police response to societal and crime problems is focused upon two related approaches: (1) Utilitarian approaches to crime control and reduction in which the end justifies the (warrior's) means; and (2) officer individuation through a warrior mythos, rather than an emphasis on collectivity. Given a singled-minded focus upon the heroic battle over evil, the police have embraced a warrior ethos in part because they view the result of such an ethos—enforcing the law and stopping crime—as justifying the illiberal and undemocratic means by which that result is achieved. In other words, the idea is that "warring" with the community is justified if it stifles crime and criminals. As we will see in chapter 3, there has been an attempt to address the warrior problem by shifting to a guardian mythos. However, such a shift simply entrenches the second problem by reinforcing officer individuation at the expense of collectivity. The upshot is that both the warrior mythos and the guardian mythos breed a culture in which crime reduction is privileged over other fundamental values—such as legitimacy, security of person within the community, and human dignity—topics to which we will turn in chapter 4.

Consequential Policing

One of the undiagnosed problems of contemporary policing is the convergence of the warrior mythos with a crude form of consequentialism that becomes manifest through militarism. As the name implies, consequentialism is simply the idea that normative properties (for example, properties regarding what we should do) depend only on consequences. The standard example of consequentialism is utilitarianism, which includes classic proponents such as Jeremy Bentham, John Stuart Mill, and Henry Sidgwick.[17] The views of classic utilitarianism might be described as hedonistic. This variant of consequentialism claims that an act is morally right if and only if that act maximizes the good. It is hedonistic given the claim that pleasure is the only intrinsic good and that pain is the only intrinsic bad. Of course, policing has not taken consequentialism to its logical conclusion—namely, that nothing is intrinsically wrong—but the warrior mythos has moved policing closer to the position that analysis of consequences is all that matters. To set the stage, consider the philosophical backdrop for this approach to policing.

Utilitarianism generally takes the view that we ought to maximize total happiness, not just our own (as in the case of ethical egoism). This is appealing for natural reasons, especially in the context of large-scale social policy issues that affect many people: When determining the right thing to do, utilitarianism simply requires us to figure out what will produce the most good or happiness. Moreover, everyone's happiness counts, and that seems appropriate when addressing large-scale public policies. But this is also a weakness—particularly in the context of policing and punishment—because the utilitarian analysis is not about what people deserve given their moral agency and human dignity. Rather, the utilitarian calculus is about what sort of policing and punishment (or lack thereof) produces the most happiness. This means that excessive policing and punishment—or policing and punishing people differently, even though they commit the same crimes—are not only on the table but justified under a general utilitarian analysis.

Of course, philosophical theories of utilitarianism come in all shapes and sizes and need not be so crude. *Act utilitarianism* stands for the position that an act is right if and only if it produces at least as much total happiness as would any alternative act open to the actor. On the other hand, *rule utilitarianism* states that an act is right if and only if it conforms to rules that would produce as much happiness as would any other set of rules. But what about cases in which breaking (or fudging) rules would maximize happiness? It is not difficult to imagine how this worry is relevant to policing given the warrior's singled-minded focus upon enforcing the law and stopping crime in an eternal struggle against evil. If the only legitimate purpose of a system of criminal justice is to promote the general welfare, then policing and punishment are not about what people deserve; rather, they are about promoting the most happiness. So even if some law enforcement tactics oppose rights and values such as legitimacy and human dignity in some communities, such tactics would be justified under a utilitarian analysis given that the tactics promote a gain in total happiness. For example, under this sort of analysis, perhaps there is nothing wrong with occupying a neighborhood with military equipment, using SWAT teams (discussed below) indiscriminately, using discretion to strictly enforce minor offenses, and downplaying the value of legitimacy and community trust—as long as such tactics promote, say, the goal of deterring people from committing crime.

Taking a step back, we can see how a utilitarian promise to efficiently promote justice on a large scale might fall short. Consider classic critiques of utilitarianism from within political philosophy. Recall that act utilitarianism says that an act is right if it produces the most happiness; goodness is happiness, and so right acts maximize goodness. This means that a distribution of social goods—such as security and crime reduction—is just if it maximizes happiness compared with other theories. But this would seem to deliver results that are intuitively unjust. Suppose there are three neighborhoods—A, B, and C—with three crime problems. Intuitively, the police should treat the people in each neighborhood equally when addressing each neighborhood's respective crime problems. But what if neighborhood A gets one-tenth more units of pleasure—so to speak—from crime reduction than neighborhoods B and C? Perhaps this is because the residents of neighborhood A include many well-to-do families who receive tremendous pleasure from the prompt enforcement of even minor infractions, such as loitering and skateboarding in undesignated skate zones. Then perhaps the police would want to give slightly more attention (or less attention, depending upon what generates most pleasure) to neighborhood A. But then why not give all the attention (or, again, none of the attention, depending upon the criminal activity and what maximizes happiness) to neighborhood A?

There are obvious reasons why this utilitarian calculus strikes us as wrong, including negative utility. In other words, how do we respond to the sadness and discontent that will result in neighborhoods B and C (even if focusing upon neighborhood A generates the most happiness)? And what about decreasing marginal utility? For example, suppose the police continue to maximize happiness by prioritizing neighborhood A: They enforce popular laws that keep neighborhood A "clean," while using their discretion to overlook violations of less popular laws when such violations perpetuate neighborhood A's wealth and happiness. Eventually, utility will drop if the police continue to heap benefits upon neighborhood A, while neighborhoods B and C become fixed within a status quo of cyclical unhappiness. The upshot is that utilitarianism can justify all sorts of policies that strike us as straightforwardly unjust.

Things do not fare much better under rule utilitarianism, though for different reasons. Recall that rule utilitarianism asks us to first think about what the ideal rules would be in utilitarian terms, and then asks us to conform to those rules. For example, what would be the best rule in society regarding reducing crime, such that it would promote utility? Naturally, one might suggest rules that promote tactics that are effective at reducing crime. But we might also have a competing rule about the goal of reducing crime legitimately. So even if in some cases it would increase happiness and security by pursuing tactics that denigrate police legitimacy, we ought not do that because promoting legitimacy is the best rule for society. This also avoids the problems of act utilitarianism regarding not having to make every decision a moral decision. For instance, we do not need rules about whether the police should wear blue or grey uniforms, only rules about the most important things. However, there is a big problem with rule utilitarianism: Why would a utilitarian commit to it? It simply does not maximize happiness in many cases, and thus it is highly susceptible to abuse. An apt example might be when the police can easily maximize happiness through crime reduction by pursuing policies that denigrate legitimacy and rights with respect to some persons and communities.

This is roughly the objection of prominent political philosophers over the last half century. Liberal egalitarians such as John Rawls argue that utilitarianism does not take seriously the distinction among persons—the person as an individual.[18] If utilitarianism is based upon reasoning such that we try to maximize happiness overall, that means that we will sometimes have to set aside the interests of some in favor of the interests of others. This is problematic because persons are individuals and our legal and political traditions view each person (theoretically) as inviolable in terms of justice. In one sense, this tradition (roughly what one might call the liberal tradition) suggests that each person—individually—should be considered with respect to the requirements of justice. This general idea has a prominent association with social contract theory and Enlightenment philosophers such as John Locke, Jean-Jacques Rousseau, and Immanuel Kant. Social contract theory is steeped in the assumption that justice is based upon what free and rational people would accept in an initial situation of equality. In contemporary terms, this view is often associated with Rawls's theory of *justice as fairness*.

Rawls argues that people would—hypothetically, such as in an imaginary (and highly artificial) state of nature—reject utilitarianism.[19] This is because people who view themselves as equal would not adopt principles of justice based upon a view that could disadvantage some persons for the benefit of others (as in the case of utilitarianism, which could sacrifice the rights of some for the happiness of others). Rawls presents a complex argument, but it boils down to the view that people would (from an initial, hypothetical position of fairness) begin by adopting a principle of justice that promotes equality in the assignment of rights and duties. In other words, each *individual* person would have an equal right to society's basic scheme of liberties, which would be compatible with everyone having the same liberties.

Rawls's theory is rooted in Kant's emphasis on the value, worth, and dignity of each individual—which requires us to treat others always as an end in themselves, never just as a means to an end (a law enforcement end, for example). If we accept this sort of conception of persons—and if we have doubts about the rationality of a police role that disproportionately emphasizes utilitarianism—then ought we to rethink our conception of the police role? If so, we might begin by asking whether the police role should be based upon a broader, non-utilitarian notion of justice. Indeed, institutional documents such as the Bill of Rights are clearly anti-majoritarian and anti-utilitarian, which lends support for more non-utilitarian policies in policing administration. Nevertheless, one of the central conceptions of the police role is now based upon the convergence of utilitarianism and police militarization—a convergence leading to the warrior ethos.

Police Militarization

As we saw in the last chapter, the seeds of the police warrior mythos were sown long ago, during the very beginnings of police professionalization. This was an era in which existential angst was appropriated and channeled, resulting in the idea that eternal heroism is a central basis for the conception of the police role. Those who engaged in daring acts of individual valor were duly recognized, promoted, and emulated. Given this gradual evolution of policing from within a heroic ethos, it is impossible to pin down a single time and place at which the warrior mindset took hold. Still, some have pointed to the police's response to the turmoil and riots of the 1960s, especially with respect to new training, tactics, and equipment used to quell violence stemming from political unrest.[20] Although only a piece of the story, there is good reason to view the police's response to this tumultuous decade as a moment of crystallization for the warrior mythos. Radley Balko and other commentators have embraced this notion, suggesting that the modern police warrior was born in the Los Angeles Police Department (LAPD) following the Watts neighborhood riots of 1965. The riots were precipitated by what seemed like a routine traffic stop and arrest, though it was in fact "the culmination of years of animosity between black Angelenos and the LAPD administration ...."[21] The riots lasted six days, during which police faced overwhelming violence in the form of fires, fire bombs, and sniper fire—ultimately resulting in thirty-four deaths and millions of dollars in damage. The police relied upon the U.S. military to restore order, dispatching thousands of California National Guard troops to help stop the violence and secure the streets.[22]

Whatever the root causes—and there were many—of the police–community tension that led to riots, the police were not equipped to restore order without military assistance. LAPD Inspector Daryl Gates—who played a central role in the police's response to the riots—put it this way: "We had no idea how to deal with this .... It was random chaos, in small disparate patches. We did not know how to handle guerrilla warfare."[23] Gates thus sought guidance from the military—which at the time was engaged with guerrilla warfare in Vietnam—guidance that resulted in what Balko describes as:

> A phenomenon that over the course of ... [Gates's] career would reach virtually every city in America. It would change the face, the mind-set, and the culture of US policing from the late 1960s on, through today,

and probably into the foreseeable future. He started America's first SWAT team.[24]

SWAT stands for "Special Weapons and Tactics," and such weapons and tactics were considered a necessary response given the violence of the Watts riot and similar events. The central problem—well-documented by Balko and others—is that the police's use of SWAT teams became commonplace, spreading far beyond the high-risk situations for which they were created. Indeed, SWAT usage increased from 3,000 deployments annually in the early 1980s to 40,000 deployments annually by 2001. Balko provides this example: "the city of Minneapolis, Minnesota, deployed its SWAT team on no-knock warrants 35 times in 1987. By 1996, the same unit had been deployed for drug raids more than 700 times that year alone."[25]

But police militarization did not stop at SWAT teams. It rather expanded within policing across the board. I often teach criminal law to undergraduates, and one of the cases I use when covering "attempt crimes" is the North Hollywood, California, bank robbery of 1997. The bank robbers engaged in a lengthy shootout with police following the robbery, which was prolonged because the criminals' gear included automatic rifles and body armor—far superior than the police's gear. During a traffic stop prior to the bank robbery and shootout, some of the criminals' gear had been confiscated and then returned by police because there was insufficient evidence to pursue an attempted bank robbery charge before the robbery was committed (hence the inclusion of this case under attempt crimes). Unfortunately, the criminals subsequently claimed their gear and eventually used it to commit the North Hollywood robbery.[26] The robbery and shootout—coupled with the growing prominence of active shooter incidents—greatly contributed to the trend of equipping (non-SWAT) officers with military-grade weapons and equipment. Anecdotally, in addition to the standard Glock.40 (model 22) handgun that I was issued as an FBI Special Agent, I was also given a shotgun and an M4 carbine—the latter being an assault rifle used by U.S. military infantry. I was not on the FBI's SWAT team and I did not personally consider the M4 to be a practical tool (given the risk of collateral damage from M4 rifle rounds in most law enforcement situations, as well as the relative rarity of situations in which M4 rounds would be useful), and yet the assault rifle became a standard part of my equipment given the statistical possibility that I would find myself in a North Hollywood type of shootout.

The militarization of policing is not limited to firearms. As I write this sentence in February 2020, here are two recent newspaper headlines: "Riot police in armored vehicle roust homeless mothers from illegally occupied Oakland house" (*The Washington Post*, January 15, 2020) and "New London acquires war-ready armored vehicle" (*The Day* (Connecticut), February 3, 2020). The first story reports:

A BearCat armored vehicle rolled down the still-sleepy residential street. Officers broke through the reinforced front door with a battering ram and sent a small, camera-equipped robot into the home to check for any potential threats .... [D]eputies aimed to arrest a small coalition of homeless parents who were trying to live inside the long-uninhabited home without paying rent.[27]

The second story describes how New London Police Department acquired armored vehicles—including a "Cougar" truck and high-water rescue trucks—from the military through the federal government's surplus vehicle program.[28] Under the 1033 Program administered by the Defense Logistics Agency's Law Enforcement Support Office, local law enforcement agencies are able to acquire military equipment such as the Cougar—which is a type of Mine-Resistant Ambush Protected (MRAP) vehicle designed to withstand improvised explosive device (IED) ambushes.[29] Legal scholar Barry Friedman describes how "equipment was distributed like Halloween candy":

> North Carolina got sixteen military helicopters and twenty-two grenade launchers; Tennessee got thirty-one MRAPs and seven grenade launchers; Florida did particularly well, garnering forty-seven MRAPs, thirty-six grenade launchers, and more than seven thousand rifles. Then there were the schools: five districts in Texas and five in California received material, including MRAPs and grenade launchers. Mississippi's Hinds Community College and The University of Central Florida each got grenade launchers; Hinds got two M16s as well.[30]

These weapons and vehicles—coupled with the dark-colored, tactical uniforms, including helmets, goggles, and body armor—can give communities the impression that they are being occupied by a formidable, military force. For example, after the unrest that followed Michael Brown's death in 2014, American columnist Jamelle Bouie described how "[t]he most striking photos from Ferguson, MO aren't of Saturday's demonstrations or Sunday night's riots; they're of the police."[31] It is thus true that the concern over such gear is often simply a matter of *appearance* and *community perception*, but that is not an irrelevant concern (even though the gear and tactics are sometimes vital given the danger of high-risk law enforcement operations). Accordingly, the real problem is the *unnecessary* use—use as a matter of course—of military vehicles and equipment inasmuch as such use elicits fear and distrust within communities. I personally have never lived in a neighborhood in which it is common to see military vehicles driving down the street carrying police officers dressed in tactical gear, but I can imagine how it would feel to live in such a community.

This militarization of the police has coincided with an era in which courts have bolstered the police's warrior ethos. Consider one recent example. In *Utah v. Strieff*, the U.S. Supreme Court limited the scope of the Fourth Amendment's exclusionary rule—the legal rule preventing evidence collected in violation of one's constitutional rights from being used in a court of law.[32] In *Strieff*, Utah police began surveilling a suspected drug house and observed Edward Strieff leaving the house. Upon stopping and detaining Strieff on the street, officers discovered that Strieff had an outstanding warrant for a traffic violation. The officers thus conducted a search incident to his arrest and found drug paraphernalia on Strieff's person. Even though the officers lacked "reasonable suspicion" to detain Strieff (making the detention unlawful),[33] the Supreme Court ruled that the drug evidence seized during the detention was admissible because "the discovery of a valid arrest warrant was a sufficient intervening event to break the causal chain between the unlawful stop and the discovery of drug-related evidence on Strieff's person."[34]

This rationale implies that the police will not abuse their authority by unlawfully stopping civilians with the goal of checking for outstanding warrants and—if a warrant exists—securing admissible evidence from the arrest. More broadly, the rationale is consistent with the view that the police are entitled to the benefit of the doubt given the value of crime reduction—an end that justifies the means, in other words.[35] In a similar way, the Court's well-known description of use-of-force decisions illuminates the perception that policing is inherently dangerous and that legal handwringing increases the danger: "police officers are often forced to make split-second judgements … in circumstances which are tense, uncertain, and rapidly evolving."[36] The upshot is implicit judicial support of the view that policing is fundamentally a profession in which warriors engage in dangerous missions to stop crime—missions entitling the police to vast leeway and discretion in their tactics.

The Warrior Ideal

One surprising view on these issues is that the police warrior "ideal" is not the problem, but rather that the ideal has been corrupted.[37] There are significant flaws with this view that tend to distract from the problems that are inherent in the warrior mythos. We should begin by acknowledging the difficulty of getting to the heart of the warrior ideal. W.B. Gallie's discussion of "essentially contested concepts" helps illuminate the difficulty. The basic idea is that fundamental disagreement exists regarding some concepts in political philosophy (such as "democracy") that are "essentially contested" because they are "not resolvable by argument of any kind," yet still sustainable by "perfectly respectable arguments and evidence."[38] There is something similar going on in disputes about the "warrior" concept in policing. The police have a variety of responsibilities—from the use of (deadly) force to simple acts of communication with members of the community. The diverse police functions allow one to present a variety of reasonable (though contestable) evidence regarding various conceptions of the police role—including warrior conceptions. One way to address disputes is to distinguish "concepts" from "conceptions." For example, Ronald Dworkin claims that "*concepts* are abstract moral ideals while *conceptions* are particular instantiations of those ideals."[39] In other words, when one appeals to the warrior concept, one appeals to what it means to be a warrior without regard to one's special view on the matter. But when one sets forth a particular warrior conception, one's special meaning of warrior is the crux of the issue. Accordingly, when we appeal to the warrior concept we pose a moral question about policing, and when we set forth a particular warrior conception we try to answer a moral question.[40]

The goal, then, is characterizing the warrior concept accurately. This will help determine the extent to which the concept is consistent with other values relevant to policing. An accurate characterization of the underlying warrior concept will also help determine the extent to which particular warrior conceptions are reasonable. Admittedly, there is no perfect method for explicating the warrior concept, though it is of course desirable to avoid ad hoc approaches. We thus need to consider the various ways that a set of characteristics associated with a particular warrior conception "C" might serve as the foundation for the warrior concept "W". There are at least four ways to pursue this task:

i as a matter of history and genealogy, [W] was generated out of [C];
ii [C] is the source of [W], in the way that the application of one legal proposition may be the source of the validity of another;
iii [W] can be derived logically from [C], either deductively or with the help of empirical premises; or
iv [C] throws some indispensable light on [W] or helps in the interpretation of [W].[41]

In short, these are possible methods for analyzing various warrior conceptions—methods that help show the moral importance of related values and how they might serve as a foundation (or at least as a more basic ground) for the warrior ideal. Such an analysis allows one to determine which rights, duties, and values are at bottom implied by the warrior concept, resulting in a reasonable account of the warrior ideal. The goal, then, is to identify various rights, duties, and values for which the warrior ideal serves as a unifying rationale—thereby establishing a fixed point that constrains the various warrior conceptions.

I should reiterate that many people—both officers and academics—view components of warrior policing positively. For example, legal scholar and former police officer Seth Stoughton has written thoughtfully on the topic, suggesting that "[t]he Warrior principles are admirable, but in practice, policing all too often fails to live up to those ideals." This is because, "[d]espite the best of intentions, the Warrior concept promotes an adversarial style of policing that estranges the public and contributes to unnecessary conflict and violence."[42] But as an initial matter, it is difficult to see how we are justified in giving even *idealized* warrior principles the benefit of the doubt here. Why think that idealized warrior principles are "admirable" *in the context of policing*? I agree that "[u]nder the Warrior worldview, police legitimacy is found in criminal law, the unique ability of officers to enforce it ...," and that "public support is not viewed as an essential part of policing ...."[43] But this simply raises the distinction between the *special (or positional) requirements* of the warrior on the one hand and the police officer on the other hand. The logical place to find common ground between police and warriors is in their *general moral requirements*—a different matter altogether.

Special moral requirements are grounded in (or arise within) those special relationships that we have (or freely make) with particular groups.[44] This would include promissory or contractual obligations, which are voluntary in nature—such as when I create a moral obligation by promising to pick up my neighbor at the airport. Special moral requirements also include associative obligations, which are often non-voluntary in nature—such as any moral obligations I have to my mother, brother, children, and friends given my special association with them. Positional duties are a subset of special moral requirements. If, say, a police officer fails to do her duty as police officer (or a soldier fails to do her duty at war), then she is morally blameworthy. This is because she voluntarily entered her position and undertook—in full knowledge of the details of the situation—the duties of that position.

Special moral requirements may be contrasted with general moral requirements, which are non-voluntary and bind us simply in virtue of natural duties to others regarding their personhood and moral equality (irrespective of any special roles or relationships entered).[45] There could be a variety of theories about what grounds general moral requirements. This might include human dignity (a person's priceless worth, or high-ranking, equal, social status), or natural rights (which are typically said to be natural because they exist in a pre-institutional state of nature based upon, say, the human capacity for reason). Such general moral requirements might include human rights, which could be grounded in those natural rights that enable persons to live with dignity.

Of course, there may be overlap between general and special moral requirements, as when the police have a general moral requirement not to brutalize persons—which is also prohibited by their special, positional duty as police. Or, in the case of soldiers at war, we would say that the soldiers have a special moral requirement not to direct acts of war against non-combatants (innocent civilians) or to subject enemy combatants to acts such as mass rape. And such positional requirements of conducting war (*jus in bello*) overlap with a soldier's general moral requirements with respect to all persons (for example, prohibitions against wrongs described as *mala in se*—wrong in itself—independent of institutional prohibitions). The point is that the police very likely have a lot in common with warriors and soldiers given our general moral requirements. On the other hand, it is much less clear that they share the same special (positional) moral requirements. With these preliminary matters in mind, let us now consider the values and principles that are said to illuminate the warrior ideal—as well as special (positional) and general moral requirements that are relevant to the police and warriors.

First, consider Stoughton's account of "the many positive attributes associated with the Warrior concept … [which include] *honor, duty, resolve, and a willingness to engage in righteous violence.*"[46] With respect to honor, the idea is that "[w]arriors serve others, not themselves, and do so only for honorable ends. Warriors pursue justice—the triumph of right over wrong—and they seek to defend the weak from those who would take advantage of them."[47] As a matter of history and genealogy, it seems wrong to describe the warrior concept as being generated out of such conceptions of honor. Consider the warrior culture of the Huns, whose name historian Denis Sinor describes as having become "synonymous with that of cruel, destructive invaders."[48] The reputation of Hun warriors as cruel and merciless seems to have a strong historical basis, as when Sinor quotes fourth-century St. Jerome:

> [The Huns] filled the whole earth with slaughter and panic alike as they flitted hither and thither on their swift horses … and they took pity neither upon religion nor rank nor age nor wailing childhood. Those who had just begun to live were compelled to die and, in ignorance of their plight, would smile amid the drawn sword of the enemy.[49]

Although we could seek to distinguish "good" warriors from "bad" ones, the warrior concept is the wrong paradigm given the vastly different positional requirements between warriors and police. Historian Michael Kulikowski's *The Tragedy of Empire* shows how the fall of the Roman Empire was exacerbated by rivalrous Roman generals who depended upon Hun and Goth warriors to fuel their destructive conquests.[50] The warrior culture was not driven by honor or serving others (or the Roman state), but rather the warriors' loyalty was simply to the Roman generals who were paying them.[51] More generally, one could of course add to this the voluminous accounts of warrior cultures from around the world, such as the use of fear and terror that was vital to warriors of the thirteenth-century Mongol Empire or the brutality of early Celtic warriors and invaders—not to mention the contemporary tactics used systematically by American soldiers, including the abuse, humiliation, torture, and execution of prisoners of war during the conflicts in Iraq and Afghanistan (such as at the Abu Ghraib prison) in the 2000s.[52]

Things do not improve for the police warrior conception from here. Consider the suggestion that the code or standard of honor that constrains warriors is "created not by the law ... but by the norms of the Warrior brotherhood itself."[53] This is troubling for the obvious reason that the warrior code—thus conceived—is not governed by the rule of law, but rather a "brotherhood."[54] With respect to the rule of law, it is of course important to note that discretion is necessary in policing. To use a simple example again, it is impossible for the police to enforce violations of speed limit laws against all motorists. Discretion is thus a necessary aspect of policing, but it is limited by other rule of law principles. For instance, police discretion must not pervert the law, such as when the police have undue discretion to enforce the law by breaking the law. In the same way that the President of the United States has limits in his discretion to deviate from the law in times of national emergency, the police have limits in using their law-breaking discretion to enforce the law.[55] This would include, say, the FBI's use of "otherwise illegal activity," which permits agents to break the law (or have informants break the law) when such law-breaking would benefit an investigation.

The limits of discretion—limits steeped in the rule of law—include the special (positional) moral requirements one accepts when one becomes a law enforcement officer. These requirements include the professional prerogative power to use discretion within the limits of one's position (not under "color of law," or the pretense of law), as well as within the broader limits of policy and law that rest upon a society's political and moral norms. The limits and constraints placed upon police—related to honor or not—have no legitimate basis within a warrior "brotherhood." Quite the contrary: It is often the "brotherhood" mentality that hides dishonorable acts of those within the brotherhood. Recall the phenomenon known as the "blue wall of silence," which is the informal code among some police officers not to report on a colleague's misconduct—instead claiming not to have seen anything or pleading ignorance of another officer's wrongdoing. The broader point is that it is far from clear that the conception of "honor" described earlier is a source of the warrior concept, nor is it clear that the warrior concept may be derived logically from such a notion of honor. The upshot is that the proposed notion of honor does not shed light on the warrior concept, but rather suggests—if anything—that the warrior ideal is inconsistent with both special (positional) and general moral requirements that are relevant to policing.

The proposed conception of *duty* does not fare much better in explicating the warrior concept and its relation to policing. For instance, it is said the warrior's honorable mission "has no end," but rather warriors "must dedicate themselves to a cause, a calling, that they will never see completed."[56] To emphasize this point about duty, Stoughton invokes eighteenth-century samurai, Yamamoto Tsunetomo: "[T]he way of the warrior is death."[57] The police do sometimes die tragically in the line of duty. And perhaps invoking a samurai is mostly rhetorical. On the other hand, implying that *death is the way of the police (warrior)* is indicative of the underlying police identity crisis introduced in chapter 1. There are many ways to respond to one's existential reality, including the special dangers associated with policing. However, one's response becomes disordered and disproportionate when it unjustifiably affects one's general and special (positional) moral requirements owed to others. The problem is exacerbated in policing inasmuch as law enforcement officers are taught to view their role—which includes the statistical possibility of death—as one of heroic warriors in an eternal battle of good versus evil. This disproportionate response to the police role is more akin to a desire to affirm and make sense of one's life on an existential level—not an acceptance of the positional moral obligations of one's profession. In short, conceiving of duty as a response to the existential reality of policing—a defense against death—is a form of heroic individuation that obscures (not illuminates) the police role. Perhaps this conception of duty says something about the warrior ideal generally. However, it does not logically follow—given competing values such as legitimacy, security of person, and human dignity, discussed more in chapter 4—that the police role is grounded in such a conception of duty.

Turning to the idea of *resolve*, warriors are said to have the "mental tenacity to survive life-threatening situations and overwhelming odds," as well as "the resolve to ... enforc[e] laws they personally oppose and protect [] individuals whom they personally despise."[58] Consider the first facet of warrior resolve: mental tenacity to survive life-threatening situations and overwhelming odds. Without downplaying the difficulty and danger of policing, it is helpful to point out that death in the line of duty is a rarity. It has been reported that there are more than 900,000 sworn law enforcement officers in the United States, with an average of 158 deaths in the line of duty per year over the last ten years.[59] According to data collected by FBI, "89 law enforcement officers were killed in line-of-duty incidents in 2019. Of these, 48 officers died as a result of felonious acts, and 41 officers died in accidents."[60] It has thus been observed that:

> [S]tatistically, law enforcement does not make the list of the ten most dangerous jobs in America. Commercial fishing is worse, as are roofing and construction. Studies of patrol officers' service calls have shown that less than five per cent are related to violent crimes.[61]

To be sure, even one death is a death too many—and all deaths are heart-wrenchingly tragic—but it is important to be clear that policing in communities is different from warring on battlefields.

It is unusual for law enforcement to face overwhelming odds such as the North Hollywood bank robbery noted above, or the Miami bank and armored car robbery noted in chapter 1. Resources of course vary widely among agencies, with the FBI (in my experience) bordering on overkill in terms of the resources and personnel used in any operational activity. But more generally, the statistics regarding pervasive police militarization and SWAT use undermine the implication that police routinely face operational situations involving overwhelming odds. All of that said, mental tenacity is certainly a valuable attribute in most any profession, especially professions that involve dangerous risks and odds such as policing. The point is rather the limits of forcing a merger between the police role and the warrior concept—even if idealized. There are of course areas of overlap, but the analysis so far indicates that many presumed facets of the warrior concept are either ad hoc or unrelated to policing conceptually and logically.

Now consider the second facet of warrior resolve: warriors enforce laws they personally oppose and protect individuals they personally despise. This is commendable, though unfortunately ad hoc absent an account—historical, logical, or otherwise—that such a conception of *resolve* is a ground for the warrior concept. It is unclear how the warrior ideal may be derived in part from the principle of putting aside personal bias in the protection of laws and people. Accordingly, this sort of resolve—even if justified—does little to aid our understanding of the warrior concept. On the contrary, it suggests that the warrior ethos has little to do with the special, positional moral requirements of policing—requirements such as stopping and preventing crime in accordance with the rule of law. Enforcing laws and protecting people without bias is a vital part of the police role. This is because values such as legitimacy, the rule of law, and the limits of discretion, are fundamental to justice. So rather than forcing these values into an idiosyncratic warrior conception—and then linking that conception with the police role—it makes sense to simply frame the police role in terms of the collective pursuit of justice in society. That will be done in chapter 4, but let us conclude this section by examining the idea that the warrior ideal entails exclusivity and a "willingness to engage in righteous violence."[62]

Recall from chapter 1 the popular police warrior training employed across the country. Writer Justin Peters took—in 2020, a year that included many high-profile police killings—an online version of police trainer Dave Grossman's course, "On Combat" (available via the Grossman Academy website for $79), and described it this way: "[The training] teaches its students to fear and resent the people they serve, to willfully mistake this contempt for bravery, and to believe that heroism is conferred by the barrel of a smoking gun."[63] The book, *On Combat*, provides a foundation for the training and is likewise quite popular in law enforcement circles, especially the sheep, wolf, sheepdog, warrior metaphor.[64] I myself bought a copy after completing my training at Quantico. As many have observed, the book emphasizes "the gift of aggression" and the idea that warriors must *want* to engage in violence when called.[65] This desire to engage in "righteous violence" is deeply connected to another presumed facet of the warrior ideal: *exclusivity*. [66] In *On Combat*, the authors write that warriors are "able to survive and thrive in an environment that destroys 98 percent of the population."[67] Stoughton adds:

> The solidarity of this brotherhood ... allows the profession as a whole to associate itself with the heroic deeds of individual officers, further enhancing the appeal of membership—when officers are initiated into the Warrior brotherhood, they stand shoulder to shoulder with people who have done great things.[68]

This sentiment is emblematic of the issues raised by the heroic ethos in chapter 1, thus bringing full circle the connection between police heroes and warriors. The idea is that the warrior concept entails an exclusive *desire* to engage in the violence permitted by one's role as warrior, including because such violence associates one with the heroic warrior mythos.

The upshot is a conception of the police that is set apart from society ("us vs. them"), rather than a conception in which the police are engaged in the collective pursuit of justice within the community. The warrior's simplistic good–bad dichotomy is described by Stoughton this way:

> By adopting the Warrior concept, officers separate themselves and the darkness of their working reality from real society—they are on the fringes, in the trenches, fighting the disorder that threatens to spill over to the 'good' neighborhoods and the families worth protecting.[69]

As he and others have recognized, then, the warrior concept "discourages officers from thinking of themselves as members of the public."[70] Exclusivity thus poses a significant problem for policing. It is precisely this same problem that should dissuade us from merely shifting to a different, individuated archetype steeped in heroism, namely: the police *guardian*. We will examine the police guardian conception in the next chapter—including the status of "them" in "us vs. them." But let us now shift gears by considering how the warrior concept might become manifest in practice. This will further illuminate the extent to which the warrior concept is a poor model given the special (positional) moral requirements of the police role.

Objections and Positional Requirements

Philando Castile, a 32-year old Black man, was driving his car in a suburb of Saint Paul, Minnesota, on the evening of July 6, 2016. A police officer pulled him over for having a brake light out. Squad-car video shows the officer approaching Castile's car (which included his girlfriend and her 4-year-old) and asking for a driver's license and insurance proof.[71] Castile appears to give something to the officer through the driver's side window. Castile is then heard saying, "Sir, I have to tell you, I do have a firearm on me." Before Castile finishes that sentence, the officer has his hand on his own gun and is pulling it out of the holster. There is shouting, and the officer screams, "Don't pull it out!" before he fires seven shots into the car. Before being shot, Castile had replied, "I'm not pulling it out." Castile—an elementary school lunchroom worker—had a lawful permit to carry his handgun, which was subsequently found in his pocket on his dead body. As noted in the book's introduction, one might compare this to the police's treatment of Kyle Rittenhouse, the (white) man who carried an "assault-style" rifle past the police during the protests following the police's shooting of Jacob Blake in Kenosha, Wisconsin in 2020. Rittenhouse was in the process of leaving a scene at which he killed two people and injured another with his rifle—yet the police saw no reason to question him. One wonders whether Rittenhouse somehow did not meet the profile of the "wolf" who police are trained to battle.

The Minnesota police officer who shot and killed Castile had attended a popular police training course called "The Bulletproof Warrior." These courses instruct officers to be less hesitant to use lethal force, urging them to be willing to use it more quickly, and teaching them how to adopt the mentality of a warrior.[72] As we have seen, the historical development and content of the police warrior culture is much larger and complex than any one training course. But "the Bulletproof Warrior" example—and its connection to the officer who killed Castile—is representative of the police identity crisis that has been examined so far.

The police identity crisis introduced in chapter 1 is based in part upon the confluence of existential fear and an unjustified hero trope that draw upon antiquated notions of masculinity. The history of the police's pursuit of the heroic mythos has made a deep mark on the state of policing today. In particular, we have seen how the heroic identity—and the problems associated with that identity—have contributed to a contemporary "brotherhood" of police warriors that is inconsistent with other policing values. The problem is not that the warrior "ideal" has been corrupted. Even an idealized warrior concept does not shed light upon a justified conception of the police role given the historical, conceptual, and logical problems of the police warrior concept. In any event, the police warrior identity is not based upon an idealized concept in practice, but rather a crude conception of manliness.

A former Los Angeles Police Department captain described it this way: "That testosterone, that male swagger—it was contagious."[73] In a recent documentary, *Do Not Resist*—the police trainer describes how one of the police's job perks is having "very intense sex" after surviving and returning home from a fight with the "bad guys." In the same documentary, SWAT team members describe how the thrill and fun of executing a search warrant in a person's home is akin to the thrill and fun of taking a person's virginity. New SWAT team members are called "SWAT Pops" on their first warrant: "Their first time, they're always smiling ear-to-ear and feel like they're on top of the world."[74] Intruding upon a person's most personal space—the home—requires the officer to "try[] not to smile because it's so much fun and ... so cool."[75] And as discussed in the last chapter, former FBI trainees (women) have sued the bureau, asserting that it ran a "good-old-boy network," while the Justice Department investigated claims that the FBI forced out other trainees (men) for not being "masculine enough."[76] These trends contribute to the deep erosion of police legitimacy within society generally and communities specifically. I have joined the chorus of commentators suggesting that the police's focus upon a warrior conception is at the heart of this erosion. I now want to further consider how the warrior conception conflicts with the positional moral requirements of law enforcement officers—requirements that are in turn constrained by general moral requirements owed to all persons.

I begin with an objection suggesting that the police are not the problem, but merely the face of broader political and legal injustice within society. Consider the police's enforcement of unpopular and (arguably) unjustified laws, such as those regarding the "war" on drugs. How can we justify the police's enforcement of such laws considering deep disagreements in society about, say, the use of marijuana and other controlled substances? One might argue that the central issue is that the state's actions are not justified and thus our focus should be on the relationship between illegitimate *laws* and modes of their enforcement—rather than my focus upon conceptions of the police role (warrior or otherwise).[77] This sort of objection is why I take the view that political theories should view justice holistically, rather than in a piecemeal fashion that focuses only on the police, or only on particular laws, and so on. Indeed, it is important to think about how policing (or corrections, or sentencing, or welfare policies) fit in with our broader conception of justice, not just whether practices within each of these domains is justified independent of other domains.

The broader issue in play is the distinction between *justification* and *legitimacy*, and how that distinction is relevant to the police role.[78] *Justification* concerns questions regarding whether one arrangement is better than another. Flossing leads to good health and is thus justified given the value we place upon good health. On the other hand, *legitimacy* raises questions about whether there is authority to impose one arrangement over another. Flossing might be justified, but my neighbor doesn't have the authority to require me to floss—even if she happens to be a dentist. What about the police's authority (legitimacy) to enforce laws with which one might disagree? There are deep questions about whether existing liberal states are in fact legitimate, given that few of us consented to the state's authority, for example. However, this does not mean that states (and laws) are not justified. The state may very well be better than the alternatives, even if it is not legitimate strictly speaking. Accordingly, a reasonable response to the problem of illegitimate laws (and modes of their enforcement) might be something such as this: The state ought to take remedial action to reduce the extent to which it imposes unfair and illegitimate institutions on others—thus transitioning closer to a broad ideal of justice.

In the case of the police, this would mean performing obligations in a way that is consistent with the broad outline of a liberal ideal of justice—rather than in a way that is focused upon an individuated police archetype (hero, warrior, guardian, and so on). At the most general level, this would include policing that is consistent with governance by the rule of law and the justified use of discretion. It would also include policing that respects personhood, especially one's equal social status, moral agency, and human dignity. Focusing upon an ideal of justice constrains the police's response to injustice in the actual world such that the response is consistent with the pursuit of justice in other domains (legislation, corrections, courts, and so on)—given that all domains of justice will be constrained by tenets such as the rule of law and personhood. One can imagine how this might look with respect to the police's enforcement of potentially illegitimate laws.

Even if there is deep disagreement about, say, drug laws, the police can use their discretion to: (1) Prioritize the most grievous injustices—assaults, rapes, murders, and affronts to one's security of person generally—over marijuana violations; (2) prioritize the most grievous drug violations, such as those resulting in violence; and (3) enforce all laws (drug laws or otherwise) in accordance with the rule of law and in a way that respects one's personhood. Adhering to the rule of law might mean that the police do not use their discretion in a way that perverts the law, such as unnecessarily breaking the law to enforce the law (e.g., unjustified drug buys) and not enforcing the law prejudicially (e.g., based upon ethnicity, class, and so on). Respecting personhood might mean that the police do not use informants in a way that is an affront to the informant's moral worth and high-ranking social status (conceptions of human dignity), such as coercing informants to engage in otherwise illegal activity and subjecting informants to dangerous operations (e.g., unnecessary drug buys that open the informant to the risk of serious bodily injury).[79] The basic legal and philosophical tenets of a liberal theory of justice provide a unifying theme for these considerations in policing—a theme of promoting reciprocity and human dignity, while discouraging unconscionable agreements (between police and informants, for example), extralegal punishment, and unfettered discretion.[80]

Questions about the enforcement of unjust laws thus boil down to the balance between special and general moral requirements noted earlier. Recall, for example, that if a police officer fails to do her duty as a police officer, then the officer is morally blameworthy. She voluntarily entered her position in full knowledge of the details of the situation, to perform the duties of that position. But such special moral requirements are constrained by general moral requirements, which bind us simply in virtue of our personhood and moral equality—irrespective of any special roles or relationships. Consider Rawls's proceduralist argument regarding unjust laws:

> The injustice of a law is not, in general, a sufficient reason for not adhering to it any more than the legal validity of legislation (as defined by the existing constitution) is a sufficient reason for going along with it. When the basic structure of society is reasonably just, as estimated by what the current state of things allows, we are to recognize unjust law as binding provided they do not exceed certain limits of injustice.[81]

Although professional discretion is a necessity, Rawls is suggesting that it is generally impermissible to use discretion to *deviate from rule of law principles*; rather, such deviation is only permissible when the limits of injustice have been exceeded. Given the complex nature of policing, it would be a practical impossibility to outline a bright-line rule regarding when the police may use their professional discretion to disregard their positional requirements to enforce (unjust) laws. However, there are clear cases that provide general guidance and support broad guidelines.

For example, the police may have had a special, positional duty to enforce Jim Crow laws (and the Nazis may have had similar positional duties during WWII), but those duties were negated by our general moral duties to others in virtue of personhood and moral equality. The Nuremberg trials were not about breaking German law, but rather about breaking laws of nature or inter-personal morality (general duties owed to others). Compare those cases with sheriffs who pledged—in 2019—to not enforce new laws restricting the use of assault weapons because they believed the laws violated the Second Amendment.[82] It is difficult to imagine anyone seriously comparing a sheriff's refusal to enforce a new gun regulation (in a country that has a population of 330 million and 400 million guns in circulation) with laws that deny one's personhood. The point is that regardless of whether one agrees with, say, U.S. drug and firearms laws, we must consider whether the police's (theoretically) *equal* enforcement of those laws would be a breach of some general moral duty owed to all people.

I myself believe there are serious problems with drug laws, but it is not clear that enforcing those laws (fairly) would be a breach of some *general* moral duty owed to all people—or at least nowhere near as clear as enforcing Jim Crow or Nazi laws. Why? Because drug laws may be enforced without bias (again, theoretically) in accordance with the rule of law such that no one is viewed as privileged or as having a higher or lower social status. Although it may be impossible to discern a bright-line rule, I have elsewhere defended a broad framework (*the prerogative power test*) for determining when the police may deviate from rule of law of principles.[83] The test suggests that the police may use their prerogative power to deviate from the rule of law in accordance with the following constraints:

1 *Purpose constraint*: The power must be wielded for public good/national security;
2 *Prudential constraint*: A legislative action is not viable;
3 *Personhood constraint*: The power must not be an affront to liberal personhood;
4 *Emergency constraint*: The power must be reserved for emergencies that involve:

   a   An acute threat of death or serious bodily harm, and
   b   The threat cannot be averted without wielding the power.[84]

The test is strict for good reason. No one seriously questions the need and justification for discretion in policing; to be sure, limited discretion is consistent with the rule of law. But the actual deviation from rule of law principles should have a high bar given that governance by law—rather than governance by the discretion of government officials—is foundational to liberal societies. We may disagree that the state has the authority to regulate society through drug laws because such laws limit our freedom, but the state limits our freedom in all sorts of (potentially unjustified) ways in exchange for a potential increase in security. Again, the solution is for the state to take remedial action to reduce the extent to which it imposes unfair and illegitimate institutions on others—thus transitioning closer to the ideal. But with respect to the police, it is just not clear that they have a *general* moral requirement to all persons that overrides their *positional* duty to (fairly) enforce the host of laws that people view as unjust. We are thus brought back to the police themselves and *how* they pursue their role—as heroes, warriors, guardians, and so on.

All of this is a long way of saying that there is good reason for the police to pursue their role in ways that go beyond a utilitarian (the end justifies the warrior's means) focus on security and crime reduction. Specifically, the coming chapters—especially chapter 4—argue that the police should seek public justification for their power in order to enhance legitimacy. One practical way to do this is a renewed emphasis on established policing strategies—such as community policing—that seek community support and buy-in through public reason. This is especially important given that the police are indeed tasked to enforce many laws (such as drug laws) that are considered unjust. An emphasis on reciprocal police–community relationships helps address problems associated with the police's role in enforcing these unpopular laws. Such relationships also help balance what might be described as *specific authority* on the one hand and *general authority* on the other. Warrior policing emphasizes the fact that law enforcement officers have the power to demand specific authority in any given encounter in which such authority is necessary. For example, in the 1968 landmark case, *Terry v. Ohio* (regarding "stop and frisk" tactics), the Supreme Court noted "officers' perceived need to maintain the power image of the beat officer, an aim sometimes accomplished by humiliating anyone who attempts to undermine police control on the streets."[85] Putting aside the obvious problem of the police's use of humiliating tactics, focusing solely upon specific authority obscures the value of enhancing a broader, general authority. As we will see, justice-seeking policing incorporates the goal of general authority by pursuing public justification and engaging in strategies that promote legitimacy within communities. We conclude this chapter with final observations regarding how the warrior concept impedes both the positional and the general moral requirements of the police role.

Conclusion: Fear and Force

In *On Killing: The Psychological Cost of Learning to Kill in War and Society*, police trainer Dave Grossman draws upon Alfred de Vigny's writing about the Napoleonic Wars to illustrate the dual nature of warring: being a soldier requires preparation to be both a victim and an executioner.[86] Despite the differences between soldiering and policing that have been discussed, this sentiment is of course true of policing. Police run the risk of being killed, but they also run the risk of killing of others. These risks—coupled with the existential fear that underscores them—bolster an ethos driven by "manly" heroism drawing upon fearless, reflexive courage in the face of danger. Paradoxically, law enforcement officers are programmed to view almost every encounter in their law enforcement role with fear. I again recall my first training lectures at Quantico regarding how we or others could die on the job, as well as watching videos of actual officers dying on the job.

It is one thing to acknowledge and prepare officers for this reality, but it is quite another to imply that every interaction with the public could be a life and death battle of good versus evil. Stoughton draws out the point well:

> Under this warrior worldview, officers are locked in intermittent and unpredictable combat with unknown but highly lethal enemies ....

Imagine ... you have been told (repeatedly) that your survival depends on believing that everyone you see—literally *everyone*—is capable of, and may very well be interested in, killing you.[87]

From a neuropsychological and neurological perspective, the feeling of fear signals the sympathetic nervous system to go into survival mode, propelling one into a heightened state of physiological arousal known as *fight or flight*.[88] Of course, understanding and preparing for the functioning of these bodily systems is important. But such an understanding is not mutually exclusive with a move away from the warrior concept. Such a move can create space to focus upon the positional and general moral requirements of the police role. These requirements involve critical thinking that draws upon evidence, experience, and knowledge, not merely reflexive action in the face of danger.

Nancy Sherman makes a similar point in her book, *Stoic Warriors*.[89] Building upon the Stoic philosopher Seneca ("false shapes of evil when there are no signs that point to any evil"), Sherman observes that "anxiety about the future can derail agency."[90] The sentiment is especially important in policing, given that the police role—as with the solider role—involves both the fear of being killed and the fear of killing. And in the same way that there is just conduct and killing in war (*jus in bello*), there is just conduct and killing in policing that is constrained by the positional and general moral requirements of policing. As Michael Walzer puts it in *Just and Unjust Wars*, war is still a "rule-governed activity, a world of permissions and prohibitions."[91] If we assume this is true of war, it stands to reason that it is true in the context policing within a domestic community of equal members with equal rights. It is in this way that we come full circle to the police's positional and general moral requirements: Policing is a rule-governed activity based upon permissions and prohibitions of the position—as well as based upon the general requirements owed to others given their humanity. While the role of human rights in policing will be addressed more fully in chapter 4, the point here is simply that the moral requirements of policing are based upon both positional and general grounds— grounds that are obscured by an emphasis on the warrior concept.

There have been some recent shifts away from the warrior mindset. For example, in late 2019, the Baltimore Police Department described their new use-of-force policy as a "major cultural shift" because it "emphasizes ... actions to quell situations before they escalate."[92] Notably, Baltimore's use-of-force policy includes a "critical thinking" component, stating:

> Prior to using force, members shall use a critical thinking and decision-making framework to analyze and respond to incidents. This framework will allow members to uphold the sanctity of life and protect

themselves by decelerating and stabilizing a situation to minimize the likelihood of a Use of Force incident.[93]

Equally notable is the policy's statement of core principles, including *Sanctity of Human Life*: "Members shall make every effort to preserve human life in all situations; and *Value and Worth of All Persons*: "All human beings have equal value and worth and members shall respect and uphold the value and dignity of all persons at all times."[94] To promote these core principles, the department's critical thinking component requires officers to "1. Assess the situation, threats, and risks; 2. Gather relevant facts about the incident; 3. Consider police powers and BPD policy; 4. Identify options and determine the best course of action; and 5. Act, review, and re-assess the situation."[95] When this policy was released, some of my students worried that it would create additional legal issues for officers (regarding whether a shooting or some other use of force was justified) given the new critical thinking requirement. Expanded policies always have the potential to increase liability (there are simply more rules of which officers can run afoul), but it is not clear why that is a bad thing.

As we have seen, law enforcement officers are taught (as early as the first days of academy, as in my case at the FBI Academy) that they will be engaging in daily battle with unknown but highly lethal enemies. Accordingly, a greater emphasis on reason and critical judgment is a welcome counterweight. This only sounds impractical if one assumes that critical thinking must occur in a split-second, or immediately before a decision is made about the use of force. But that is a bad assumption. Indeed, officers can be trained to specifically avoid tactics that *unnecessarily* increase the likelihood of the use of force (thus reducing the likelihood of ever reaching the point of a split second-decision to use force). For instance, police suspects are in some cases harmed (or killed) because an officer engages in bad tactics that actually *give rise* to a situation in which lethal force is perceived to be necessary.[96] Perhaps the officer aggressively (and unnecessarily) approaches a suspect without maintaining cover or concealment (or distance), or chases a fleeing suspect alone, without any hope of receiving back-up from other officers.

Although such decisions may sometimes be necessary (when say, a suspect is endangering another person), these tactics are often the result of poor critical judgments that inevitably give rise to split-second use-of-force decisions. Such judgments and tactics are unjustified given the weight that police assign to the sanctity of human life and the value and worth of all persons (even persons who are suspected of committing a crime), which outweighs arrests and other law enforcement actions in many cases. Contrary to the warrior concept, then, the emphasis should be on positional moral requirements—such as department policies to which officers agree to adhere—as well as overlapping general moral requirements regarding the respect and rights owed to all persons. We now examine whether these requirements can be better realized by conceiving of the police as guardians.

Notes

1. Jonathan Stevenson, *Trump's Praetorian Guard*, THE NEW YORK REVIEW OF BOOKS (Oct. 22, 2020). See Tim Lau & Joseph Nunn, *Martial Law Explained*, BRENNAN CENTER OF JUSTICE (Sept. 10, 2020) for an overview of the concept of martial law (noting that "the concept has no established definition"). After Joe Biden won the presidential election in November 2020, President Trump nevertheless claimed victory and that the election was stolen from him. He refused to concede and subsequently held a rally with thousands of his supporters on January 6, 2021, demanding that Congress and Vice President Pence reject Biden's victory. Trump then encouraged the crowd to "fight like hell" and walk to the Capitol, where Biden's victory was being certified. The mob of Trump's supporters violently stormed the Capitol, leading to an evacuation, lockdown, and five deaths. The deaths included a Capitol Police officer, as well as a rioter who was shot by Capitol Police while trying to breach a barricaded door. Trump was subsequently impeached (his second impeachment) on January 13, 2021, for incitement of insurrection. See Dan Barry, Mike McIntire, & Matthew Rosenberg, *'Our President Wants Us Here': The Mob That Stormed the Capitol*, N.Y. TIMES (Jan. 9, 2021).
2. *Id.*
3. *See* Stephen Vladeck & Benjamin Wittes, *DHS Authorizes Domestic Surveillance to Protect Statues and Monuments*, LAWFARE (July 20, 2020).
4. *Id.*
5. Shawn Boburg, Meg Kelly, & Joyce Sohyun Lee, *Swept up in the federal response to Portland protests: 'I didn't know if I was going to be seen again,'* WASH. POST (Sept. 10, 2020).
6. U.S. CONST. amend. X. See generally LUKE WILLIAM HUNT, THE RETRIEVAL OF LIBERALISM IN POLICING 107–14 (2019), for a discussion of the police power.
7. *See* Jennifer K. Elsea, *The Posse Comitatus Act and Related Matters: The Use of the Military to Execute Civilian Law*, CONGRESSIONAL RESEARCH SERVICE (Nov. 6, 2018).
8. Libor Jany, *Minneapolis police union offers free 'warrior' training, in defiance of mayor's ban*, STARTRIBUNE (April 19, 2019). Jeronimo Yanez, a former Minnesota officer, shot and killed Philando Castile after a traffic stop in 2016. Yanez had attended a training course called "The Bulletproof Warrior." He was acquitted in the shooting of Castile. Mohamed Noor, a former Minneapolis officer, was charged with killing a woman after responding to the woman's 911 call for assistance near her neighborhood home. *Id.*
9. *Id.*
10. *Id.*
11. *Id.*
12. *See* Seth W. Stoughton, *Law Enforcement's "Warrior" Problem*, 128 HARVARD LAW REVIEW FORUM 225 (2015).
13. LARRY F. JETMORE, THE PATH OF THE WARRIOR: AN ETHICAL GUIDE TO PERSONAL & PROFESSIONAL DEVELOPMENT IN THE FIELD OF CRIMINAL JUSTICE 110 (2005) (quoting Theodore Roosevelt, 26th U.S. President, Citizenship in a Republic (April 23, 2010)) (emphasis added).

14 Johnson described the war on crime this way: "If we wish to rid this country of crime, if we wish to stop hacking at its branches only, we must cut its roots and drain its swamping breeding ground, the slum. Nothing short of total victory will be acceptable." ELIZABETH HINTON, FROM THE WAR ON POVERTY TO THE WAR ON CRIME: THE MAKING OF MASS INCARCERATION IN AMERICA 80 (2017) (quoting Johnson).
15 Michael Kramer, *Frying Them Isn't the Answer*, TIME, March 14, 1994.
16 Justice Policy Institute, "Clinton Crime Agenda Ignores Proven Methods for Reducing Crime," April 14, 2008.
17 *See, e.g.*, JEREMY BENTHAM, AN INTRODUCTION TO THE PRINCIPLES OF MORALS AND LEGISLATION (1789); JOHN STUART MILL, UTILITARIANISM (1863); and HENRY SIDGWICK, THE METHODS OF ETHICS (1874).
18 The other side of the political spectrum—libertarianism—embraces an almost identical critique of utilitarianism.
19 I say artificial because—to the extent that Rawls borrows the idea of the state of nature—it is much different than the idea presented by seventeenth-century philosophers such as Thomas Hobbes and John Locke. Hobbes and Locke conceptualized the state of nature as dangerous and violent (or least highly inconvenient). Still, Hobbes did conceive of people as largely equal and Locke argued that everyone is born equally with a set of (natural) rights that allow them to govern themselves. There is thus a direct connection between early ideas about the state of nature and Rawls's borrowing of those ideas—even if Rawls's artificial conception of beginnings and fairness (behind a veil of ignorance that leads to a state of fairness) has much additional scaffolding.
20 *See, e.g.*, RADLEY BALKO, THE RISE OF THE WARRIOR COP (2014); Seth W. Stoughton, *Principled Policing: Warrior Cops and Guardian Officers*, 51 WAKE FOREST LAW REVIEW 611, 631 (2016).
21 BALKO, *supra* note 20, at 52.
22 *Id.*
23 DARYL GATES, CHIEF: MY LIFE IN THE LAPD 104 (1992).
24 BALKO, *supra* note 20, at 53.
25 RADLEY BALKO, OVERKILL: THE RISE OF PARAMILITARY POLICE RAIDS IN AMERICA 11, https://www.cato.org/sites/cato.org/files/pubs/pdf/balko_whitepaper_2006.pdf
26 PAUL H. ROBINSON, CRIMINAL LAW CASE STUDIES (5th ed., 2015).
27 Katie Shepherd, *Riot police in armored vehicle roust homeless mothers from illegally occupied Oakland house*, WASH. POST (Jan. 15, 2020).
28 David Collins, *New London acquires war-ready armored vehicle*, THE DAY (Feb. 3, 2020).
29 *See* Greg Smith, *New London police department's new military vehicle panned by some*, THE DAY (Feb. 5, 2020).
30 BARRY FRIEDMAN, UNWARRANTED: POLICING WITHOUT PERMISSION 95 (2017).
31 Jamelle Bouie, *The Militarization of the Police*, SLATE (Aug. 13, 2014).
32 Utah v. Strieff, 579 U.S. ___, 136 S. Ct. 2056 (2016); see Mapp v. Ohio, 367 U.S. 643 (1961), in which the U.S. Supreme Court held that the exclusionary rule applies to the U.S. states (in addition to the U.S. federal government).
33 *See, e.g.*, Terry v. Ohio, 392 U.S. 1 (1968).
34 *See* Strieff, *supra* note 32.
35 *See, e.g.*, Hein v. North Carolina, 574 U.S. ___ (2014) (holding that a police officer's reasonable mistake of law can provide the individualized suspicion required by the Fourth Amendment to justify a traffic stop).
36 Graham v. Connor, 490 U.S. 386, 396–97 (1989).
37 See Stoughton, *supra* note 20, at 651, for a thoughtful (and comprehensive) statement of this position.

38 W.B. Gallie, *Essentially Contested Concepts*, 56 PROCEEDING OF THE ARISTOTELIAN SOCIETY 167, 169 (1956). See HUNT, *supra* note 6, at 55 (2019), for a discussion of Gallie's work as it relates to liberalism.
39 HUNT, *supra* note 6, at 56 (citing Ronald Dworkin, *A Special Supplement: The Jurisprudence of Richard Nixon*, THE NEW YORK REVIEW OF BOOKS (May 4, 1972)).
40 *Id.* at 57.
41 Jeremy Waldron, *Is Dignity the Foundation of Human Rights?*, in PHILOSOPHICAL FOUNDATIONS OF HUMAN RIGHTS 125 (Rowan Cruft, S. Matthew Liao, & Massimo Renzo eds., 2015). Waldron suggests that these are "four possible accounts of what it might mean to say that one concept, α, is the foundation of another concept, β." *Id.* Analogously, I suggest that such accounts might help us determine whether a set of characteristics associated with a particular warrior conception "C" might serve as the foundation for the warrior concept "W".
42 Stoughton, *supra* note 20, at 651.
43 *Id.* at 652.
44 *See, e.g.*, JOHN RAWLS, A THEORY OF JUSTICE 97–99 (rev. ed., 1999) (1971).
45 *Id.*
46 Stoughton, *supra* note 20, at 631–32 (emphasis added).
47 *Id.* at 632–33.
48 Denis Sinor, *The Hun Period*, in THE CAMBRIDGE HISTORY OF EARLY INNER ASIA 177 (Denis Sinor ed., 1990)
49 *Id.* at 182 (quoting St. Jerome).
50 MICHAEL KULIKOWSKI, THE TRAGEDY OF EMPIRE: FROM CONSTANTINE TO THE DESTRUCTION OF ROMAN ITALY (2019).
51 *Id.*
52 *See, e.g.*, Joseph Hincks, *'Now People Can Read the Truth.' A Former FBI Agent's Memoir on the War on Terror Is Declassified After 9 Years*, TIME (Sept. 7, 2020).
53 Stoughton, *supra* note 20, at 632–33.
54 Incidentally, one wonders about the vast historical record of women as warriors, given that even my seven-year-old son is aware of the tradition of women as warriors from (fictional) films such as *Mulan*.
55 See HUNT, *supra* note 6, at 189–201 for a discussion of the limits of executive discretion to deviate from rule of law principles.
56 Stoughton, *supra* note 20, at 633.
57 *Id.* (quoting YAMAMOTO TSUNETOMO, HAGAKURE: THE SECRET WISDOM OF THE SAMURAI 42 n.2 (Alexander Bennett trans.), 2014).
58 *Id.* at 634.
59 *National Law Enforcement Officers Memorial Fund*, https://nleomf.org/facts-fi gures/law-enforcement-facts
60 *FBI Releases 2019 Statistics on Law Enforcement Officers Killed in the Line of Duty*, FBI NATIONAL PRESS OFFICE (May 4, 2020), https://www.fbi.gov/news/pressrel/p ress-releases/fbi-releases-2019-statistics-on-law-enforcement-officers-kille d-in-the-line-of-duty?utm_campaign=em
61 William Finnegan, *How Police Unions Fight Reform*, THE NEW YORKER (July 27, 2020).
62 Stoughton, *supra* note 20, at 634.
63 Justin Peters, *I Learned to Think Like a "Warrior Cop,"* SLATE (Aug. 28, 2020).
64 DAVE GROSSMAN & LOREN W. CHRISTENSEN, ON COMBAT: THE PSYCHOLOGY AND PHYSIOLOGY OF DEADLY CONFLICT IN WAR AND IN PEACE (2007).
65 Stoughton, *supra* note 20, at 634.
66 *Id.* at 636.

67 GROSSMAN & CHRISTENSEN, *supra* note 64, at 179.
68 Stoughton, *supra* note 20, at 636–37 (citing Barbara E. Armacost, *Organizational Culture and Police Misconduct*, 72 GEO. WASH. L. REV. 453, 453–54 (2004)).
69 Stoughton, *supra* note 20, at 638.
70 *Id.* at 654.
71 Dashcam video of the shooting is available at https://www.youtube.com/watch?v=9Y7sgZZQ7pw
72 Mitch Smith & Timothy Williams, *Minnesota Police Officer's 'Bulletproof Warrior' Training Is Questioned*, N.Y. TIMES (July 14, 2016).
73 Kimberly Kindy, *Creating Guardians, Calming Warriors*, WASH. POST. (Dec. 10, 2015).
74 DO NOT RESIST (Craig Atkinson, 2016).
75 *Id.*
76 Adam Goldman, *Women Sue F.B.I., Claiming Discrimination at Training Academy*, N.Y. TIMES (May 29, 2019).
77 I thank Jake Monaghan for raising this worry during my conference presentation at the Central Division Meeting of the American Philosophical Association in Chicago in February 2020.
78 See the vast work of A. John Simmons on this distinction.
79 See HUNT, *supra* note 6, at 140–48, discussing otherwise illegal activity and the use of informants.
80 *See generally id.* My first book examined how liberalism is a unifying theme for these values.
81 *See* RAWLS, *supra* note 44, at 308.
82 *See, e.g.*, Jason Wilson, *Washington state: at least 20 county sheriffs refuse to enforce new gun laws*, THE GUARDIAN (Feb. 22, 2019).
83 *See* HUNT, *supra* note 6, at 189–200.
84 *Id.* at 197. The test is based upon John Locke's theory of prerogative power, coupled with the doctrine of executive emergency power explicated in U.S. Supreme Court jurisprudence. I first invoked this test as a model for addressing questions regarding the police's power to engage in Otherwise Illegal Activity ("OIA"), a power that is strictly speaking legal but that involves breaking what would otherwise be a vast array of substantive laws in a vast array of non-emergency situations. It seems plausible that the framework is also relevant in the present context given that the framework is based upon a holistic conception of the liberal tradition, recognizing an institutional context (including through the prudential constraint), a substantive context (including through the purpose and emergency constraints), and a philosophical context (including through the personhood constraint).
85 Terry v. Ohio, 392 U.S. 1, 14 n. 11 (1968) (quoting LAWRENCE P. TIFFANY ET AL., DETECTION OF CRIME 47–48 (Frank J. Remington ed., 2d ed. 1967)).
86 DAVE GROSSMAN, ON KILLING: THE PSYCHOLOGICAL COST OF LEARNING TO KILL IN WAR AND SOCIETY 86 (1995) (quoting JOHN KEEGAN & RICHARD HOLMS, SOLDIERS: A HISTORY OF MEN IN BATTLE (1986)).
87 Stoughton, *supra* note 12, at 227–29.
88 *See* JUDITH LEWIS HERMAN, TRAUMA AND RECOVERY 34 (1992).
89 NANCY SHERMAN, STOIC WARRIORS: THE ANCIENT PHILOSOPHY BEHIND THE MILITARY MIND (2005).
90 *Id.* at 114–15 (2005) (quoting Seneca).
91 MICHAEL WALZER, JUST AND UNJUST WARS 36 (1977).
92 Phillip Jackson, *Baltimore police introduce a new use-of-force policy that emphasizes training and a 'cultural shift'*, BALTIMORE SUN (Nov. 26, 2019).

93 Baltimore Police Department, *Policy 1115, Use of Force* (Nov. 24, 2019).
94 *Id.*
95 *Id.*
96 *See, e.g.*, Jeffrey Noble & Geoffrey Alpert, *State-Created Danger: Should Police Officers Be Accountable for Reckless Tactical Decision Making, in* CRITICAL ISSUES IN POLICING 481–95 (6th ed., Roger Dunham & Geoffrey Alpert eds., 2010).

Chapter 3

Guardians

Whom and What to Guard?

Firefighters and police respond to a 911 call regarding a disoriented man laying on the sidewalk in a residential neighborhood in Washington, D.C.[1] The man begins to vomit when the first responders arrive and the police are informed that the man is "possibly intoxicated" and "fell and hit his head." The scene is not secured and the man is taken to the hospital as an "ETOH" (ethanol alcohol) case. Given that the man seems to be a vomit-stained drunk, he is not taken seriously at the hospital until—some hours later—he shows symptoms of a serious head injury. He is eventually taken into surgery but dies of a blood clot that caused his brain to swell. The man is David Rosembaum, an award-winning *New York Times* journalist who had retired weeks earlier after working almost forty years at the paper's Washington Bureau. He had been hit in the head with a pipe and robbed. Legal scholar Adam Benforado describes how this case can be divided between two distinct periods:

> When his nametag read JOHN DOE ETOH, firefighters, EMTs, nurses, and doctors neglected rules and procedures, ignored responsibilities, and went through the motions. The police, for their part, did not interview potential witnesses, try to identify the victim, canvass the neighborhood, collect any evidence, or question why an apparently intoxicated person had no wallet. The headphones that were found next to John's body in the grass were simply left at the scene. When the lead officer was asked whether he had filled out the mandatory incident report, he replied, "No, not for a drunk."[2]

On the other hand, everything changed after the man was identified as a prominent journalist. Fortunately for the police (given their failure to secure the crime scene), one of the men who robbed and assaulted Rosembaum turned himself in and confessed to the crime.

Benforado draws upon research in psychology to explain the inadequate response to "John Doe," particularly the way we jump to conclusions given "automatic processes in our brain" ("System 1") rather than "our more deliberate and effortful mental processes (System 2)."[3] He suggests that—in Rosembaum's case—these processes are connected to the vomit on Rosmbaum's jacket, which seemed to immediately elicit *physical* disgust in the first responders.[4] This, in turn, may be linked to *moral* disgust and "dehumanization that is all the easier when the victim lacks a name and cannot communicate, aside from the occasional moan."[5] This response is not a one-off phenomenon, but rather associated with a conception of "outsiders" generally—such as those whose presence is said to harm "people living their Suburban Lifestyle Dream."[6]

We might consider the large swaths of undocumented immigrants who have been characterized as drug dealers, criminals, and rapists who come from "shithole" countries to threaten our way of life.[7] This sort of rhetoric is often accompanied by concrete law enforcement action, including crackdowns by U.S. Immigration and Customs Enforcement (ICE)—the federal law enforcement agency under the U.S. Department of Homeland Security (DHS). Some of these undocumented immigrants have lived in the U.S. for decades, with children who are U.S. citizens or who are recipients of Deferred Action for Childhood Arrivals (DACA). One such woman described how her routine check-ins with ICE changed in 2016:

> [T]he tone of ICE agents at the field office was totally different. "All of a sudden, they talked to me rude …. Like I'm nobody, like I'm not a human being. They don't respect [immigrants] and I think they were waiting for a chance to let us know." She wanted to remind ICE that this is supposed to be a nation of immigrants ….[8]

As historian and Latin American scholar Adam Goodman notes, these people are often transferred to ICE after being arrested by local police for minor offenses: "Officials have long used everyday policing, immigration raids, and mass expulsion drives to remove unauthorized immigrants from the country, but they have also relied on rumors and publicity blitzes surrounding these initiatives to spur self-deportation."[9] To be sure, we should acknowledge that undocumented immigrants break the law when they enter the U.S. without authorization. However, we should also consider whether the punishment is disproportionate given that many immigrants cross the border to reunite with family or to satisfy the needs of employers looking for labor. The disproportionate response raises questions regarding the extent to which some groups of people are dehumanized by law enforcement officials, as in the case of John Doe ETOH.

Given this backdrop, one might find hope in the fact that police culture has sought to reframe the police identity in recent years. In the aftermath of police abuses and community protests, officials and academics sought (not without resistance) a replacement for the police warrior conception.

Interestingly, many of these practitioners and scholars settled upon the idea of police "guardians." An example is Ekow N. Yankah's insightful work regarding what constitutional democracies require of the police.[10] Yankah's writing is especially valuable because it provides a much-needed philosophical study of the various dimensions of police legitimacy, including the shift from a "warrior culture" to a "guardian culture."[11] His basic idea is that:

> [P]olicing is justified not primarily by the invocation of individual rights—retributivist warriors roaming the land; rather, police are best viewed as public officials—or guardians—justified by the political value of franchise to protect the laws that make our shared civic polity possible and protect our claims to civic equality.[12]

This chapter embraces the underlying idea that policing is a component of our shared polity, not an exercise of individual police warriors ridding the polity of wolves. Unfortunately, however, the guardian trope is flawed in both conception and execution.

Executing the shift from a warrior to a guardian identity raises both moral and practical questions. Yankah imagines "a world largely populated by police guardians ... in lighter blue uniforms—focused solely on order maintenance and assistance."[13] This world is said to both reflect what most police officers actually do, as well as lessen the tension in encounters between the police and people of color.[14] In Yankah's case, the goal is to provide political justification for this view (not "iron out all potential wrinkles" such as meeting the "needs of vastly different jurisdictions"), but it is worth noting the practical difficulties of transforming police into non-armed caretaker guardians *in America*.[15] Yankah himself makes the point that

> America is not New Zealand; Americans are a remarkably armed nation for one, inherently changing the background danger levels for police. If the difference in gun possession necessitated, caretakers could still be armed with weapons, though without the power to arrest.[16]

Practically speaking, then, perhaps the shift to this form of "guardian" policing is either relatively unrealistic (in America) or relatively similar to the status quo (while still beholden to officer individuation through a guardian trope).

Accordingly, this chapter departs from the guardian conception in part because of a practical assumption about police officers. As Eric Miller puts it,

> Police officers are executive agents empowered by the state to use physical force to coerce recalcitrant individuals to comply with public laws and other lawful directives. While this is not all they do, it may be their most distinctive feature.[17]

This view seems right on a number of levels, raising a host of practical questions regarding how a shift to guardian policing would look in theory and in practice.

One of the more fundamental questions is the true nature of the guardian conception and whether it is justified in the first place.[18] The guardian conception of the police role is especially interesting because it has been linked to the guardians in Plato's *Republic*. Although the police have been referred to as guardians for decades, an example of the renewed interest in the metaphor is the collaboration between the Harvard Kennedy School and the National Institute of Justice (NIJ) (the research, development, and evaluation agency of the U.S. Department of Justice), which resulted in an *Executive Session* paper in 2015: "From Warriors to Guardians: Recommitting American Police Culture to Democratic Ideals."[19] The paper begins with the following: "In Plato's vision of a perfect society—in a republic that honors the core of democracy—the greatest amount of power is given to those called the Guardians."[20] The paper becomes even more peculiar from there, conflating Plato's philosophy with the policing strategy of Sir Robert Peel: "Perhaps it is time to revisit the wisdom of Plato and Sir Robert Peel and strive to become the trusted guardians of democracy."[21] To be sure, contemporary criminal justice has much to learn from Plato's and Peel's work. And while protecting democracy is a noble goal, it can be misleading to invoke Plato and Peel in this way. The problem begins with an unusual reading of Plato, but this textual quibble soon develops into pressing practical problems.

The task of this chapter is thus to clarify some of the central characteristics of the Platonic guardian. The hope is that accomplishing that task will help lay the groundwork for a more holistic, justified conception of the police role in chapter 4. A holistic conception of justice entails protecting the rights of all persons in society, including the impoverished and those who have broken the law or who are suspected of breaking the law. The issue is timely, especially given exclusionary policing initiatives such as treating homelessness as a *law enforcement* problem—rather than, say, a housing or a broader economic problem.[22] If the police are to be viewed as guardians, these and other policy initiatives raise questions about who and what are worthy of being guarded. Some of the ideas stemming from the guardian conception are important, but they are consistent with neither a practical understanding nor a philosophical understanding of the guardian concept. The upshot is a conception that is idiosyncratic and inapt, exacerbating the police identity crisis through an emphasis upon police archetypes in the pursuit of justice.

Plato's Guardians

Plato's *Republic* is a dialogue seeking to construct a picture of the ideally just city-state ("Kallipolis") through the process of philosophical reflection. But it is much more than that. It is also a discussion of the nature and psychology of individual persons and how that nature and psychology correspond to political society. Socrates describes it this way in the dialogue: "let's first find out what sort of thing justice is in a city ... [i]f we could watch a city coming to be in theory, wouldn't we also see its justice coming to be, and its injustice as well?"[23] Accordingly, we might describe the *Republic* as an exercise in *ideal theory*: it presents a theory of justice that is based upon idealized assumptions about a society, as well as the society's citizens and social conditions. Such a theory represents the best state (or city) because the theory represents an ideal. In one sense, then, it might seem appropriate to model contemporary police upon Plato's guardians—who play a central role in protecting the city. If Plato's guardians represent an archetype within an ideal city, then perhaps they are an ideal model for the police. Unfortunately, despite what can be learned from Plato, embracing the guardian archetype within contemporary policing is deeply problematic.

There are three core problems: First, one must contend with the widely disparate views and critiques of democracy in Plato's work. Second, one must consider the suggestion that vast, consolidated power should be left in the hands of Plato's guardians ("the greatest amount of power is given to those called the Guardians," as the Harvard/NIJ article suggested). Third, one must consider the inherent nature of Plato's guardians, including their warrior facet.[24] It is true that Plato's guardians are meant to foster good will toward their fellow-citizens, which might be analogous to the community and procedural justice policing discussed in Chapter 4. But it is also true that Plato's guardians are meant to be harsh toward strangers, who one might equate (roughly) to today's criminal suspects, and, more generally, those who are considered outsiders.

Let us begin with the claim—noted above—that police culture should turn to "Plato's vision of a perfect society ... [for] a republic that honors the core of democracy ...."[25] Even if we assume the claim does not mean to conflate Athenian democracy with contemporary democracy, the claim faces an uphill battle from the start because Plato's *Republic* is typically viewed as a critique of political democracy—as well as the moral psychology of the democratic character.[26] Indeed, Plato considers four principle political vices that rank below justice and the just soul: timocracy, oligarchy, democracy, and tyranny, corresponding to the four respective character types. He concludes that the democrat is only slightly better than the tyrant. This inauspicious start gets even worse given that Plato ranks the democrat *below* the oligarch, who is painted in an exceedingly bad light (abusive, preoccupied with money, and other unpleasantness).[27] Viewed as a sort of dilettante with wildly inconsistent desires, it is suggested that the democrat will eventually degenerate into a ruthless tyrant—the lowest character of all.

Plato's critique of democracy is quite explicit, describing the democrat's and oligarch's weakness in similar terms. This weakness is centrally about the inadequate accounting of necessary and unnecessary appetites. A necessary appetite is one that is practical and useful, such as an appetite that promotes health. An unnecessary appetite is one that is superficial, unnecessary, and potentially harmful.[28] Given that both fail to properly account for these appetites, Plato suggests that the oligarch evolves into a democrat when all appetites are treated equally. So while the oligarch subjugates everything to necessary appetites, the democrat's desires are disorderly and lack priority. From here, it is only a short jump to the tyrant who gives full dominion to *lawless* unnecessary appetites (rather than *lawful* unnecessary appetites). It is thus bewildering for contemporary police culture to embrace Plato as the harbinger of democracy. Perhaps *we* think that democracy should be exalted in society generally and by the police specifically, but that is not Plato's conception of an ideal society—nor is it his conception of the guardian's role.

In some ways, Plato's critique of the democrat (and by extension democracy) is consistent with the critique of policing's unprincipled consequentialism in the last chapter. Plato writes that the democrat is "always surrendering rule over himself to whichever desire comes along, as if it were chosen by lot. And when that is satisfied, he surrenders the rule to another, not disdaining any, but satisfying them all equally."[29] Analogously, the state's desires are given free rein such that all appetites are treated equally and pursued without regard to constraining principles and values.[30] If the state's desire for security and crime reduction is at the fore, then those appetites might be maximized in spite of other desires that are grounded in values and principles that compete with security. As Terence Irwin has argued, reasoning about *ends* is a central facet of the four characters—including the democrat—in Plato's *Republic*.[31] To be sure, one should take care not to equate Plato's conception of democracy with, say, the principles of twenty-first-century liberal democracies such as the U.S. But Plato's worry about mob rule is still relevant—even in constitutional democracies that include constraints upon majority rule. The broader point is that Plato has so far proven to be a poor spokesman for democracy.

How, then, might we salvage Plato's vision of democracy and the democrat? Dominic Scott has suggested that if we "abandon the attempt to treat all the democrat's desires as appetites ... [t]here are spirited *and* rational aspects ... [that] seem to constitute redeeming features."[32] Scott reaches this conclusion based upon Plato's conception of a tripartite soul (rationality, spiritedness, and appetitive):

To feel an appetite for something is to pursue it just because it offers one pleasure, not because one independently sees any goodness in it. By contrast, the rational part, at least in the case of the just soul, is able to form a desire for something based on the realization of its goodness. One may immediately ask how this binary distinction relates to the presence of the third part of the soul, but spirit seems to straddle the divide: when it is functioning properly, it responds to reason with a sense of the rightness of the course of action, for instance— hence its associations with pride, shame, and indignation.[33]

The democrat's desires are all like appetites or "quasi-appetitive":

Appetites are *by their nature* not based on considerations of the good. If it is functioning correctly, reason can and ought to seek the good. Similarly, spirit can and ought to ally itself with the value-judgements of reason. In deviant cases, however, it is possible to have a desire of reason for knowledge, and a desire of spirit for honour, without basing these desires upon considerations of the good. So long as such desires are orientated towards certain kinds of goals— honour or discovery— they can count as spirited or rational.

It is in this way, then, that we might provide a more nuanced account of the democrat: One who goes after a great many desires—good and bad ones—though not always for the right (just) reasons. Unlike the just person who is governed holistically by evaluative reasoning, Plato's democrat (and the democratic city-state) fail to maintain a harmonious, unified balance of desires.[34] It is thus unsurprising that Plato is broadly dismissive of democracy.

In point of fact, Plato's well-known conclusion of the ideal political society is one ruled not by democrats, but by *philosopher-kings*:

Until philosophers rule as kings or those who are now called kings and leading men genuinely and adequately philosophize ... [and] the many natures who at present pursue either one exclusively are forcibly prevented from doing so, cities will have no rest from evils ... nor ... will the human race.[35]

Perhaps Plato's most famous words, this excerpt has been the source of voluminous commentary. One prominent theme within this commentary is that Plato's political philosophy is not only undemocratic, but also a path to totalitarianism. Consider how Plato writes that just as unsatiated lust for wealth is the cause of an oligarchy's undoing, unsatiated lust for freedom is the cause of democracy's undoing.[36] Indeed, according to the *Republic*, such an emphasis on freedom means the following:

A resident alien or a foreign visitor is made equal to a citizen, and he is their equal .... The utmost freedom for the majority is reached in such a city when bought slaves, both male and female, are no less free than those who bought them. And I almost forgot to mention the extent of the legal equality of men and women and of the freedom in the relations between them.[37]

Given these and other passages from the *Republic*, we must at least take seriously the charge of totalitarianism—which goes something like this: Society should be governed by philosopher-kings, who cannot be held accountable to the citizenry even though they have the power to promote their conception of the good by paternalistically maintaining social classes and limited liberties. This charge is similar to the well-known (and divisive) critique by Karl Popper and others, specifically the way that philosopher-kings might wield power over others.[38] The worry essentially boils down to the fact that Plato is straightforwardly disdainful of democracy and individual liberty in the passages above. And this supports the idea that the *Republic's* rulers would impose a narrow vision of society without adequate regard for the freedom and interests of individuals within the polity.

One response is that—as with Plato's later dialogue, *Laws*—the *Republic's* presumed totalitarian attributes merely seek to (paternalistically) maximize the happiness of all persons in society.[39] Be that as it may, such a response nevertheless runs afoul of the same problems addressed in the last chapter with respect to consequentialist warrior policing. For example, a polity might embrace a warrior ethos because the result of such an ethos—maximizing happiness by enforcing the law and stopping crime—justifies an illiberal and undemocratic means by which that result is achieved. This does not mean that Plato was unconcerned with the good of individual persons, but it does mean that we cannot jump to the conclusion that Plato is the obvious voice for democratic policing.

The conclusion is quite clearly the opposite: Plato's ideal city (Kallipolis) is based upon the consolidated ruling power of philosopher-kings—without recourse to other options—resulting in the city being an affront to democratic principles (and policing). This point might be somewhat tempered by the idea that all members of the polity would agree that philosopher-kings should rule: "the ruler and the ruled ... share the same belief about who should rule."[40] This is based in part on the role that guardians play in keeping Kallipolis safe and secure, but the benefits bestowed by Plato's guardians do not dispel the totalitarian worries. Indeed, one of the foundational tenets of contemporary liberal theories of justice is that of *legitimacy*. Regardless of whether a polity is *justified*—in other words, whether the polity's benefits make it better than the alternatives—liberal theories of justice are fundamentally based upon the concept of legitimacy. By legitimacy I mean that those who rule have *authority* to rule, independent of the benefits bestowed on others by their rule. In a sense, the *Republic's* political philosophy dispenses with robust conceptions of legitimacy in light of the supposed virtue of the philosopher-kings. This vast authority is contrary to both democratic principles and democratic policing, especially given the well-documented abuses of unchecked executive power in contemporary society and contemporary policing.[41]

From this brief sketch of Plato's *Republic*, we can see how it is inapt to suggest that police culture should turn to "Plato's vision of a perfect society ... [for] a republic that honors the core of democracy ...."[42] Plato was in fact skeptical of many facets of democracy and the democratic character. We can now turn to the specific idea that police culture should "revisit the wisdom of Plato ... to become the trusted *guardians* of democracy."[43] Despite Plato's reservations about democracy and the democratic character, let us consider his conception of guardians and how they may or may not relate to contemporary police culture. Guardians make up the class of people who—as the name suggests—guard the city and its constitution. To begin, some of those who promote contemporary guardian policing might be surprised to learn that Plato's guardian classes are deeply communist (not to mention eugenical) in nature:

> First, none of them should possess any private property beyond what is wholly necessary. Second, none of them should have a house or storeroom that isn't open for all to enter at will. Third, whatever sustenance moderate and courageous warrior-athletes require in order to have neither shortfall nor surplus in a given year they'll receive by taxation on the other citizens as a salary for their guardianship. Fourth, they'll have common messes and live together like soldiers in a camp.[44]

There is thus a division of classes in which some possess private property (e. g., the producer class to facilitate production), but other classes do not. Whatever one might think about this sort of class division, we can see that guardians are also conceived as soldiers—which is a way to explicitly liken them to warriors. And the detailed education of this guardian class—with its careful censorship of stories and materials to which trainees may be exposed—is in many ways authoritarian in nature.[45] This gives rise to two pressing questions: First, contemporary police culture suggests that we follow Plato's "vision ... [in which] the greatest amount of power is given to those called the Guardians."[46] However, on what basis would we want to grant vast, consolidated power to police thus conceived? Second, reform in education and training is vital in contemporary policing. But on what basis would we want to model training upon a regimen that is in a sense authoritarian in nature—and thus demeaning to the police? Of course, contemporary police are not actually looking to use the *Republic* as a concrete training guide, but even invoking it rhetorically seems deeply confused.

This becomes apparent when we address the questions above, beginning with a few brief passages regarding the guardians' nature and demeanor to others. The *Republic* frames the education of guardians as an issue of great importance. Plato describes how the first task "is to select ... the kind of nature suited to guard the city."[47] The guardian's work is viewed as the work of a watch-dog, and a guardian's nature is thus said to be like a "pedigree young dog."[48] As with watch-dogs, the guardian "needs keen senses, speed to catch what it sees, and strength in case it has to fight it out with what it captures .... And each must be courageous if indeed he's to fight well."[49] More fundamentally, guardians need to be "spirited" in order to fulfill their watch-dog requirements. But there is a worry about a class of such intense, high-spirited fighters: Although strong physical attributes are necessary for the guardian's work, might these attributes cause the brave watch-dogs to treat *each other* savagely?[50] Plato's answer is that the guardians must be educated such that they are "gentle to their own people and harsh to the enemy."[51] Plato thus suggests that a guardian's disposition must be both "gentle and high-spirited," which is why guardians are like a "pedigree dog" who is "gentle as can be to those he's used to and knows, but the opposite to those he doesn't know."[52]

This is an odd model for contemporary policing. Of course, no one doubts that the police must at times use swift, powerful, and, on occasion, deadly force against law-breakers. That's not the problem here. The problem is the way guardians distinguish their treatment of persons based upon whether the person is a friend or enemy, familiar or unfamiliar. A rough analogy would be contemporary police who embrace an "us against them" warrior mindset. Although Plato says guardians must have the love of wisdom in their nature, it is a nature described as follows: "When [it] ... sees someone it doesn't know, it gets angry before anything bad happens to it. But when it knows someone, it welcomes him, even if it has never received anything good from him."[53] Indeed, Plato describes this as

> a refined quality in its nature and one that is truly philosophical .... Because it judges anything it sees to be either a friend or an enemy, on no other basis than that it knows the one and doesn't know the other.[54]

This conception of the guardian's desired nature is remarkable for a variety of reasons, not least its similarity to conceptions of contemporary police warriors. Recall that one of the major critiques of police warrior training is that it is "fear-based," teaching officers to view community members with apprehension given the possibility that they are wolves.

The underlying worry was in fact raised by Aristotle, who astutely rebuked Plato's conception of the guardian character:

> But it is a mistake to describe the Guardians as cruel towards strangers; it is not right to be cruel towards anybody, and men of great-souled nature are not fierce except towards wrongdoers, and their anger is still fiercer against their companions if they think that these are wronging them, as has been said before. And this is reasonable, because they think that in addition to the harm done them they are also being defrauded of a benefit by persons whom they believe to owe them one.[55]

Aristotle's point is well taken, especially in light of contemporary breakdowns in police–community relationships. In a sense, Aristotle illuminates the central problem of warrior (and guardian) police conceptions: Such individuated archetypes entail a *fear of the other*—a stranger who the police must battle and guard against. Rather than an emphasis on justice through collectivity, contemporary police archetypes promote a subtle xenophobia: suspicion that emphasizes the differences between the warrior (or the guardian) and those with whom the warrior-guardians must interact and serve. One of the obvious reasons xenophobic suspicion is unjust in contemporary liberal societies (especially with respect to policing) is that it creates hierarchical social statuses. In other words, some groups are granted a high-ranking social status (a conception of human dignity) that entitles them to a variety of rights and privileges, including being protected by the police with dignity and respect. Others, however, are treated as having an inferior social status, one that allows them to be dealt with harshly given suspicion and stereotypes regarding their otherness. It should go without saying that this sort of cruelty to strangers is morally and politically unjustified based upon a great many reasons. In contemporary liberal societies, these reasons include basic tenets regarding the dignity and equal, high-ranking social status of *all* persons, as well as a commitment to governing all persons in accordance with rule of law principles. Such reasons extend beyond the particularized context of liberal societies given their foundation in human rights.

Let us conclude this section with Aristotle's implication that—if a guardian is to be just—the guardian's "anger is still fiercer against their companions if they think that these are wronging them."[56] This foreshadows the problem of individuation in policing: the manner in which the police are identified as distinguished from the rest of the community. In the last chapter, we considered how the warrior concept has been described as creating an archetype that lends itself to an exclusive brotherhood:

> The solidarity of this brotherhood ...allows the profession as a whole to associate itself with the heroic deeds of individual officers, further

enhancing the appeal of membership—when officers are initiated into the Warrior brotherhood, they stand shoulder to shoulder with people who have done great things.[57]

Somewhat paradoxically, then, archetypes such as warriors and guardians allow the police to distinguish themselves by identifying with an exclusive group or "brotherhood." This emphasis upon one's exclusive membership—one's sharing in the archetype's mythos—contributes to unjustified moral codes such as protecting members of the brotherhood at all costs. This includes informal codes among some police officers such as the "blue wall of silence," which encourages officers not to report on (or not to tell the truth about) a colleague's misconduct.

Aristotle turns this code on its head:

> [A just person's] anger is still fiercer against their companions if they think that these are wronging them .... And this is reasonable, because they think that in addition to the harm done them they are also being defrauded of a benefit by persons whom they believe to owe them one.[58]

To put it a bit differently, when a police officer does wrong he is harming the "brotherhood"—the group of intimates to which the officer is tied via special obligations. This sort of wrong is thus a way of defrauding the group—a failure to uphold one's obligations—and does not deserve some sort of special protection. Of course, wrongs by the police are most significantly affronts to justice and thus wrongs to the entire community. We now turn to a closer examination of the contemporary guardian conception, as well as how that conception inherently emphasizes officer individuation over the collective pursuit of justice.

The Guardian Category Mistake

We have seen some of the difficulties with treating Plato's political philosophy as a philosophical blueprint for democratic, guardian policing. To be fair (to Plato), it was never appropriate to treat the *Republic* as either a model for political societies or a model for policing within those societies. This is especially true given that Plato was in many ways focused upon the analogy between the city and the soul and how that analogy illuminates the connections between justice and happiness. It is still reasonable to say that Plato was not sufficiently wary of the risks associated with an unchecked, elite ruling class. This is a significant point that undercuts much of the philosophical foundation on which guardian policing has been based.

Although contemporary police culture has invoked Plato to explain guardian policing, there are of course other ways of deriving such a conception. We now turn to the contemporary manifestation of the police guardian. Naturally, contemporary police culture is not focused on interpreting Plato's political philosophy, but rather the individual characteristics of an idealized, modern, police guardian archetype. Ironically, we will see how this emphasis on officer individuation leads us back to Plato—this time to his theory of Forms. Before turning to the contemporary police guardian conception, it is worth noting how the laws and regulations within liberal societies are aimed primarily at regulating one's conduct and action—not developing one's character. Accordingly, even though there will be disagreement about which critical standard to use, liberal societies do not typically aim to make people more virtuous or good (in contrast with Plato's political theory, in which the law is intended to secure a good and virtuous life for citizens).[59]

Recall that in the last chapter we examined some critical standards that are based upon conduct and actions—including unrestrained consequentialism (acts are right if and only if they maximize total happiness or conform to a rule that maximizes total happiness). In the next chapter, we will consider critical standards that are more deontological in nature: some acts and conduct are wrong regardless of their consequences given, say, an assumption that persons are ends-in-themselves. We might also embrace a hybrid theory that is focused upon conduct and actions that are constrained by both consequential and deontological standards. But let us now consider how some contemporary practitioners and scholars conceptualize police as virtuous guardians—which includes a commitment to police conduct that is constrained by the goal of protecting of human dignity.

The commonality among such conceptualizations is an emphasis on an idealized, individual officer persona. In other words, the implication is that justified policing entails embracing a persona based upon a guardian archetype. As we saw in the last chapter, scholars have done important work on the nature of the police role—articulating strengths and weakness of various conceptions of that role. Although the warrior–guardian debate has contributed to our understanding of the police, such debates are in a sense based upon a category mistake. Here is a classic example introduced by Gilbert Ryle: "imagine[] a foreigner taken to a cricket match and having the batsman, fielders, and bowlers pointed out to him, who then asks, 'But who is left to contribute the famous element of team spirit?'"[60] These sorts of mistakes involve conceptual errors—such as errors in which something that belongs to one category is presented as if it belongs to another category. Policing is a professional role in political communities that involves law enforcement, emergency operation, social peacekeeping, and related responsibilities. More broadly, these responsibilities seek to further the central value within political societies: justice. When we ask, "but who is left to battle wolves and guard the principles of democracy," we err by presenting the police category as if it belongs to some other, separate category of warriors and guardians. This may sound like a trivial matter of semantics—indeed, sometimes a category mistake is a semantical error—but the misapplication of concepts is not trivial. And our conceptualizations of the police role are all over the map.

For example, some scholars have suggested that the police role should be based upon a dual-natured persona ("officers must have the capacity to act as both Guardians and Warriors"), while also indicating that the warrior concept "is a problem" and that "the Guardian may be a suitable replacement."[61] Many would agree. Guardian policing was embraced in President Obama's *Task Force on 21st Century Policing*, and guardian rhetoric has caught on in major media outlets—including a *Washington Post* exposé ("Creating Guardians, Calming Warriors") examining police training that seeks to create "guardians of democracy" who are trained to de-escalate conflicts.[62] To be sure, almost all of the policing strategies that fall under the guardian banner are admirable and uncontroversial. Who wouldn't want policing that "seeks to instill officers with values that encourage public engagement, foster trust, and build lasting community partnerships"?[63] But one problem is that it is simply not clear that such values emanate from the guardian concept in any natural way.

Here is a likely response to the objection: *So what. There is nothing wrong with defining guardian policing however we like.* Fair enough, but this leads us directly back to the two problems to which I have already alluded: First, if our explanation of a concept's foundation does not illuminate the concept through logic, history, or some other natural rationale, then the explanation runs the risk of merely being ad hoc. In other words, we are simply picking values we like and calling them "guardian values." Not only is this a slippery approach, but it also leads to bizarre accounts of a concept's philosophical foundation. We saw this earlier with the unusual way that Plato's political philosophy was invoked as the exemplar of democratic policing. The second problem is that referring to police in this way—an independent persona based upon a guardian archetype—exacerbates the category mistake of police individuation. As we will see below, this error encourages a conception of police as heroic individuals ("guardians") rather than government agents fulfilling their professional role in the collective pursuit of justice.

Consider the first problem more closely, including the claim that guardian policing is justified for the following three reasons:

> First, individuals in communities that trust the police are more likely to cooperate and less likely to resist officers, diminishing the risk to officers and the need for force.
>
> Second, Guardian policing seeks to avoid confrontations when it is possible to do so, which similarly minimizes the risk to officers and civilians alike.

Third, Guardian policing increases the police agency social capital with the community, reducing suspicion of police actions and mitigating the negative effects of high-profile incidents, such as an egregious use of excessive force.[64]

These are commendable policing strategies, goals, and values. However, none are innate traits of "guardians" given that it is unclear how the guardian concept is logically connected to seeking trust, avoiding confrontations, and increasing social capital. If these goals and values lead to more effective policing—and if they promote our conception of justice—then we should simply explain that it is just for the police to seek trust, avoid confrontations, and increase social capital. It is unfitting to claim that these values form the basis of a guardian archetype—and a subcategory of policing—inasmuch as there are no natural historical, logical, or conventional connections on which to base the claim.

It is commendable that scholars and commentators have sought to flesh out the ideal of guardian policing by linking it to Peelian Principles (the consent of the governed) and describing its "first principle" as "the responsibility to protect civilians from unnecessary indignity and harm."[65] More specifically, guardian policing is said to embrace the components of warrior policing (honor, duty, resolve, and a willingness to engage in righteous violence), but be joined by five additional elements: "human dignity, empathy, patience, inclusivity, and introspection."[66] Accordingly, in addition to the problems with warrior attributes discussed in the last chapter, we are now faced with a second set of wide-ranging attributes that are said to form the foundation of the guardian concept. Let us consider them briefly one by one.

Human dignity is a difficult concept because it is used in a variety of ways in a variety of contexts, including: (1) *Kantian Dignity*: a characteristic of rational agents yielding the right to be treated as an end, not a means to an end; (2) *Aristocratic Dignity*: an outward, social facet of a person's high-ranking status; and (3) *Comportment Dignity*: the outward, social facet of a person that is consistent with societal expectations.[67] Aristocratic and comportment dignity are social in nature—social status and social expectations respectively—while Kantian dignity is an evaluative term based upon one's moral worth. Elements of both these social conceptions of dignity are relevant to a liberal conception of dignity.[68]

For instance, one facet of the liberal conception of dignity is that *all* persons possess a high-ranking legal status that comprises a set of rights—with one's equal status establishing the content of certain legal rights—irrespective of one's social status or comportment.[69] Although the police may be justified in treating a person in a particular way based upon the person's comportment (say, resisting arrest), it must be done in a manner that does not denigrate the rights comprised by the person's high-ranking, equal, legal status. Or consider "Kantian Dignity," which is a conception that transcends social status and is based upon one's inherent human (rational) capacities: Persons are not valued merely by their contingent social status or rank, but rather their intrinsic value. This might be connected to policing in a variety of ways. For instance, while the police's use of informants is perhaps an indispensable investigative tool, there are moral limits to the police's power to use persons (informants) as a means to a law enforcement end. Examples might include situations in which an informant has no real choice about whether to assist the police (calling into question the informants "consent" to assist the police), as well as situations in which the informant is subjected to inherently dangerous situations that would otherwise be addressed by the police in their law enforcement role.[70] As we will see in the next chapter, human dignity is often construed as the foundation of one's human rights. As such, human dignity is neither alienable nor violable.

In light of this understanding of dignity, it is unusual to hear guardian policing described as policing that "minimizes" affronts to dignity when "indignity is unavoidable."[71] Given the understanding above, human dignity is not something that the police may violate—even if the violation could have been worse without the police's thoughtful minimization. Perhaps some of the confusion arises from the distinction between human dignity and undignified behavior (or indignities). For example, consider the phenomenon of so-called "dwarf-tossing," in which persons are tossed into the air as a sort of game.[72] In some cases, the person being thrown wants to be thrown—perhaps because one can make money by permitting others to use one in this way. Of course, some will find the activity undignified even if the person consents to being thrown. But people have the right to engage in all kinds of undignified behavior, from dwarf-tossing (if you think that is undignified) to entering hot-dog-eating contests and then vomiting profusely. That said, given the liberal commitment to one's personhood—which includes a commitment to one's dignity—the state (via the police) is not justified in enforcing the law in a way that is an affront to one's dignity. This includes one's high-ranking, equal social status (a conception of human dignity), which comprises things such as equal legal and human rights. It also includes the value ascribed to one's capacity for various natural qualities that make one a moral agent—not merely a means to an end. While one may have the right to participate privately in things such as undignified games, the state (police) is precluded from using one in a way that is an affront to one's liberal personhood (including human dignity). The distinction is thus between engaging in undignified behavior on the one hand (a person drunkenly resisting arrest, for example) and, on the other hand, the state denigrating one's status and worth (the police treating the person who drunkenly resists brutally and like a *worthless animal*).

In addition to mitigating indignities, the requirements of police guardians are also described by commentators as including empathy, patience, inclusivity, and introspection.[73] The next chapter considers inclusivity more fully, but here, suffice it to say that inclusivity (meaning a pluralistic, reciprocal society in which all members play a role in the collective pursuit of justice) is fundamental to liberal societies and thus liberal policing. Consider now the other attributes: empathy, patience, and introspection. They are certainly all commendable, and they would likely be described as attributes of a "good person" (not just a good police officer). It is difficult to find any objection to the idea that it would be good if police officers had a better ability to understand the thoughts and feelings of themselves and others, as well as a calm capacity to accept delays and difficulties. The worry is that such virtues—empathy, patience, and introspection—are more focused upon constructing a particular police persona or archetype, rather than the requisite principles of justice that police must pursue as agents of the state. Admittedly, there might be a fine line between the pursuit of justice based upon political morality and the pursuit of making the police more virtuous people. Despite the potential overlap, the underlying distinction is important because it is a distinction between individuation (a particular persona and police archetype) and collectivity (the collective pursuit of justice within political society).

Police Archetypes and Individuation

It can be illuminating to consider the analogy between informal police archetypes and psychological theories of archetypes. The psychoanalytic tradition was known for theories of archetypes, which may be described roughly as universal mental images and symbols. Marilyn Nagy characterizes Carl Jung's archetype—and its philosophical influences—this way:

> The archetype itself ... is the 'introspectively recognizable form of a priori orderliness' ... and is not derivable from any known antecedents' ... [Jung's theory of archetypes] resembles nothing so much as Plato's vision of a universe ordered by the enteral forms ....[74]

By *a priori* one typically means justification that is independent of experience. The classic example is the claim that "all bachelors are unmarried." The idea is that if one is justified in believing this, one is *a priori* justified in believing it (without empirical evidence). Conversely, if one is justified in believing a statement such as "all bachelors in America must register with the Selective Service," then one is *a posteriori* justified in believing it inasmuch as its truth or falsity can be established with empirical evidence. One can begin to see the connection to Plato inasmuch as Plato's theory of "Forms" (or "Ideas") is based upon the notion that there are abstract objects that exist eternally and changelessly beyond the transient world of the senses.

Given this interpretation of archetypes, then, one might think that archetypes are based upon innate (originating in the mind) knowledge—in contrast to the idea that the mind is a blank slate that is filled in by experience (a position endorsed by philosophers such as John Locke). However, there is unlikely to be a single, definitive interpretation of the Jungian archetype given the vast and evolving work from within that tradition.[75] With respect to Plato's influence, Jung writes that archetype "is an explanatory paraphrase of the Platonic eidos [form or idea]."[76] And this sort of eternal *idea* is conceived as "the formulated meaning of a primordial image by which it was represented symbolically." The archetype thus provides symbolic meaning to experience that is perhaps analogous to Plato's forms, with Jung writing: "In Plato ... an extraordinary high value is set on the archetypes as metaphysical ideas, as 'paradigms' or models, while real things are held to be only copies of these model ideas."[77] One might thus question whether Jung's archetypes are innate given that they are symbolic and representational, which are noninheritable features inasmuch as symbols and representations are formed from lived experience.[78]

I know: This all sounds fairly weird and far-removed from policing, but I think the psychoanalytic backdrop leads to an interesting payoff. Although many have embraced an interpretative model in which Jung's archetypes are construed as some sort of inherited, innate predisposition, it is also possible to interpret archetypes less anachronistically. For example, some have suggested ways we might interpret archetypes more closely with biological and developmental research: "archetypes are the emergent properties of the dynamic developmental system of brain, environment and narrative."[79] Alternatively, we might view archetypes as *culturally* emergent forms: "symbolic forms which are repeated across a range of societies because the human experience of birth, life and death has have so much in common, whatever the cultural context."[80] From this perspective, archetypes may be viewed in terms of a self-organization process of human cultural activity and experience, namely: the mental, emotional, and pathological aspects of life. Archetypes are thus open to historical and cultural analysis regarding the symbolism of mental phenomena.[81]

Consider Petteri Pietikainen's novel interpretation—which follows Ernst Cassirer's work on symbolic forms—of the Jungian archetype:

> [A]rchetypes can be understood as 'symbolic forms' ... we can interpret them not as quasi-biological entities but as culturally determined forms, which operate functionally in the same way that the other symbolic forms do: they give an organized and coherent structure to different manifestations of man's cultural activity, and at the same time they express the 'spirituality' of man. Symbolic forms are not

transmitted genetically from generation to generation, because they are in their very essence *cultural* products: the medium that transmits symbolic forms is culture, not biology.[82]

The idea here is that—by analogy and on a much smaller scale—police culture is based in part upon a mythical tradition of archetypal heroes, warriors, and guardians that develops through cultural transmission. By taking this sort of commonsense approach to police culture, we are able to construe these police archetypes in the context of broader cultural phenomena. For example, "the police" make up a cultural community (what has been called a "brotherhood") that includes particular ideas, beliefs, and behaviors that are mentally distinct from other communities. The police are thus influenced by particular archetypes—such as those associated with heroes, warriors, and guardians—in their relation to outsiders or what is referred to as "the other." As Pietikainen notes, "[t]o approach these mentalities with the help of archetypes as symbolic forms would be of descriptive value ... it may help to see our familiar surroundings ... and our attitudes towards the world ... in a new light."[83] And this means that even the unconscious archetypal characteristics of heroes, warriors, and guardians may function on a societal plane as symbolic forms that guide cultural experiences and interactions.[84] For Pietikainen, the upshot is that if archetypal ideas, images, and ways of experience are culturally determined, then they are subject to modifications and variations.[85] And for present purposes, this means that we can not only gain a clearer picture of the police by examining their archetypal characteristics, but we can also hope to modify the culture in which those characteristics become manifest.

These themes are intricately related to the process that the psychoanalytic tradition refers to as "individuation," a term that I have so far been using informally. Jung described it explicitly:

> [T]he process by which a person becomes a psychological 'individual,' that is, a separate, indivisible unity or 'whole'. ... [I]t is a process or course of development arising out of the conflict between the two fundamental psychic facts [of conscious and unconscious].[86]

Accordingly, one might characterize individuation as the course by which the "self" develops, which includes both conscious experience and unconscious processes relating to life and death. Consider Anthony Storr's apt analysis:

> In Western man, because of the achievements of his culture, there was an especial tendency towards intellectual hubris; an overvaluation of thinking which could alienate man from his emotional roots. Neurotic symptoms, dreams and other manifestations of the unconscious were often expressions of the 'other side' trying to assert itself. There was,

therefore, within every individual, a striving towards unity in which divisions would be replaced by consistency, opposites equally balanced, consciousness in reciprocal relation to unconsciousness.[87]

This sentiment brings us full-circle to the heroic mythos in policing that was discussed in chapter 1. Police culture has channeled fear and existential angst, implying that eternal heroism (often manifested through warrior and guardian personas) can account for fear and serve as a central basis for the conception of the police role.

To be sure, these references to the psychoanalytical tradition are informal and intended to be suggestive only. I do not mean to imply that police reform should include a session on the couch for all officers to explore their subconscious (though it probably wouldn't hurt). But even though I draw on the psychoanalytic tradition by analogy, I think it can be an illuminating analogy. Warrior and guardian policing promotes a sort of artificial and informal archetype individuation, drawing upon the human experience of life and death viewed through the lens of cultural heroism. This sort of Platonic–Jungian concept is not an appropriate conception of the police role inasmuch as our idealizations in political philosophy, policy, and police culture should emphasize the ideal of *justice* (and ways to pursue that ideal) rather than the *ideally virtuous police persona*. If this is the case, then we need to shift to a new model for conceiving of the police. To continue with the psychoanalytic analogy, consider Jean Knox's account of paradigm-shifting "now" moments with respect to a person's self-concept:

> A metaphor which might illustrate the emergence of a 'now' moment is that of a set of scales with a gradually increasing weight on one side as new secure internal working models are gradually formed ... and a gradually diminishing weight on the other side as old models lose their determining power. A 'now' moment might represent the point at which the scales suddenly shift from the old to the new internal working model.[88]

Of course, the metaphor is not exactly apt in the context of police, but it is still worth considering given that police have been weighed down by individual models focused upon hero, warrior, and guardian personas. Police culture might shift instead to a model that is focused upon seeking a holistic conception of the central value in political society: justice. That discussion begins below and in the next chapter.

Conclusion: Democratic Policing and its Limits

The first three chapters have raised worries about police culture's deep focus upon the pursuit of an ideal, individual persona—whether hero, warrior, or guardian. The chief worry is that such a focus distracts from the goal of pursuing justice in society collectively. This is an inherent problem within contemporary police culture, which is apparent when considering the key differences between pursuing an ideal police archetype on the one hand and an ideal of justice on the other. The ideal of justice is in a sense stable, at least assuming we can agree upon a broad outline of principles that are fundamental within the context of liberal societies. An ideal of justice thus offers a fixed point—a target for which to aim when facing injustice in society. But for several reasons, it is difficult to take this approach in the context of individuated police archetypes: First, our laws, regulations, and policies do not idealize persons and police, but rather principles of justice that become manifest in those laws, regulations, and policies. The core legal and philosophical tenets of the liberal tradition—and its actual institutions—are not based upon the pursuit of an ideally virtuous persona.

Even assuming, *arguendo*, that the pursuit of an idealized police archetype may be consistent with the pursuit of an ideal of justice, the pursuit of such a persona is often ad hoc. Conceptions of police heroes, warriors, and guardians are not typically based upon history, logic, or a principled conceptual analysis. We saw this in the case of basing contemporary police guardians on Plato's guardians—who were in fact harsh rulers (at least to outsiders) in a semi-authoritarian city-state. This sort of "noble puppy" characterization is both inconsistent with democratic policing and demeaning to the police. At best, conceptions of contemporary police guardians are grounded—in a somewhat contrived manner—in more fundamental principles of justice. But if that is the case, then it stands to reason that we should simply let the more fundamental principles of justice be the police's guiding lights. Before turning to this idea in the next chapter, we conclude this chapter with some thoughts on contemporary democratic policing. This will bring us full circle back to Plato, who—as we have seen—was quite clear about the limits of democracy.

One important component emphasized by Plato is the guardian's education and training. Of course, police training is no less important today, but what are the characteristics of contemporary democratic policing? How do those characteristics relate to the more fundamental ideal of justice? In short, democratic policing is policing that includes the entire community, not just the police acting alone in secrecy. Legal scholar Barry Friedman puts it this way: "Democratic policing is the idea that the people should take responsibility for policing, as they do for the rest of their government, and that policing agencies should be responsive to the people's will."[89] We should add a few more concrete tenets to this definition. We might begin with the *rule of law*, by which I mean governance by law rather than blanket discretion to deviate from the law.[90] The police of course need special powers to fulfill their law enforcement role. However, that power (and the discretion to use the power) is limited by legal, political, and philosophical norms of liberal governance. This includes the police themselves acting in congruence with the law and using their discretion in a way that does not pervert the law.[91]

Next, with respect to laws, regulations, and policies that govern the police, Friedman makes the apt point that democratic policing means "the public has an opportunity to participate in the formulation of those rules, and the rules are available for all to see."[92] The next chapter expands upon these points in the context of predictive policing. As we will see, predictive policing relies upon data and computer algorithms to predict where crime will occur; it is thus policing by algorithm. One problem is that there is often little transparency regarding the data, algorithms, and strategies used by the police. Not only does this lack of transparency erode community trust, it also makes it difficult for the community to participate in governance and hold the police accountable.

For better or for worse, this description of democratic policing will naturally invoke the idea of community-oriented policing: roughly, policing that seeks to promote legitimacy by incorporating the community in the task of solving crime problems. In a sense, community policing is known as much for its failures (real and imagined) as for its idealistic goals and principles. We will consider the philosophical foundation—and justification—for community policing in the next chapter, but we should begin here by noting the historical context (and successes and failures) of this policing style. One problem is that community policing is often viewed simply as an assortment of independent initiatives that are tacked onto the police's central role of stopping crime. In other words, community policing has been conceived as a piecemeal strategy rather than a holistic approach to policing. The central reason for this is that the values and goals of community policing (especially police legitimacy through community inclusivity) take a backseat to any competing law enforcement and crime reduction goals. This will be a running theme in the next chapter and was apparent in the last chapter: Utilitarian approaches to crime control and reduction in which the end justifies undemocratic (or less democratic) means. The strategies that result in reduced crime have justified illiberal means by which those results are achieved.

To be sure, we all want to reduce crime. But many effective approaches to crime reduction— consider New York City's infamous "stop and frisk" initiatives—can come at the expense of values associated with community policing. As we have seen, the conception of police as heroic warriors—or even guardians defending society from outsiders—emphasizes law enforcement at the expense of other democratic values. The 2015 President's Task Force on 21st Century Policing put it this way: "law enforcement cannot build community trust if it is seen as an occupying force coming from outside to impose control on the community."[93] If we frame this sentiment in terms of democratic policing, it means that the public should have a say in the police's policies and rules for controlling crime. Democratic policing means that the police pursue security and crime reduction in their role as members of the community, not set apart from the community as exclusive heroes, warriors, and guardians. Recall the police's procurement of military equipment discussed in chapter 2, which Friedman describes as happening "behind the backs of civilian authorities, and without accessing the need for the equipment."[94] Likewise, tactics such as "predictive policing" might be effective, but the public should have a say in how those tactics are imposed on the community.

The extent to which the public is left in the dark with respect to fundamental questions about police tactics is indeed staggering. Seth Stoughton and Brandon Garrett have written thoughtfully about this problem, especially in the context of the police's use of force.[95] They write that "[m]embers of the public may assume that police rules and procedures provide detailed direction about when officers can use deadly force ... [and] that the U.S. Constitution protects citizens against completely unjustified uses of deadly force."[96] But this would be a mistaken assumption according to Stoughton and Garrett, leading them to their position that "courts, law enforcement, and the public all desperately require a revitalized constitutional standard regulating police use of force."[97]

This position is based in large part upon the Supreme Court's interpretation—especially the 1989 case, *Graham v. Connor*—of the police's power to use force under the Fourth Amendment.[98] In *Graham*, the Court held that "[t]he 'reasonableness' of a particular use of force must be judged from the perspective of a reasonable officer on the scene, rather than with the 20/20 vision of hindsight." According to the Court, this is because

> [t]he calculus of reasonableness must embody allowance for the fact that police officers are often forced to make split-second judgments—in circumstances that are tense, uncertain, and rapidly evolving—about the amount of force that is necessary in a particular situation.[99]

As Stoughton and Garrett astutely point out, the Court's rationale misses a crucial point: "whether officers acted as soundly trained police officers in the moments leading up to ... [a] shooting."[100] As discussed in the last chapter, there is insufficient consideration of how the police manage and deescalate situations such that split-second shooting decisions do not arise in the first place. But if we take a step back, we can see a more fundamental problem: The police and the public's almost *exclusive* reliance upon Supreme Court interpretation is decidedly *undemocratic*.

This is because it is not the job of the Supreme Court (or other courts) to solve problems within policing. The Supreme Court is responsible for interpreting the Constitution, not creating detailed use-of-force policy manuals for the police. An almost exclusive reliance on courts is thus undemocratic because courts lack accountability (compared with legislatures and police agencies), as well as because the public shirks its democratic responsibility when unduly relying upon courts.[101] Does this mean we should ignore the Supreme Court or disregard its rulings? Of course not. But it does mean that we should take a more holistic, democratic approach to policing generally and police use of force policies specifically. After all, much of the police's power is governed by administrative rules and regulations (internal policies regarding tactics, for instance), rather than sweeping Fourth Amendment interpretations by the Supreme Court. It is thus fitting that Stoughton and Garrett approach police use of force reform from a variety of angles. Their suggestions are welcome innovations to police reform efforts, especially because they reach beyond courts: empirical evidence regarding police policies, Department of Justice Consent Decrees (investigations and agreements between police departments and the federal government regarding police misconduct), police training and tactics, and factors regarding qualified immunity and litigation of offending police.[102] This sort of concrete work regarding the future of police policy is vital.

These themes will be relevant in the next chapter, which seeks a moral foundation for policies regarding the limits of the police's use of force in liberal societies. I wrap up this chapter by returning to Sir Robert Peel's principle 7 introduced in chapter 1:

> Police, at all times, should maintain a relationship with the public that gives reality to the historic tradition that the police are the public and the public are the police; the police being only members of the public who are paid to give full-time attention to duties which are incumbent on every citizen in the interests of community welfare and existence.[103]

If we embrace Peel's account of policing, then we embrace a robust account of democratic policing—an account in which both the police and the public share collective responsibility and accountability. But we cannot simply conclude with this sort of high-minded, democratic fervor. On the contrary, it is rather fitting to conclude this chapter by acknowledging—with a nod to Plato—the shortcomings of democratic policing. Friedman echoes Plato's worries about democratic chaos and dysfunction:

> Democratic governance has bequeathed to us a destructive war on drugs. Democratic institutions tend to act precipitously under pressure—which has been all too evident at times in the fight against terrorism. And, importantly, majority rule does not always bode well for the treatment of minorities, racial, religious, or otherwise. The majority tends to want lower crime rates, and doesn't care who is inconvenienced—or worse—to get them.[104]

These worries do not mean that we should abandon the benefits of democratic policing that have been examined. But they do lend support to a more fundamental emphasis on the basic legal and philosophical tenets of a liberal conception of justice. This will require an examination of the moral foundation for justice-promoting strategies such as community policing. As we will see, these are strategies grounded in collectivity, legitimacy, and human rights. We turn to them now.

Notes

1. See ADAM BENFORADO, UNFAIR – THE NEW SCIENCE OF CRIMINAL INJUSTICE, chapter 1 (2015), on which I rely for a summary of the facts of this case.
2. *Id.* at 8–9.
3. *Id.* at 10.
4. *Id.* at 12–13.
5. *Id.* at 16–17.
6. Annie Karni, Maggie Haberman, & Sydney Ember, *Trump Plays on Racist Fears of Terrorized Suburbs to Court White Voters*, N.Y. TIMES (July 29, 2020).
7. Eugene Scott, *Trump's most insulting — and violent — language is often reserved for immigrants*, WASH. POST (Oct. 2, 2019).
8. Tina Vasquez, *The New ICE Age: An Agency Unleashed*, THE NEW YORK REVIEW OF BOOKS (May 2, 2018).
9. ADAM GOODMAN, THE DEPORTATION MACHINE: AMERICA'S LONG HISTORY OF EXPELLING IMMIGRANTS (2020).
10. Ekow N. Yankah, *Pretext and Justification: Republicanism, Policing, and Race*, 40.4 CARDOZO L. REV. 1543 (2019).
11. *Id.* at 1555.
12. *Id.* at 1618.
13. *Id.* at 1628.
14. *Id.*
15. *Id.* at 1629–33. Yankah notes that "there is little reason to suppose that caretakers backed by state authority will be ineffective without routine arresting authority. The small army of private security guards who enforce order at malls and in various neighborhoods are so ubiquitous and reflexively obeyed that it rarely occurs to most that they are empowered with much less authority than a state official." *Id.* at 1633.
16. *Id.* at 1635.
17. Eric Miller, *Encountering Resistance: Non-Compliance, Non-Cooperation, and Procedural Justice*, UNIVERSITY OF CHICAGO LEGAL FORUM 295 (Article 8, 2016).
18. Yankah acknowledges the potential risks of the guardian concept: "reimagining police legitimacy as premised on franchise or civic equality avoids cheap nostalgia and the danger of returning to a time when police guardians meant police domination and contempt for persons of color." Yankah, *supra* note 10, at 1626.
19. Sue Rahr & Stephen K. Rice, *From Warriors to Guardians: Recommitting American Police Culture to Democratic Ideals*, NEW PERSPECTIVES IN POLICING BULLETIN (Harvard Kennedy School) (U.S. Department of Justice, National Institute of Justice, April 2015). *See also* U.S. COMM'N ON CIVIL RIGHTS, WHO IS GUARDING THE GUARDIANS? A REPORT ON POLICE PRACTICES (1981).

20 *Id.* (quoting MICHAEL NILA & STEPHEN R. COVEY, THE NOBILITY OF POLICING 7 (2008).
21 Rahr & Rice, *supra* note 19.
22 Kriston Capps, *Trump's Plan to Criminalize Homelessness Is Taking Shape*, CITYLAB (Dec. 17, 2019). This is related to broader trends regarding shifting attitudes in police culture. For example, in early 2020, the U.S. Attorney General swore in sixteen members of *The President's Commission on Law Enforcement and the Administration*, stating: "there has been … a disturbing pattern of cynicism and disrespect shown toward law enforcement. All Americans should agree that nobody wins when trust breaks down between the police and the community they serve. We need to address the divide." The suggestion is that the real policing problem is a lack of respect shown by the public to the police. Aside from the Commission's Chair (who is a former police chief), all the commission's members worked in law enforcement. This fact raised worries about whether the commission would give serious consideration to broader issues such as civil and human rights. Tom Jackman, *Attorney general launches presidential commission on law enforcement*, WASH. POST (Jan. 22, 2020). The worry was appropriate given that it came on the heels of the Attorney General stating: "If communities don't give that support and respect, they might find themselves without the police protection they need." Tim Elfrink, *William Barr says 'communities' that protest cops could lose 'the police protection they need'*, WASH. POST (Dec. 4, 2019). This is an unusual way to frame the police role given that we entrust the police to provide collective security for all persons in society—regardless of one's personal attitudes and actions.
23 PLATO, REPUBLIC II 1008 (369a) (John M. Cooper trans., Hackett 1997).
24 *See generally* RACHANA KAMTEKAR, PLATO'S MORAL PSYCHOLOGY: INTELLECTUALISM, THE DIVIDED SOUL, AND THE DESIRE FOR GOOD (2018).
25 Rahr & Rice, *supra* note 19.
26 Dominic Scott, *Plato's Critique of the Democratic Character*, XLV, 1 PHRONESIS 19 (2000). I thank Professor Scott for his illuminating seminar on Plato's *Laws*, which I had the pleasure of taking during my doctoral program at the University of Virginia in 2014.
27 PLATO, *supra* note 23, at 580a-c
28 *Id.* at 558d-559d.
29 *Id.* at 561b.
30 *See* PLATO at 558c.
31 TERENCE IRWIN, PLATO'S ETHICS 286 (1995).
32 Scott, *supra* note 26, at 25 (emphasis added).
33 *Id.* (citing PLATO*supra* note 23, at 441c and 442c).
34 *See e.g.*, PLATO, *supra* note 23, at 443c–444a.
35 *Id.* at 473c–d.
36 *Id.* at 562a–b.
37 Plato, 563a–b.
38 KARL POPPER, THE OPEN SOCIETY AND ITS ENEMIES, VOLUME I: THE SPELL OF PLATO (5th ed., 1971) (1945). *See also* RENFORD BAMBROUGH (ED.), PLATO, POPPER, AND POLITICS (1967); C.C.W. Taylor, *Plato's Totalitarianism*, 5 POLIS 4–29 (1986); Leslie Brown, *How totalitarian is Plato's Republic?*, *in* ESSAYS ON PLATO'S REPUBLIC 13–27 (Erik Nis Ostenfeld ed., 1998);

  J.L. Ackrill, *What's wrong with Plato's Republic?*, *in* ESSAYS ON PLATO AND ARISTOTLE 230–51 (1997).
39 *See, e.g.*, Gregory Vlastos, *The Theory of Social Justice in the Polis in Plato's Republic*, *in* STUDIES IN GREEK PHILOSOPHY, VOLUME II: SOCRATES, PLATO, AND

THEIR TRADITION 69–103 (D.W. Graham ed., 1995); Luke William Hunt, *The Law in Plato's Laws: A Reading of the "Classical Thesis,"* 35.1 POLIS 102–26 (2018). *But see* Donald Morrison, *The Happiness of the City and the Happiness of the Individual in Plato's Republic*, 21 ANCIENT PHILOSOPHY 1–25 (2001); Rachana Kamtekar, *Social Justice and Happiness in the Republic: Plato's Two Principles*, 22 HISTORY OF POLITICAL THOUGHT 189–220 (2001).
40 PLATO, *supra* note 23, at 431d–432a.
41 *See* LUKE WILLIAM HUNT, THE RETRIEVAL OF LIBERALISM IN POLICING (2019), for a discussion of the risks of unchecked executive power in policing and beyond.
42 Rahr & Rice, *supra* note 19.
43 *Id.*
44 PLATO, *supra* note 23, at 415d–417b. Although the guardian class is open to both men and women, there is some dispute about whether this point should be read as feminist in nature. *See, e.g.,* Julia Annas, *Plato's Republic and Feminism, in* PLATO 2: ETHICS, POLITICS, RELIGION, AND THE SOUL 265–79 (Gail Fine ed., 1999); MORAG BUCHAN, WOMEN IN PLATO'S POLITICAL THEORY (1999). For a recent discussion of Plato's communism, see Alessio Santoro, *A City of Guardians: Refocusing the Aim and Scope of Aristotle's Critique of Plato's Republic*, 36 POLIS 313–35 (2019).
45 *See, e.g.,* PLATO, *supra* note 23, at 377b–c.
46 Rahr & Rice, *supra* note 19.
47 Plato, *supra* note 23, at 374e.
48 *Id.* at 375a.
49 *Id.*
50 *Id.* at 375b.
51 *Id.* at 375c.
52 *Id.* at 375c–e.
53 *Id.* at 376a.
54 *Id.* at 376b.
55 ARISTOTLE, POLITICS, 1328a. For a broader discussion of this point, see P.A. Vander Waerdt, *Kingship and Philosophy in Aristotle's Best Regime*, 30.3 PHRONESIS 249–73 (1985).
56 ARISTOTLE, *supra* note 55.
57 Seth W. Stoughton, *Principled Policing: Warrior Cops and Guardian Officers*, 51 WAKE FOREST LAW REVIEW 611, 636–37 (2016) (citing Barbara E. Armacost, *Organizational Culture and Police Misconduct*, 72 GEO. WASH. L. REV. 453, 453–54 (2004)).
58 ARISTOTLE, *supra* note 55, at 1328a.
59 *See, e.g.,* Hunt, *supra* note 41, at 124, describing how in Plato's *Laws*, "[t]he purpose of the law is not merely to protect one's interests, but rather to make one better off in every respect .... to secure a good and virtuous life for the citizens ...."
60 A.C. GRAYLING, THE HISTORY OF PHILOSOPHY (2019) (quoting GILBERT RYLE, THE CONCEPT OF MIND (1949)).
61 Stoughton, *supra* note 57, at 617, 666.
62 PRESIDENT'S TASK FORCE ON 21ST CENTURY POLICING, FINAL REPORT OF THE PRESIDENT'S TASK FORCE ON 21ST CENTURY POLICING 1, 11–12 (2015); Kimberly Kindy, *Creating Guardians, Calming Warriors*, WASH. POST. (Dec. 10, 2015).
63 Stoughton, *supra* note 57, at 667.
64 *Id.*
65 *Id.* at 667–68.
66 *Id.* at 668.

67 Doris Schroeder, *Dignity: Two Riddles and Four Concepts*, 17 CAMBRIDGE QUARTERLY OF HEALTHCARE ETHICS 230–38 (2008). Schroeder also consider *meritorious dignity*: an all-encompassing virtue that includes one's sense of self-worth.
68 See HUNT, *supra* note 41, at 127–33, for my account of liberal personhood.
69 *See* JEREMY WALDRON, DIGNITY, RANK, AND RIGHTS (Meir Dan-Cohen ed., 2012).
70 See HUNT, *supra* note 41, at chapter 4, for a discussion of problems regarding the police's use of informants.
71 Stoughton, *supra* note 57, at 669.
72 See HUNT, *supra* note 41, at 236–42, for a discussion of "dwarf-tossing" cases.
73 Stoughton, *supra* note 57, at 669–72.
74 MARILYN NAGY, PHILOSOPHICAL ISSUES IN THE PSYCHOLOGY OF C. G. JUNG 185 (1991).
75 See JEAN KNOX, ARCHETYPE, ATTACHMENT, ANALYSIS: JUNGIAN PSYCHOLOGY AND THE EMERGENT MIND 23 (2003) (identifying four distinct models for thinking about Jung's archetypes).
76 C.G. JUNG, THE COLLECTED WORKS OF C.G. JUNG (H. Read, M. Fordham, G., & W. McGuire eds., trans. R.F.C. Hull, 1954) (1934).
77 *Id.* at vol. 8, para. 275 (1919).
78 KNOX, *supra* note 75, at 35.
79 George B. Hogenson, *The Baldwin effect: a neglected influence on C.G. Jung's evolutionary thinking*, 46.4 JOURNAL OF ANALYTICAL PSYCHOLOGY 591, 607 (2001); *see also* Peter Saunders & Patricia Skar, *Archetypes, complexes and self-organization*, 46.2 JOURNAL OF ANALYTICAL PSYCHOLOGY 255–413 (2001).
80 KNOX, *supra* note 75, at 63.
81 Petteri Pietikainen, *Archetypes as symbolic forms*, 43.3 THE JOURNAL OF ANALYTIC PSYCHOLOGY 325–43 (1998).
82 *Id.* at 333.
83 *Id.* at 339.
84 *Id.*
85 *Id.* at 342.
86 JUNG, *supra* note 76, at vol. 9i, para. 490 and 522–4 (1939).
87 ANTHONY STORR, THE ESSENTIAL JUNG 18 (1983).
88 KNOX, *supra* note 75, at 186.
89 BARRY FRIEDMAN, UNWARRANTED: POLICING WITHOUT PERMISSION 27 (2017).
90 *See* HUNT, *supra* note 41, at 47–52 for an overview of the rule of law.
91 *See* LON L. FULLER, THE MORALITY OF LAW 38–44 (1969) (describing the precept, "congruence between the rules as announced and their actual administration"); and JOSEPH RAZ, THE AUTHORITY OF LAW 218 (1979) (describing the precept, "[t]he discretion of the crime-preventing agencies should not be allowed to pervert the law").
92 FRIEDMAN, *supra* note 89, at 27.
93 PRESIDENT'S TASK FORCE, *supra* note 62, at 1.
94 FRIEDMAN, *supra* note 89, at 96.
95 Brandon Garrett & Seth Stoughton, *A Tactical Fourth Amendment*, 103.2 VIRGINIA LAW REVIEW 211 (2017). *See also* SETH W. STOUGHTON, JEFFREY J. NOBLE, & GEOFFREY P. ALPERT, EVALUATING POLICE USES OF FORCE (2020).
96 Garrett & Stoughton, *supra* note 95.
97 *Id.*
98 Graham v. Connor, 490 U.S. 386 (1989).
99 *Id.*
100 Garrett & Stoughton, *supra* note 95, at 215.

101 *See* FRIEDMAN, *supra* note 89, at 73 (stating that "even if the ... [the courts] could—and did—write such rules [regarding detailed policing policies], that still is not the same as democratic control of policing. Indeed, the courts are even less democratically accountable than the police themselves.").
102 *See* Garrett & Stoughton, *supra* note 95, at 244–99.
103 *Sir Robert Peel's Nine Principles of Policing*, N.Y. TIMES, April 15, 2014.
104 FRIEDMAN, *supra* note 89, at 307.

Chapter 4

Algorithms and Justice

The Conflation of Fact and Value

A former colleague who worked on crime pattern mapping included the following quotation at the bottom of every email he sent: "It doesn't matter how beautiful your theory is; it doesn't matter how smart you are; if it doesn't agree with the [data], it's wrong."[1] This is a variation of a remark made by quantum physicist Richard Feynman. Feynman was part of a group of scientists who received the Nobel Prize for Physics in 1965 for work in quantum electrodynamics. Even if you don't know anything about quantum physics—and I do not—it is easy to understand the significance of the quotation at the bottom of the professor's email. Feynman's remark is an abbreviated account of the scientific method: Scientists formulate hypotheses about the way the world is, as well as predictions about the world given those hypotheses; then they test the hypotheses through experiments that allow them to observe whether the world in fact conforms to their predictions.[2] I learned a slightly more rigorous version of the scientific method in my fourth-grade science class, but this simple account is enough to highlight the important role of experimental data. Without data, we can only guess about the way the world is. And when we do have data—and the data conflicts with our theory about the world—then our theory about the world is often wrong.

But there are important limits to what data can tell us, and sometimes those limits are overlooked. Some of the students with whom I have worked were interested in exploring criminal justice through quantitative research—research that investigates the world through statistical data. One such student wanted to write a thesis about the use of emerging policing strategies (such as advanced technology policing) in socially disorganized communities (communities with environmental conditions that affect crime rates).[3] The student's hypothesis was that data would show that the use of these policing strategies was more prevalent in communities with greater social disorganization. This is a phenomenon that can be observed and measured. It simply required the student to examine the use of different policing strategies in a community given variables that indicate the community's degree of social disorganization. I asked the student whether the project would stop there—a description of the way the world is—or, in addition, whether the project would address normative questions. In other words, I wanted to know whether the student planned to explore the extent to which it would be good or desirable (or just) for the police to use particular strategies in some communities rather than others. But is it not *obvious* that sophisticated policing strategies should be used in communities that are more socially disorganized and crime-ridden?

It depends upon whether the goal of a particular strategy is one that we value, as well as whether the strategy is pursued in a way that is consistent with our values. Data does not answer these sorts of questions—questions about which strategies the police should or should not use. Rather, we (human persons) make normative arguments about policing in light of our desires for society. To be sure, data can help inform our judgments in the context of policing. If data indicates that a particular policing strategy greatly reduces crime, then we might be more likely to argue in favor of the strategy given that we value crime reduction. But the data itself is silent with respect to what we ought to do. Neil Postman made a related point in his work on public culture and discourse:

> We have enough [prejudices] of our own, as for example, the equation we moderns make of truth and quantification. In this prejudice, we come astonishingly close to the mystical beliefs of Pythagoras and his followers who attempted to submit all of life to the sovereignty of numbers.[4]

How close are we to these mystical beliefs in policing?

Suppose data indicates that Community X can eradicate motor vehicle theft by instituting the following law: "The mother—or next closest relative—of any person who steals a motor vehicle in Community X shall be incarcerated in prison for no less than three years." The data may show that Community X's law will dramatically reduce motor vehicle theft, but Community X must decide whether it is right to pursue the policy in light of the value of crime reduction and any competing values. Community X would likewise have to determine whether other, more draconian tactics would be justified in the effort to reduce crime (perhaps torture as a punishment would drastically reduce crime). The tactics need not be so outrageous, and it is certainly true that less extreme strategies *seem* more justified given data that they reduce crime. The point is simply that data does not tell us whether we should take a particular course of action. My student had overlooked this basic point—the distinction between facts (data) and values—a point that I and others gloss over sometimes, too. More accurately, there is often an assumption that we should pursue a policing strategy because data indicates that the strategy will promote the value of crime reduction. The problem arises when we simply assume that the tactic is justified given data that the tactic promotes the value of crime reduction. But that is not always a good assumption. This is because data is neutral with respect to pursuing crime reduction versus competing values—such as legitimacy. The data does make evaluative arguments, but rather we must argue in favor of various police tactics given our analysis of the tactic's promotion (or erosion) of crime reduction *and* any competing values.

This distinction is the basis of the famous *is–ought problem*, which is often attributed to David Hume as the inability to derive normative arguments (ought) from descriptive statements (is).[5] In *A Treatise of Human Nature* (1739), Hume writes of the surprising way that ethical discourse makes the "imperceptible" change from propositions connected to "*is*, and *is not*" to propositions "connected with an *ought*, or an *ought not*."[6] Although this is often a subtle shift in terms, the move is deeply significant because "*ought*, or *ought not*, expresses some new relation" and thus needs explanation regarding "how this new relation can be a deduction from others, which are entirely different from it."[7] In short, the problem is that we sometimes assume there is an obvious or natural relation between *how things are* (given data about the world) and *how things should be* (given value judgments), leading us to hastily deduce an "ought" from an "is" without justification. I draw upon Hume here to make a broad, rhetorical point, but one must be careful not to define Hume's moral theory by one excerpt. As David Wiggins has noted:

> Hume's interest in morality was that of a moral scientist or as one would now say moral psychologist. His first question is not the question of the vindication of duty (that question can arise later), but the question of how natural beings such as ourselves can have arrived at the point where we can even think the refined and complex thoughts we do think about morality and its requirements.[8]

Hume's work generally—and the *is–ought problem* specifically—do not mean that we are without recourse in our ethical discussions, but they do mean that providing a basis for the move from one proposition to another can clarify those discussions.[9]

The goal of this chapter is straightforward: To sketch a conception of the police role that is consistent with the basic values of a constitutional democracy in the liberal tradition.[10] The conception itself is also straightforward: Seeking justice within the domain of policing. The hope is that clarifying the police role will likewise clarify any constraints upon our policing strategies—even if there is good evidence that particular tactics are effective law enforcement strategies. The underlying problem—conflating *is* and *ought* in our policing—is not limited to inconsequential mistakes made within the ivory tower. The problem is pervasive, affecting government policy at every level of policing—local, state, and federal. And the problem is made more difficult because it can be an almost imperceptible problem: Impressive advances in technology promising "law and order" based upon hard data result in assumptions that it is right for the police to use the technology—without regard to competing values. We need not imagine a hypothetical community that is contemplating law enforcement through torture and the imprisonment of one's mother. We need only look at the policing strategies in so-called liberal states. Sophisticated tactics—such as the police's use of crime analysis and advanced technology—seem completely benign in many cases. And such tactics are of course justified (and effective) when employed within the constraints of a justified police role.

However, as we have seen in prior chapters, the police are in the midst of an identity crisis that exacerbates unjustified law enforcement tactics. Although I have examined problems resulting from this police identity crisis, the implication is not that the police should have *no* identity. A conception of the police centered on the pursuit of justice is a good thing; mindlessness in the face of technology is not. In other words, it is a false dilemma to suggest that policing must *either* be subsumed by technocratic judgments encoded in some obscure piece of software, *or* be based upon a police ethic steeped in the wise discretion—as it were—of hero, warrior, and guardian policing. This chapter suggests a third option—an option that departs from both policing that is unduly technocratic and policing that is unduly individualistic. Before turning to a new conception of the police role, consider how the allure of data has driven us beyond our liberal constraints.

Policing by Prediction

The ambition to wield science for political purposes is hardly new. Take Sir William Petty, who began his career as an anatomy professor at Oxford University in the middle of the seventeenth century. One of the more interesting things about Petty—particularly as seen through his work, *Political Arithmetic*—was the development of natural philosophy into social science.[11] This extension of early modern scientific theories—couched within a mechanical worldview—reduced people and communities to "elementary particles, homogeneous and politically vacuous units at the disposal of the crown."[12] In short, Petty's project was based upon the idea that social policy could be guided by the scientific manipulation of people and places as *material stuff*. Such an idea is in some ways anathema to what might now be called "liberal values." But why? Is there reason to think that scientific rigor is somehow inappropriate when developing social and political policies? No, that is not the worry, for scientific rigor is an enlightening attribute in any domain. The worry is rather the implication that we can quantify what it means to be a person in society. If the essence of persons and communities can be captured in statistical terms governed by absolute mathematical rules, then we are merely part of a complex system that is as predictable as the moving parts in a machine. However, statistics do not provide a meaningful perspective given one's vantage point on the ground, so to speak. Or to put it a bit differently, statistically relevant information does not necessarily determine action.

For example, in one sense it would be meaningless to collect statistics regarding the number of people within a community who have had a negative encounter with the police. This is because such encounters are not understood within a particular family—say, the Johnson family—as an expression of something quantitative. The Johnsons' son, Joe, might belong to a demographic that is most likely to have negative police encounters, but—within the Johnson family—Joe is certainly not viewed as a statistic. He is just Joe, who had a police encounter on the way home from school that left a lasting impression one summer evening. On the other hand, statistics are indeed meaningful when we step back from Joe's perspective and view his experience through the lens of mass society. By abstracting away from Joe's experience and examining the world from an impersonal perspective, it is possible to learn something about society as a whole: Joe becomes a numerical representative of society. It is in this way that governments pursue social policies based upon human predictability. The trouble with viewing persons as numbers is that it can tend to overshadow the individualized perspective of those to whom social policies are meant to apply.[13]

This is the worry with the emerging strategy known as *predictive policing*: "the application of analytical techniques— particularly quantitative techniques—to identify likely targets for police intervention and prevent crime or solve past crimes by making statistical predictions."[14] The technique might bring to mind Steven Spielberg's 2002 film, *Minority Report*, in which a futuristic, high-tech police department ("PreCrime") apprehends criminals based upon the precognition of psychics (or "precogs"). The central philosophical issues raised in the film have to do with high-tech societies debating free will versus determinism. However, the problem of real-world predictive policing is not only about the technology behind the strategy (though there are problems with the technology that must be addressed), nor is the problem about free will *per se*.

Indeed, there are a variety of tactics that may be described as "predictive policing," including those that fall within the two broad categories of *person-based* predictive policing (when the police target and investigate specific individuals based upon algorithmically generated predictions) and *place-based* predictive policing (predicting when and where a crime will occur based upon an algorithm).[15] By algorithm I mean a "formally specified set of instructions used to analyze data and automate decisions," which can be more generally described as the "process by which computers make automated, predictive decisions about a dataset."[16] Given the growing prominence of place-based predictive policing—and the fact that it might *seem* less problematic than person-based predictive policing—this chapter focuses upon the ethics of place-based predictive policing. Ultimately, person-based and placed-based predictive policing raise many of the same ethical quandaries.

High-tech tools generally have the potential for good when used within the context of a justified police role. We see this to varying degrees with respect to a wide array of recent police tools, from in-vehicle computers to body cameras. The core problem with predictive policing is that it is used in a way that (paradoxically) bolsters the individualized police roles (especially the warrior role) discussed in the prior chapters: relegating policing to technocratic judgments encoded in software creates an identity vacuum, motivating a reactionary emphasis on the heroic warrior–guardian mythos. The problem is exacerbated by the reflexive, unchecked use of predictive policing that transforms persons into numerical representatives in society, sending police to nameless geographic spaces (literal 500-by-500 foot area boxes). Although the implementation of predictive policing tactics varies widely, police are often sent to these boxes with the expectation that they are likely to encounter crime and should try to stop it before it happens—warriors on a mission, so to speak—with little other instruction. What is often left out of this strategy is the personal viewpoint of the numerical representatives—the actual persons being predictively policed.

A first step in coming to grips with predictive policing is to situate it within the broader field of *crime analysis*, which "utilizes various data sources and analytical techniques to support crime prevention, crime reduction, and criminal apprehension efforts of police agencies."[17] The study of data as a way to reduce crime is nothing new. But the rapid advances in analytical technology raise two fundamental normative questions: Given that a new analytical technology provides new law enforcement tactics, (1) on what basis should the police use those tactics and (2) what are the constraints of that use?

The first question has a straightforward answer: Strategies such as predictive policing should be used to the extent that they are effective. And by effective we typically mean effective at reducing crime. Crime reduction itself is an uncontroversial goal that is justified in liberal societies. This is because security is one of the core values promoted by what is described as the social contract: Persons are in a reciprocal arrangement with the state under which each party to the arrangement has rights and duties. The legitimate provision of security is one reason that this sort of collective arrangement is practically and morally justified. We desire to be safe, secure, and free from crime, and so we enter into a cooperative enterprise that promotes that desire. This means that the state is justified in part based upon whether it fulfills our desire for security effectively.[18] But as implied in the second question above, there are competing values that constrain the way the state reduces crime and provides security. Obvious (and extreme) examples would be tactics such as illegitimate punishment and torture: Even if such tactics would reduce crime, they are constrained by the worth and status that we ascribe to each individual person. Before examining competing values, consider the extent to which predictive policing is effective at reducing crime.

Predictive policing originated from within a crime analysis strategy that is considered by many to be extremely effective: CompStat ("comparative statistics"). The central characteristic of CompStat is data-driven analysis of crime problems and assessment of a police department's efforts to solve those problems. CompStat's development and implementation is typically credited to William Bratton, who first became the Commissioner of the New York Police Department in 1994. The strategy is multifaceted and known for its use of computer database crime statistics (regarding murder, rape, theft, and so on) and police encounters (for example, arrests, stops, and so on) for a given geographic area (such as district or precinct). The data within the district is analyzed during meetings, which informs a police department's use of its resources to solve crime problems. Bratton subsequently became Chief of the Los Angeles Police Department (2002–2009), where he supported an enhanced version of CompStat ("CompStat Plus") and began referring to predictive policing: "We [LAPD] will move from near real-time analysis to true real-time analysis and then to a 'predictive policing' posture wherein more accurate and reliable probability modeling will be utilized to forecast potential crime trends over an increasing time span."[19] That was in 2008, but the evidence suggests that predictive policing is still in its infancy.

PredPol—a company self-described as "the market leader in predictive policing"—began as a research project at UCLA, where researchers worked with the Los Angeles Police Department to test their algorithms using crime data.[20] Officer Sean Malinowski was part of the team who led the LAPD's early use of PredPol. He put the decision to pursue predictive policing this way:

> [I]f we have a way to use mathematics to find out where we need to be in order to prevent crime, let's use it .... The only training you need to give the officers is what the map means and how to use the map.[21]

Others have taken a different view. The Richmond (California) Police Department canceled its contract with PredPol in 2016. Richmond saw a negligible impact on crime, and the department decided to instead focus on community relationships and trust as a way to improve crime intelligence. "I don't think you can get anything like that out of software," said Richmond Officer Felix Tan.[22] Ironically, the LAPD announced that it would discontinue its use of the PredPol predictive policing program—not for philosophical reasons, but rather due to financial constraints regarding the 2020 coronavirus pandemic.

In any event, the LAPD Chief of Police advised (in 2020) that "he believed the underlying principles behind PredPol were valid and that he'd be looking at other systems that crime analysts have to identify where crime is occurring."[23] It is difficult to say what sort of commitment the LAPD—not to mention other departments using predictive policing—will have with respect to pursuing community policing strategies in conjunction with future predictive policing efforts. Indeed, "a handbook on data-informed community policing ... was published on the LAPD's website" just the day before the chief announced an end to its use of PredPol.[24] To be sure, we should be careful not to equate concerns about PredPol with general concerns about predictive policing or the use of statistical analysis. These are not the same and each may raise a unique set of issues. For example, some reformers might not like PredPol in particular, but think that predictive policing is not bad *per se* (even if it is overly focused on lower-level property crime, which the police need to move past in a systematic way). My point is simply that the general worry—policing by numbers, so to speak—should be thought of less as an over-generalization and more as a fundamental way that technology is linked to the underlying police identity crisis.

Here is one way to frame the issue: If the goal of predictive policing is simply to reduce crime by having a larger police presence in particular areas, then predictive policing is inadequate and potentially harmful. Without a justified conception of the police role, the officers who physically occupy particular neighborhoods exacerbate (perhaps unwittingly) a feedback loop (in other words, when an algorithm tells police where to go, crime data is affected by the algorithm itself leading to a self-reinforcing loop) through biased data collection that results in biased predictions.[25] So predictive policing may not only fail to address the nature of crime rates, it also has the potential to perpetuate misleading data about crime rates. Policing strictly by numbers can lead to biased practices that harm particular communities—including through the goal to increase punitive police interactions as a way to "get the numbers up."[26] In order to be consistent with our political and legal values, a strategy must be pursued that views the police role more holistically. This begins with the recognition that crime problems cannot be resolved by numbers alone.[27]

To be sure, no one is suggesting (yet) that numbers and predictive policing can completely solve all our crime problems, but "data-driven" policing has become an almost unchecked obsession that has the potential for significant problems.[28] Consider legal scholar Sandra Mayson's *Bias In, Bias Out*, which examines the racial impacts of using algorithmic risk assessment to estimate future crime.[29] Mayson claims that the source of racial inequality in this sort of risk assessment is the nature of prediction itself because prediction looks to the past to make guesses about the future. For Mayson, then, *any* method for prediction will project past injustices into the future *given* a racially stratified world. This leads to the apt conclusion that redressing racial disparity in prediction requires fundamentally changing the criminal justice system's conception of risk.[30] In a parallel way, this chapter contends that *one* remedy is to fundamentally address the police identity crisis—including the vacuum created by the trend of almost single-mindedly focusing on technology. While numbers are of course important, it is also important to have a comprehensive conception of policing that incorporates the social dynamics between the police and the communities they serve.

Such a conception plays very little role in predictive policing itself. One of (place-based) predictive policing's core analytical objectives is identifying the geographic location of future crime.[31] The ability to predict the location of a crime seems like a good idea in principle. Who wouldn't want to head off crime by responding to the location it will occur before it occurs? But there is something troubling about how this goal is carried out: The predicted location is often determined exclusively by the analysis of data from computer software—without human reflection, in other words.[32] This is significant because it solidifies the divide between data and values. But rather than bridging the divide by incorporating more (human) analysis and value judgments, the police are directed to locations robotically based upon a computer algorithm.[33] In a sense, then, predictive policing is the embodiment of the *is–ought problem*. The philosophical problem underlying this trend belies a significant practical and professional problem, with criminologist Rachel Boba Santos putting it this way:

> These methods [of predictive policing] represent a clear distinction from traditional crime analysis techniques that include the analyst critically analyzing and making conclusions based on qualitative efforts such as reading crime and arrest reports, synthesizing intelligence, visually inspecting maps, as well as using statistical and mapping techniques, such as percent change, linear regression, and density mapping.[34]

This profound move away from human judgment is exemplified most clearly in the popular technique that I'll refer to as *prediction box*.

Prediction box is a predictive policing technique that has been described as "forecast[ing] individual crimes in the immediate future in order to direct patrol officers into 500-by-500 foot areas (i.e., boxes) that are at a higher risk of a crime occurring during a particular 8, 10, or 12 hour shift."[35] In other words, the *prediction box* technique directs the officers on each shift to report to—and move through—a specific geographic box with the goal of preventing a specific crime from occurring in that box.[36] The box is computed in part based upon data regarding time, date, and location of reported crimes without subsequent human analysis. This means that officers are given a map with an arbitrarily-bordered box covering an area within their jurisdiction.[37] New data is uploaded into the computer frequently, resulting in updated boxes for each shift.[38] Remarkably, there is one basic human judgment that is essential for police to use the *prediction box* technique: The decision of whether or not to purchase the computer software so that the prediction box maps can be printed for each police shift.[39] That's it—no additional human judgment is necessary.

Indeed, policing by *prediction box* can mean that officers are advised simply to "go to the box."[40] The hope seems to be that crime prevention will *just happen* when police patrol the box. This may sound overly robotic, but it is what many police departments desire. Santos notes that "[i]n my conversations with police chiefs, even those who have not yet implemented predictive policing refer to the process described here as the implementation they hope to achieve."[41] Again, the problems resulting from what I am calling a police identity crisis do not mean that the police should have *no* identity. The *just go to the box* approach is dehumanizing to the police—not just the community—inasmuch as it belittles their skills and strips them of agency (and perhaps responsibility) in the pursuit of justice.[42] But if that's the case, imagine how it feels to the community members within the box. Police are being sent to patrol the areas in which people live, work, and play. The central reason they are sent to these areas is the expectation that crime is imminent and should be prevented. So even if the police have other roles beyond stopping crime (communicating, assisting, and partnering with the community in a non-law-enforcement capacity, for example), those roles are eclipsed given the basic nature and goal of the *prediction box* technique.

This is the core problem of "sophisticated" police techniques such as predictive policing. It is not always the technology or tactic itself that is the biggest threat, but rather that the technology obscures the broader nature of the police role. In short, data is defining and directing police in a way that results in other value judgments (beyond a narrow focus on the value of crime reduction) falling by the wayside. If departments send police to patrol areas where there is an expectation that crime will occur, they should also clarify the nature of the police role in that specific area and the constraints upon that role. The police may very well encounter crime that requires the use of their law enforcement power inside the box. But they are not entering a battlefield as warriors on a mission. They are entering a community or neighborhood consisting of individual persons who are entitled to a conception of justice that goes beyond data-driven law enforcement.

Prediction Problems

> I think analytics should be a tool in the box, not the actual toolbox .... I know just because you had five steals doesn't mean you are a great defensive player.... I can still take that information, watch the players perform, and see how they got those numbers. ... [B]asketball has become homogenous because people follow, not because it is the right thing to do.
>
> (Jalen Rose)[43]

The point I have tried to make so far is that predictive policing tends to follow a one-size-fits-all path to justice. It is—quite literally—policing that can be purchased off-the-shelf. Although that may seem efficient, it shouldn't be controversial to suggest that a standard computer software package is not always the best way to guide the policing within a unique community. The crime problems that exist within Los Angeles are of a different nature than the crime problems within Portland, Dallas, Denver, Chicago, and New York—not to mention much smaller cities. However, it is not clear that predictive policing can be appropriately adapted to the unique characteristics of the communities in which it is applied. This is because predictive policing is inherently statistical policing applied to the mass without regard to the perspective of the particular community and individual citizen. From a technological standpoint, Santos notes that the lack of transparency regarding a computer's prediction software means that "crime analysts and police departments cannot determine if the models being applied to their data are actually relevant to their own jurisdiction's environment and levels of crime before or even after they have purchased access to the software."[44] The upshot is that predictive policing in the abstract tends not to pursue justice holistically. Of course, some aspects of predictive policing might be justified in conjunction with additional policing tactics that promote a justified police role. But as things stand, it is questionable whether predictive policing is justified at all.

One big problem is the data itself, with researchers frequently describing how predictive policing relies upon bad statistics.[45] Although predictive policing often relies upon data regarding crimes that are reported by victims, "the imperfect report writing by officers ... coding of variables, systematic errors and other factors may systematically bias the data and may not be transparent in an automatic transfer and analysis of large amounts of data."[46] These trends weigh in favor of a move away from blind reliance on statistics, and a move toward human analysis and value judgments.[47] One might object that if crime statistics and predictive policing algorithms are faulty and biased, it is often *because* they are the aggregate result of millions of human actors exercising their (faulty and biased) human analysis and value judgments. To be sure, I do not mean to suggest that we should appeal to some sort of abstract, ideal, bias-free, and fault-free exercise of human judgment. Rather, I more modestly suggest that our pursuit of human analysis and tactics such as community policing should be conducted in conjunction with concrete, restraining strategies that emphasize procedural justice in policing—a topic addressed in the chapter's conclusion.

For present purposes, the general idea is that a greater emphasis must be placed upon qualitative context in order to paint a more complete picture of the data. This includes seeking a deeper understanding of the specific communities and individuals being policed. It also requires us to consider normative questions regarding interactions between the police and the individuals served by the police. The larger point is that predictive policing is not the cutting-edge crime solution for which many hoped. The popular computer science saying is apt here: "garbage in, garbage out." In other words, the input of poor quality policing data will result in the output of poor quality predictions.[48] On a more fundamental level, are police departments even getting their money's worth from predictive policing software? One of the few studies of the *prediction box* technique was conducted by Temple University and the Philadelphia Police Department in 2015–2016.[49] The 500-by-500 foot boxes were predicted by Hunchlab predictive policing software; the results were less than overwhelming. The study found that the *prediction box* technique did not reduce violent crime. Although the technique appeared more effective with respect to property crime, the results were statistically insignificant.[50] Of course, police departments should try to salvage the good from the bad, but they should also be careful not to waste precious resources on predictive policing that has little positive impact and the potential for a significant negative impact.

Indeed, any crime reduction that results from predictive policing in its current form is unlikely to be worth the tradeoff of other values. This brings us full-circle to the central problem: Without a holistic policing strategy based upon a justified police role, the problems of the heroic police warrior identity are exacerbated by predictive policing's data-driven community interactions. Rather than promoting values such as legitimacy, predictive policing can reinforce the problems with which we have become all too familiar: a lack of community trust, an increase in excessive force, and a rise in biased tactics that threaten constitutional rights. Research has begun to acknowledge how predictive policing turns a blind eye to privacy and civil rights given that biased data means biased predictions.[51] This is especially apparent when data analysis is used to predict specific persons (person-based predictive policing) who are likely to be involved in crime— even if as a victim. In a much-discussed Chicago program, citizens who were deemed to be at risk of gun violence were placed on a list.[52] However, "[c]ommanders were not given specific guidance on what treatments to apply to [those on the list]; instead, they were expected to tailor interventions appropriately."[53] The problem with such tactics is that they do not seem to be an accurate predictor of potential victims, but rather who will be arrested upon receiving a visit from the police.[54]

The potential threats to one's constitutional rights under the Fourth Amendment are equally troubling. The Fourth Amendment states:

> The right of the people to be secure in their persons, houses, papers, and effects, against unreasonable searches and seizures, shall not be violated, and no Warrants shall issue, but upon probable cause, supported by Oath or affirmation, and particularly describing the place to be searched, and the persons or things to be seized.[55]

Modern Fourth Amendment jurisprudence has focused largely upon two seemingly distinct parts of the amendment: the "reasonableness clause" ("right ... to be secure ... against unreasonable searches and seizures") and the "warrant clause," which lists specific requirements for the issuance of a valid warrant.[56] More broadly, many view the Fourth Amendment's underlying goal as constraining the discretionary authority of government officers.[57] Legal scholar Thomas Davies put it this way in a prominent article on the Fourth Amendment's history:

> The Framers aimed the Fourth Amendment precisely at banning Congress from authorizing use of general warrants; they did not mean to create any broad reasonableness standard for accessing warrantless searches and arrests. Likewise, they did not intend it to guide officers in the exercise of discretionary arrest or search authority; instead, the Amendment's ban on too-loose warrants served to reaffirm the common law's general resistance to conferring discretionary authority on ordinary officers.[58]

More recently, this sentiment was echoed in *United States v. Jones*—a case in which the police used a GPS tracking device outside the parameters set out by a search warrant.[59] The goal of the Fourth Amendment is described in a concurring opinion this way: "to curb arbitrary exercises of police power and prevent 'a too permeating police surveillance.'"[60] One problem is that the police's discretion has grown exponentially, with respect to electronic surveillance discretion and beyond.[61] This growth in discretionary authority—along with the rise of predictive policing techniques—is a recipe for disaster without the constraining force of a legitimate conception of the police role.

Consider the proliferation of the police's use of tactics such as "stop and frisk"—a brief detention that includes patting down the person being detained. A police "stop and frisk" is constitutional only if the police have *reasonable suspicion* (based upon "specific and articulable facts") that a person has committed, is committing, or is about to commit a crime and has a reasonable belief that the person "may be armed and presently dangerous."[62] However, the New York Police Department—for example—

documented 685,724 stops (and 381,704 frisks) in 2011, and, of those frisked, a weapon was found only 1.9% of the time; moreover, over 70% of those stopped and frisked in the ten precincts with the lowest Black and Latino populations were Black and Latino.[63] Predictive policing techniques have the potential to exacerbate these disparities by expanding the criteria used to justify a "stop and frisk."[64] For instance, the police could rely upon predictive policing data—and courts could affirm their reliance—as an additional (and unjustified) factor that helps establish "reasonable suspicion" to "stop and frisk" a person.[65] Legal scholar Andrew Ferguson illustrates with this example:

> If a particular block suffers a statistically high number of car thefts over a month period, a predictive model might forecast that the same block will be the locus of a subsequent theft. Blind adherence to the predictive forecast might mean that an individual observed with a screwdriver on that block, in combination with the forecast, might result in reasonable suspicion for a stop. However, if prior to the stop police had arrested the gang responsible for all the prior car thefts, improved the lighting in the area, and posted police on the street, reliance on the prediction should be irrelevant. The reason why the future crime is predicted to happen no longer holds. Incorporating predictive policing into the reasonable suspicion analysis of the court then would not be appropriate.[66]

As troubling as this scenario may sound, the deeper point is the way that predictive policing affects the nature of the police role—including a framework for justified police discretion. Statistical analysis can obscure the broader nature of policing by encouraging strict adherence to the predictive model. The power of predictive policing is thus its basis in data: How can anyone argue with hard data? But that's just it: Data doesn't argue. Data provides a snapshot of the world. Sometimes it is a high-resolution snapshot that allows us to see the world more clearly. In other cases, the snapshot is poor quality, providing a misleading illustration of the world. Either way, the data does not provide answers to normative questions regarding what the police ought to do. The data undoubtedly informs these questions, but the answers themselves are based upon arguments regarding the data's value and its relation to other values. These value arguments are deeply entrenched in broader conceptions of justice that constrain and define a legitimate police role.

This role is developed in the next half of the chapter. The hope is that clarifying the nature of the police role will point to solutions to some of the concerns that have been raised. The overarching concern is straightforward: Predictive policing has been heralded as a scientific quick-fix to crime problems requiring little human capital. This is misleading and distracts from the systemic, cultural problems that require critical analysis in policing—and that raise basic questions regarding the fundamental nature of the police role. Assuming that the use of predictive policing techniques will continue to increase, it stands to reason that we should incorporate a legitimate police role into police training generally and predictive policing training specifically. This role minimally entails an emphasis on strategies that include public reason, human rights, and civil rights. Admittedly, this task is rife with practical difficulties. In the short-run, it is far easier to address crime problems by purchasing off-the-shelf software than critiquing, clarifying, and promulgating the basic conception of the police role.[67] But given the growth of predictive policing around the world, it is a fitting time to examine the police—not just the prediction.

Justice through Human Rights

Law enforcement institutions come in all shapes and sizes at all levels of government—local, state, and federal. So they shouldn't be painted with too broad a brush. However, almost all government bureaucracies share an attribute that seems wrong at first glance: Bureaucracies dehumanize people by viewing them as numbers. This is not as bad as it sounds.[68] It is rather a necessity that comes with the administration of large numbers of people. It is almost impossible to imagine a police department—or any government agency—without statistics. This is because it is necessary to think of people as numbers, statistics, and data, in order to produce things such as crime analysis products—not to mention other valuable social goods such as universal welfare safety nets. But there is a danger in embracing a statistical perspective without constraint. The value of inductive reasoning and making generalizations cannot be overstated, but as Frederick Schauer has noted, "much of the history of unfortunate discrimination is a history of the erroneous belief in statistical relationships that turn out to have no basis in fact."[69] In the context of policing, one of the chief dangers of reducing people to numbers is that it enables an "us versus them" mindset. This happens when the *us* (the police) views the *them* as a mass of statistics that may be dealt with in a less than human way. This sort of dehumanization is perhaps most obvious with soldiers—or warriors—at war. Dehumanization is in part what allows us to push a single button that results in the death of hundreds or thousands of people. The death toll is in large part a matter of statistics, which inform the next action on the battlefield.

The police are not warriors. They might be required to use (deadly) force, but they are not at war with the communities they serve. One way to clarify this idea—introduced in chapter 2—is to temper the policing perspective that communities are an undifferentiated mass. This does not mean that we should dispense with statistics or stop using data in our policy decisions. But it does mean that we should emphasize the humanity of the communities that police serve, as well as the police's role of promoting the human rights of those in the community. Human rights mean different things to different people and are typically emphasized in an international context—such as the justification of a state intervening in the affairs of another state. More broadly, human rights are viewed as the most basic, minimal rights because they are owed to every person. Accordingly, one might view the first step of seeking a moral foundation for the police role as accounting for each person's human rights—or at least the human rights that are within the police's purview to protect.[70] These rights will of course overlap with more concrete civil rights.

Consider the police's use of chokeholds, a tactic that is not against the law—but that has been against police policy in New York since 1992. In 2013, the New York City Civilian Complaint Review Board (CCRB) recorded 233 complaints involving chokeholds, which was 4.4 percent of the police abuse allegations it received. In 2003, chokehold allegations made up only 2.3 percent of the excessive-force complaints.[71] Those numbers don't seem terribly high, and, as the saying goes, perhaps they reflect a small number of bad (police) apples. On the other hand, there are tragedies behind the numerical trends. For example, Anthony Baez—a security guard—was playing football with his brothers when their football accidentally hit parked police patrol cars in the Bronx during the early morning of December 22, 1994. The police asserted that the men were disrupting the neighborhood and arrested Baez for disorderly conduct. Baez had an asthmatic condition, and—during a struggle that ensued upon his arrest—Baez died from asphyxia related to the alleged use of a chokehold.[72]

Or consider the more recent case of Eric Garner, who the police arrested for the charge of selling loose cigarettes illegally (without tax), a crime for which he had been arrested multiple times. When Garner pulled away from being handcuffed, it was reported that

> [t]he officer immediately threw his arm around [Garner's] neck and pulled him to the ground, holding him in what appears, in a video, to be a chokehold. The man can be heard saying 'I can't breathe' over and over again as other officers swarm about.[73]

Garner was a large (unarmed) man with health issues, meaning that he may have been perceived as a physical threat that required swift force (irrespective of health issues, of which the police may have been unaware). A grand jury decided not to indict the officer who killed Garner. Recall that there was no law prohibiting the officer's use of a chokehold. But that does not address why the police used their discretion to arrest Garner for a minor offense that immediately escalated to the use of an unauthorized (against policy), lethal chokehold.

Even if such tactics are not against the law—but only against police policy—they still raise questions about a person's most basic, human rights.

As we have seen, the police are now sent to communities based upon a prediction that a crime will occur. In addition to this expectation of crime, they should also arrive with a conception of how the police role relates to the human rights of the individual persons within those communities—persons such as Anthony Baez and Eric Garner and others who might be suspected of crimes. Unfortunately, human rights can have a tendency to seem a bit pie-in-the-sky to some realists who understand the difficult nature of policing. For instance, it may not help that some human rights advocates have argued that a free, annual vacation is a human right.[74] I can imagine my former police colleagues reacting to such a notion: *Sure, let's give this gentleman a holiday in Bermuda after we book him for shooting at me.* These worries make it beneficial to begin by examining how basic human rights are connected to more concrete legal rights—particularly those related to policing.

Recall how the Fourth Amendment to the U.S. Constitution protects the "right of the people to be secure in their persons ... against unreasonable ... seizures." A police officer's use of force (deadly, or otherwise) constitutes a seizure and must be reasonable. As discussed in the last chapter, courts have construed the "reasonableness" of force based upon "the perspective of a reasonable officer on the scene, rather than with the 20/20 vision of hindsight."[75] This allows for broad deadly forces polices. Here is the policy I learned while training to be a Special Agent at the FBI Academy at Quantico: "Special agents may use deadly force only when necessary—when the agent has a reasonable belief that the subject of such force poses an imminent danger of death or serious physical injury to the agent or another person ...."[76] One can see how the policy language tracks the broad "reasonableness" of the Constitution and case law: The use of deadly force is based upon (1) *necessity*, which is defined as (2) a *reasonable belief* that (3) *serious harm* will occur (4) *imminently*.

Taken as a whole, this may sound like a high standard. Afterall, deadly force can be used only to address a danger of serious harm—such as death. But almost everything hinges on the reasonable belief that deadly force is necessary. And this is shaped in part by the officer's conception of the police officer role: Regarding questions about the necessity of force and risk of serious harm, what perspective would be taken by a reasonable officer? This will vary depending upon whether reasonable officers are conceived primarily as heroes, warriors, guardians, or something else. A reasonable perspective for a warrior may very well be different from the perspective of others, in part because police warriors are often taught—somewhat paradoxically—that it is reasonable for violent reflex to trump rationality.[77] The larger point is that the Fourth Amendment embodies perhaps the most fundamental human right: *security of person*. And the extent to which that right is respected by the police is in part based upon the conception of the police role. First, though, what does it mean to say that security of person is a human right?[78]

A good place to start is the classic account of rights developed by American jurist Wesley Newcomb Hohfeld.[79] We can begin with what have become known as *first-order rights*: Rights that a person has to certain things, or rights for one person to do certain things for another person. First-order rights include *liberty rights* (or privileges), which are based simply upon a person's freedom to do something or have something. For example, I have a liberty right to stop at a water fountain in a public park and drink the water. Under most circumstances, I have complete freedom to drink the water because I have no duty—legal, moral, or otherwise—to not drink the water. First-order rights also include *claim rights*, which are obligations that a person has to enable another person to do something or to have something. I have a claim right against other people at the park regarding their not stopping me from drinking from of the water fountain. Other park-goers have a duty to enable me—or at least not stop me—from drinking water from of a public water fountain.

Simply put, *second-order rights* are the sort of rights that impact first-order liberty and claim rights. These include what are known as *powers* and *immunities*, such as legal rights. A power is the ability to alter a first-order right, as when the police prevent me from drinking from a public water fountain because they are securing a crime scene in the park. I have a liberty right to drink from the fountain and a claim right against the police and others from stopping me. However, the police have the power to alter my rights given their legitimate legal authority to investigate crimes. An immunity involves an *inability* to alter first-order rights, such as when the police try to prevent a person from drinking from a public water fountain because the person is wearing a shirt stating, "fuck the police." The police have the power to alter my rights based upon legitimate legal authority. However, one's rights are immune from such alteration in this case given one's legal right to free expression under the First Amendment to the U.S. Constitution.

Where do human rights and the police fit into this framework? This is a difficult question to answer in part because there is disagreement about the nature and foundation of human rights. For example, there are three ways (at least) to think about the foundation of human rights: (1) Derived from human dignity; (2) derived from natural rights; (3) derived from practical political conceptions.[80] Some political and legal philosophers—such as Jeremy Waldron—think of dignity as a status concept—a status that results in a particular package of (human) rights that a person has in virtue of being human.[81] This is a promising foundational account of human rights, though it raises questions about the nature of the status (presumably some sort of universal, equal, high-ranking social–legal status), as well as questions about the extent to which dignity constrains the list of potential human rights.

Alternatively, one might construe human rights as a facet of the natural rights tradition—including the Kantian and Lockean traditions—suggesting that certain pre-institutional natural rights simply count as "equal and inalienable" rights of human persons.[82] This sort of human rights theory is particularly relevant in the realm of policing, given that the Lockean tradition (for example) defends a natural right to be free from the non-consensual coercion of political and legal institutions.[83] This principle of course raises the idea of a natural right to *legitimate* institutions—meaning that we should at a minimum mitigate the illegitimacy of actual institutions (including the police institution). Finally, one might build upon Rawls's implicit critique of foundational theories of human rights—as Charles Beitz has done—arguing for a "practical" conception of human rights based upon the pressing concerns of domestic and international politics (rather than historical, pre-institutional natural rights).[84] Although there is certainly more that can be said about these and other accounts of human rights theory, consider now some of the ways that human rights theory has been applied—especially applications relevant in the domain of policing.

After the horrors of World War II, the world's nations adopted the Universal Declaration of Human Rights in 1948. In the subsequent seven decades, there has been a proliferation of human rights treaties, conventions, and organizations. Before these developments, there were documents such as the U.S. Constitution and the human rights mandate of the Bill of Rights—not to mention the philosophical tradition from which those documents took root. Where to begin? There are a few characteristics about human rights that seem relatively uncontroversial. First, human rights are *universal* because they are standards of treatment applicable to all persons given their personhood.[85] It may be trivial to point out, but a right is not a human right if does not apply to all humans. The alternative is that no human rights exist because, say, some humans lack minimal cognitive potential for such rights, or because, say, presumptive human rights are in fact alienable. In any event, the universality of human rights is of course aspirational: The fact that the United States has a Bill of Rights does not mean that no person in the United States is subjected to coerced confessions and police brutality. But if we are talking about human rights, then we are generally talking about rights that should be universal.

Next, human rights are typically construed as *claim rights* because they impose duties of treatment on others.[86] This means that human rights include obligations that a person has to enable another person to do something or to have something. For example, if *security of person* is a human right, then it is a claim right on other people to respect one's liberty. This means that I have a claim right against others not to use force against me or seize me. But if I break the law, then the police have the power to alter my right and seize me—including through the use of legitimate force. On the other hand, I am immune from certain police actions because the police have no legitimate power to alter my security of person through brutality.

This raises the next general characteristic of human rights: They are often *political* rights because duty-bearers typically include those with power over right-holders.[87] Again, police brutality is an apt example here. There are many ways that one's human right to security of person may be violated—think of common crimes such as assault, rape, and murder. But security of person is uniquely violated in the political context, as when agents of the state harass, assault, and brutalize persons within the state's jurisdiction. Many states—not least the United States—have a history of violating one's human right to security of person and those violations continue to this day. It thus stands to reason that any justified conception of the police role includes the following point: The police have a duty to pursue justice in a way that respects one's human right to security of person.

So there is a natural overlap between certain human rights and certain political and civil rights. And these characteristics provide a rough framework by identifying human rights as (1) *universal* rights involving (2) a *claim* against those who have (3) *political* power over the right-holder. Given these assumptions, a good case can be made that *legitimacy* should be included as a human right, in addition to security of person. There are many different ways to think about legitimacy. Options include narrowly construed conceptions of police legitimacy, as well as broader notions of a state's legitimacy. Most conceptions of legitimacy are at their core based upon the appropriate *authority* to wield power over a person. Consider how the idea of police legitimacy is related to a state's legitimacy. A police officer executing a valid warrant acts as an agent of the state and, accordingly, an agent of the sovereign political power. This means that when the police act without requisite authority, their acts are illegitimate because they are not acts of the state. We often describe this as acting "under color of law" (acting under the pretense of authority) because the action is outside the rule of law and without authority.[88] The police do not have the *authority* to use force in a discriminatory or brutal way. Such actions are illegitimate.

Legitimacy and Security of Person through Public Reason

The preceding sections led to the basic claim that policing should be pursued in a way that promotes legitimacy. Although this idea may sound obvious, the tactics and strategies noted earlier in the chapter suggest that it is not. And this lends support to the view that policing strategies should renew focus on values beyond general security and crime reduction. A warrior role—coupled with data-driven predictive policing—may be effective at reducing crime. But in isolation, this conception of the police role overlooks the broader goal of seeking justice through promoting human rights that include security of person and legitimacy. This is especially the case with respect to people and places associated with crime predictions.

Here is where the idea of *public reason* can play a helpful role. Roughly, public reason is a concept in political philosophy standing for the idea that government principles should be justifiable to all those to whom the principles are meant to apply. Although public reason is often presented as a normative ideal in the context of idealized societies and persons, it is possible to apply the tenets of public reason to actual political deliberations—especially given a methodology based upon nonideal theory that seeks to transition to the ideal.[89] Admittedly, though, my use of public reason to defend actual police practices is clearly non-standard. This is because most political philosophers regard public reason as pertaining to how a society's basic laws and policies are articulated and debated in the political sphere, rather than yielding substantive (and specific) laws and policies in any direct way.

In what follows, then, I suggest a novel expansion of the standard view of public reason—an expansion that might serve as a unifying rationale and moral foundation for a justified police role. This is because public reason promotes legitimacy and security of person by bolstering autonomy, justice, and respect regarding differences of ethnicity, gender, sexual orientation, mental health—and, more generally, promotes human dignity.[90] I take it as a safe normative assumption that human rights—such as security of person and legitimacy—should be pursued by the police. I also consider it uncontroversial to make the empirical assumption that security of person and legitimacy have eroded in some communities. If there are particular conceptions of the police role that promote these human rights through public reason, then such roles should be pursued in addition to those focused upon crime reduction. But first consider why public reason is important in liberal societies.

There is a multitude of accounts regarding what makes a state legitimate. John Locke embraced a transactional account of legitimacy that is known through the idea of the social contract: Legitimacy is based upon our interactions with others, as when we consent to a state's authority.[91] So, for example, if a particular state is legitimate, it is because the state's citizens consented to the state's authority in some way; accordingly, the state's citizens have a duty to obey the state's laws given the weight we place upon valid consent. But we know that receiving explicit consent from everyone governed in a community is a practical impossibility. Public reason might thus be viewed as a middle ground for justifying our moral and political principles to all those persons to whom the principles are meant to apply. And that might be a way to achieve some form of legitimacy with respect to those principles.

As I have indicated, it is also possible to think of legitimacy more narrowly, as with theories of "police legitimacy." A familiar account of police legitimacy is "a property of an authority or institution that leads people to feel that authority or institution is entitled to be deferred to and obeyed."[92]

To put it a bit differently, the authority that the police exert over communities should be reasonably acceptable to those communities—namely, authority to which reasonable persons might consent. This means that a conception of the police role is justified inasmuch as it entails reciprocity between the police and the community through communication of applicable laws, regulations, and policies.

Why pursue this goal? Why seek to have our principles and policies justifiable to those to whom they apply? One answer is that it promotes values that are fundamental to legitimate polities and that are especially relevant to policing: civic relationships based upon inclusivity, autonomy, respect, justice, duty, and dignity.[93] For example, pluralistic political communities include a variety of perspectives. Consider the diversity within most any city—from ethnicity, religion, and politics, to mental health, gender, and sexual orientation. Given this vast diversity, how do community members and government agents maintain an appropriate and justified communal relationship with each other? Public reason answers the question this way: Communities regulated by laws, policies, and regulations that can be justified to each member—despite the diversity of perspectives—are related to each other in an appropriate and justified manner.[94] A simple example might be the extent to which police respect all victims equally, rather than, say, inflicting further harm by misgendering and misnaming transgender victims.[95]

This idea gets to the heart of constitutional democracy and the balance of *reciprocity* and *authority* between diverse members within a community. Achieving legitimate authority is possible through reciprocal arrangements that are reasonable to persons subject to the authority. There are a variety of doctrinal examples, including: "We the people ... to form a more perfect union ... to promote general welfare ... establish this Constitution."[96] This sort of transaction aspires to establish an agreement that promotes the general welfare of all persons. The state's authority is based upon the agreement setting forth reciprocal rights and duties. And reciprocity and authority are bolstered by public values—such as fairness, equality, and the rule of law—drawn from common sense principles of social cooperation that permit agreement between diverse groups within the state. Conversely, the denial of these public values results in political power and coercive (police) force based upon arbitrary authority lacking buy-in from the diverse members of the community—illegitimate authority, in other words.

This relational component is also relevant to how public reason encourages autonomy by promoting expression of a common will of the citizenry—and governance by law—rather than exclusive, autonomy-stifling expression by the state.[97] For example, the general principle might be illustrated through a state's endorsement of *retribution* through *extrajudicial* killings. Consider the extensive protesting (and counter-protesting) against police violence following the killing of George Floyd on May 25, 2020.

Michael Forest Reinoehl, a self-described anti-fascist, was wanted on suspicion of fatally shooting a member of a far-right group during protests in Portland, Oregon, on August 29, 2020. Although the facts may not be completely clear, it is plausible to think Reinoehl unjustifiably took the law into his hands (perhaps similar to the killings in Kenosha, Wisconsin, on August 25, 2020) when he shot someone on the street. Indeed, Reinoehl seemed to admit to the shooting in an interview, though claimed self-defense.[98] Reinoehl was subsequently shot and killed by law enforcement officers on September 3, 2020—the day that President Trump took to Twitter calling for Reinoehl's arrest and describing him as a "cold blooded killer."[99] Following Reinoehl's death, Trump was interviewed and appeared to support the view that law enforcement officers may need to take criminal justice and punishment into their own hands: "That's the way it has to be. There has to be retribution when you have crime like this."[100]

While one might strongly condemn Reinoehl's actions, it would of course be an affront to the rule of law for the head of state to ask law enforcement officers to be both judge and jury.[101] The American criminal justice system presumes that suspects are innocent until proven guilty in a court of law. If Reinoehl resisted arrest or attacked law enforcement during an arrest operation (there were conflicting witness reports), then the police may have been justified in using deadly force.[102] But promoting *punitive* action against a suspect before the suspect is proven guilty in a court of law is not justified under any circumstances. The rule of law is embodied in a variety of institutional sources, including the 14th Amendment to the U.S. Constitution: States are prohibited from depriving any person of life without due process of law. The point is simply that failures of public reason may result in failures of autonomy. And a failure of autonomy leads to an exclusive expression of political will that may be contrary to the common will and the rule of law.

Public reason thus encourages citizens to view themselves as legislators, supporting political positions that could be justified on grounds that all reasonable citizens could embrace.[103] This point is especially relevant in the area of policing, in which community members are often used as a mere means to a law enforcement end. Consider the police's extensive reliance upon informants in many communities. Unfortunately, questions about the limits of the police's use of informants and sting operations have been largely ignored.[104] Such tactics are undoubtedly justified in some cases. This might include "patriotic" informants who voluntarily provide intelligence regarding threats about which they have special access. But other uses of informants might be deemed a departure from dignity and legitimacy-promoting policing—especially cases in which the police use their leverage to coerce persons to "consent" to dangerous operations.

A tragic example is the case of LeBron Gaither, who was a sixteen-year-old student at a Kentucky public high school when he punched the school's assistant principal in the face. After being arrested for juvenile assault, the Kentucky State Police used their leverage over Gaither to make a high-stakes offer: Gaither could take his chances with a lengthy prison term or agree to become their drug informant. Faced with these options, Gaither "chose" to engage in drug sting operations for the police. Two years later, Gaither was called to testify before a grand jury against Jason Noel, a dealer who Gaither had set up in a prior sting operation. In spite of his testimony, the police tasked Gaither to make another drug buy from Noel the next day.[105] Journalist Sarah Stillman recounts what transpired:

> The meeting was to take place in the parking lot of a local grocery store; Gaither was instructed to say, "This looks good," once he had the drugs in hand. At that point, the police would move in for the arrest. If something went wrong, he was to say, "I wish my brother was here," and officers would hasten to his aid. Shortly after the sting began, however, detectives lost track of Gaither when Noel, who had learned of the teen's testimony from a grand juror, drove off with him. Gaither was tortured, beaten with a bat, shot with a pistol and a shotgun, run over by a car, and dragged by a chain through the woods.[106]

It is difficult to see how the police viewed Gaither as anything but an expendable means to a law enforcement end in this case.

We often associate informants with undercover drug deals such as in Gaither's case. But the police use informants in all areas of law enforcement—from gangs and corruption to terrorism and prostitution (including tasking informants to engage in sex acts to gather evidence about prostitution).[107] These cases illustrate the variety of ways that informants are placed into situations that could result in harm or death. What does the pervasive use of informants to engage in illegal and dangerous acts do to a community? Sociologist Alice Goffman lived and worked for six years in a Black, lower-income neighborhood in Philadelphia.[108] Through documenting the police's routine encounters with (and use of) community members, Goffman answers the general question about informants this way:

> Whether a man's friends, relatives, or girlfriend bring him to the attention of the authorities because the police pressure them to do so or because they leverage his wanted status to control or punish him, he comes to regard those closest to him as potential informants. Like going to the hospital or calling the police, spending time with friends, family, or romantic partners places men at risk.[109]

To be sure, the police are seeking the resolution of real crime problems through their use of informants. But what is missing from the equation is the value of legitimacy that is bolstered through the basic tenets of public reason. Without these values, the use of informants is a mere means to a law enforcement end. The impact on the informant specifically—and the community generally—is secondary if it is considered at all. The police use their discretionary authority to coerce informants into unlawful activity, which, among many other things, can weaken the rule of law and breed distrust in the community. Goffman describes how the use of informants divides not only communities, but also family structures within communities:

> [T]he police's strategy of arresting large numbers of young men by turning their mothers and girlfriends against them goes far in creating a culture of fear and suspicion, overturning women's basic understandings of themselves as good people and their lives as reasonably secure, and destroying familial and romantic relationships that are often quite fragile to begin with.[110]

There are justified uses of informants, but it is not clear that the police consider how the pervasive use of informants (often in relatively minor cases) can affect communities.

Given that the police's law enforcement role of reducing crime is often the primary focus of inquiries regarding informants, there can be a tendency to overlook the need to balance law enforcement with competing values such as legitimacy. I raise these considerations to foreshadow how the police's role is not limited to law enforcement, but rather includes a variety of (non-law-enforcement) roles that invoke values beyond crime reduction. The police's use of informants is a facet of their law enforcement role, though it is also relevant to other roles. And the use of informants highlights tension between strictly constitutional (i.e., Fourth Amendment, which is not typically relevant to the decision to use an informant) constraints upon the police's law enforcement role and the broader normative considerations that are relevant to policing generally—such as the role of law enforcement discretion.[111] The discretionary use of informants may be legal, but it does not follow that such discretion should always be exercised given values beyond crime reduction. An exclusive emphasis on law enforcement overlooks the broader police role illuminated through public reason.

Ultimately, then, public reason promotes the fundamental values of justice and duty. By showing that policing principles should be subject to public reason, we are in a better position to see how they regulate public life fairly and justly.[112] Public reason also affords diverse communities the opportunity to think of themselves as if they were legislators: Communities support political positions justified by appealing to reasons that all reasonable persons could endorse, and they hold government officials to the same standard.[113] The first part of this chapter addressed emerging trends in policing that focus exclusively on data and law enforcement. These contemporary trends show how departing from the tenets of public reason can contribute to stratified communities in which police are unduly focused upon crime reduction at the expense of other fundamental values. We now turn to different conceptions of the police role, those that view law enforcement as but a single (important) facet of seeking justice.

Conclusion: Public Reason through (Procedurally Just) Community Policing

Community policing is one justified way for the police to pursue their law enforcement role and promote human rights through public reason. This is because community policing pursues legitimacy by building community trust and developing public justification. Although this strategy has been around for decades, one difficulty with pursuing it effectively is a renewed emphasis on police roles that are inconsistent with community policing (coupled with emerging technocratic strategies such as predictive policing). This includes the entrenched police warrior role (and inadequate "guardian" role), which continue to focus upon so-called "law and order" tactics such as increased police militarization, re-escalation of the "war on drugs," and zero tolerance immigration policies. For example, Radley Balko has described how the "war" on drugs "utterly dehumanize[d] drug users, cast the drug fight as a biblical struggle between good and evil, and in the process turn[ed] the country's drug cops into holy soldiers."[114] Another difficulty with pursuing community policing is that recent work in the social sciences suggests that it has limited impact on crime, which tends to imply that crime reduction is the only relevant value in policing.[115] Such tension raises questions about how the police should balance different values—legitimacy and crime reduction, for instance.

So far, the police tactics that have been discussed illustrate an underlying disconnect between the police and various segments of communities. It is this disconnect that contributes to a lack of police legitimacy. One factor that can exacerbate the disconnect is an almost exclusive emphasis on the *law enforcement* role of policing. Although law enforcement is of course one of the central police roles, we have seen why it is important to balance law enforcement with other public values through public reason. If too much emphasis is placed upon law enforcement (at the expense of other police roles and values), then police are at risk of relying upon coercive force that breeds arbitrary authority. In other words, our institutions may justify tactics that merely use community members as a means to a law enforcement end, fostering illegitimacy. The value of crime reduction cannot be overstated, but neither can it be justified at the expense of legitimacy.

A modest first step toward addressing this problem is to acknowledge that policing is more than law enforcement. Then the various other police roles can be better balanced to achieve community policing that is consistent with the basic tenets of public reason. Consider below three police roles described by John Klenig that are not about law enforcement and crime reduction.[116] As I will discuss in the Epilogue, there have been recent pushes to "defund" (or even "abolish") the police, including some of the responsibilities discussed below. The idea is to reallocate police funds to other social service organizations that are more skilled at handling non-law enforcement situations. Some elements of this idea may have merit: Who wouldn't want more funding for mental health professionals so that such professionals—not the police—are put into a better position to address mental health crises? However, it is likely—for the reasons below—that policing will continue to include many non-law enforcement roles, making it vital for us to think beyond the values of law enforcement and crime reduction.

First, police are *emergency operators*: When there is an accident on the interstate, who is typically the first to respond? It is very likely the police, who assist their communities by addressing emergency situations—especially until more specialized responders arrive. Given their daily interactions with the public and the fact that they are dispersed over large geographic areas, police are particularly suited to respond to emergency situations quickly. The police thus fulfill the vital societal role of emergency operators. This role often has little or no relation to the distinct law enforcement role, drawing out one of the many ways that the police serve communities beyond providing law and order. Nevertheless, the emergency operator role requires legitimacy because emergency situations involve trust. It is thus important that the police are viewed as possessing the necessary authority that justifies deference in emergency situations.

Second, police are *social enforcers*. Police are often the first to address domestic disputes, even if such disputes do not involve law enforcement. Police use their coercive force not just to investigate crime, but also to address other human problems that require the use of force. This might include responding to an emergency or domestic situation in which a community member needs help—especially until more specialized social service officials are available to assist. As with the emergency operator role, the social enforcer role may thus have little or no relation to law enforcement—yet it reflects a vital relationship between the state and the citizenry. The social enforcer role likewise requires legitimacy because resolving domestic disputes and other non-law-enforcement social conflicts requires trust. Here again, promoting police legitimacy is justified inasmuch as the police possess authoritative, deferential roles beyond investigating and stopping crime.

More holistically, then, one might say that the police are *social peacekeepers*. This conception of the police focuses upon the police's responsibility for maintaining security (or peace) in a way that is consistent with the limits of the state's legitimate power. In other words, keeping the peace involves building trust by the appropriate use of discretionary power, including discretionary law enforcement power.[117] The police are not warriors or single-minded crime-fighters, but rather public servants who must keep the peace by partnering with the community in justified ways. And this helps to strengthen public trust and build police legitimacy, the idea behind community-oriented policing.

What remains is a simple but important conclusion: Policing is far more than solving crime problems and enforcing the law. The role of the police has changed dramatically over the last two centuries—from night watchmen and constables with little power and authority, to professional agents and agencies with vast discretionary powers at the local, state, and federal levels.[118] Still, the police have long assumed a variety of roles that serve the community beyond stopping crime, even if those roles have at times lacked broad support and visibility.[119] In a sense, the idea of "community-oriented policing" formalizes a model of policing that includes serving the community in a variety of ways that complement a variety of roles. Community policing thus entails the evaluation of police holistically in a way that includes the police's diverse set of roles.[120]

Where does reducing crime fit into community policing? Community policing and solving crime problems are not mutually exclusive, of course, yet it may turn out that community policing is not the best way to solve crime problems. But this shouldn't be surprising. Indeed, many tactics that would effectively solve crime problems are not pursued by society because the tactics fail to promote values beyond crime reduction. Putting one's mother in prison when one engages in grand larceny may be an effective way to solve the problem of grand larceny, but it is an ineffective way to promote the legal and philosophical values of liberalism regarding culpability, fairness, and so on. What, then, are the justified tactics of community policing?

Roughly, community policing is a philosophy and organizational strategy that promotes community empowerment and collective efficacy: Policing that seeks community development through community partnership.[121] A simple example would be coordination between the police and a neighborhood watch group, which might increase citizen empowerment and reduce citizen fear—thereby facilitating conditions that will help solve crime problems.[122] Generally speaking, there are three defining aspects of community policing:

1 Citizen involvement in identifying and addressing public safety concerns,
2 The decentralization of decision making to develop responses to locally defined problems, and
3 Problem solving.[123]

These aspects of community policing become manifest through a variety of specific activities, including problem solving through partnerships; police representation at community meetings and gatherings; bicycle and foot patrols; citizen police academies, citizen volunteers, and ride-alongs; and neighborhood watches. The last aspect—crime problem solving—is subject to the objection that community policing is ineffective (keeping in mind that police agencies have not always been fully committed to community policing). As we will see, however, there are reasons to pursue community policing independent of evidence that it affects the social ethos. This is especially the case inasmuch as community policing functions as a manifestation of public reason.

First, community policing pursues communication with community partners. This might begin at a very basic level, including door-to-door in-person visits, group community meetings, and communication via social media. This communicative role of community policing thus involves addressing how community members themselves can decrease crime rates—which promotes a variety of public reason tenets, including inclusivity, autonomy, and duty. Community policing often involves civilian review boards and "citizen's academies" that demonstrate respect for community members. By encouraging community involvement in police oversight, community policing helps ascribe an equal status and worth to each person, rather than the perspective that community members are simply a means to a law enforcement end.

Second, community policing entails an emphasis on ethics in law enforcement. This involves improved training that addresses how ethnicity, gender, age, and socioeconomic factors might affect an officer's interaction with the community. It also includes understanding and dealing with mental health-related issues—training that may prevent tragic cases that play out in the news with increasing regularity. Consider two cases in Florida: In the first, a seven-year-old child hit his teacher. The child was subsequently handcuffed by Florida police and taken into custody in the back of a police car. The same law enforcement protocols that would be used for a twenty-year-old were used for an emotionally dysregulated seven-year-old. In the second case, a Florida police officer shot an unarmed caretaker of an autistic man. The officer did not recognize that the patient was being handled in an effective way by the mental health worker and instead acted reflexively upon the (mistaken) belief that deadly force was necessary.[124] Training and community understanding come into play here, not just law enforcement: Who is in the community, and how should the police respond to the community given a diversity of people and problems? These examples highlight how the police's power is in large part governed by a vast array of administrative rules and regulations that should include considerations based upon the tenets of public reason through community policing—not just considerations driven by law enforcement.

To be sure, one must be careful not to be Panglossian about community policing. As noted above, a central worry about community policing is that it does not solve crime problems effectively. Some researchers have examined various community policing tactics (e.g., community meetings, newsletters, and so on), concluding that such measures do not yield evidence of significant crime reduction—a conclusion supported generally by collaborative research projects on policing.[125] What are we to make of community policing's limited impact on crime? One of the most important responses to this question is disarmingly straightforward: It doesn't matter because community policing promotes other values—beyond crime reduction—that are vital to the police's role as *justice seekers*.

For example, researchers examined the extent to which community policing promoted perceived legitimacy based upon a variety of indicators—including confidence and trust in the police—and indicated that the communities involved with community policing were in fact more likely to view the police as legitimate than communities not involved with community policing.[126] More generally, in a 2018 consensus study report, *Proactive Policing*, the committee "concluded that community-oriented policing programs were likely to improve evaluations of the police, albeit modestly."[127] The report added that

> if the policy goal of an agency is to improve its relationship with the communities it serves, community-oriented policing is a promising strategy choice, although we are unable to offer a judgment on whether the benefits are sufficient to justify the expected costs.[128]

The last part of this conclusion—whether the benefits are sufficient to justify the expected costs—is of particular interest here. This is because the assessment is likely affected by the committee's final conclusion that "[e]xisting studies do not identify a consistent crime prevention benefit for community-oriented policing programs ... [though] many of these studies are characterized by weak evaluation designs."[129] Given that there is little evidence that community policing affects crime (and, moreover, that its effect on legitimacy is relatively minor), one might argue that community policing's benefits do not justify its costs. One must thus be clear that the primary justification for community policing will not be found in the results of empirical studies. Rather, community policing's primary justification is that it is a manifestation of public reason and consistent with the basic tenets of a liberal, democratic society—whatever its utilitarian benefits or lack thereof.

A second objection to community policing is that—somewhat paradoxically—it might lead to increased bad behavior by the police. For instance, perhaps community policing increases police discretion and community engagement in a way that leads to increased illegal encounters with community members—such as expansion of police discretion to use unjustified "stop and frisk" tactics.[130] To put the point a bit differently, poorly executed community policing may exacerbate both police legal noncompliance and police legitimacy. So one might object that the relevant question is not, say, whether algorithmic techniques are biased (as discussed in the first half of the chapter), but rather whether they are likely to be less biased than the standard status quo of human bias. As noted earlier, if crime statistics and predictive policing algorithms are biased, it is often because they are the aggregate result of millions of human actors exercising their (biased) human analysis and value judgments—such as police decisions about whether to arrest, prosecutorial decisions about whether and how to prosecute, and judicial decisions about conviction and sentencing. This is a real and difficult problem, and the answer is not to appeal to a vaguely imagined bias-free exercise of human judgment in community policing. I rather suggest that our pursuit of tactics such as community policing should be conducted in conjunction with concrete, restraining strategies such as "procedural justice policing."

Although procedural justice policing is closely related to community policing, it is a distinct organization strategy that seeks to communicate to the community that the police exercise their authority legitimately. Procedural justice policing focuses more narrowly upon "giving citizens police decision processes that manifest demonstrations of police fairness and regard for a person's dignity."[131] The basic idea, then, is that procedural justice policing promotes police legitimacy both directly (the people with whom the police interact) and indirectly (the community generally). This is typically accomplished by emphasizing the following questions that highlight specific police behaviors:

1 Do they provide opportunities for voice, allowing members of the public to state their perspective or tell their side of the story before decisions are made?
2 Do they make decisions in ways that people regard as neutral, rule-based, consistent, and absent of bias?
3 Do they treat people with the dignity, courtesy, and respect that they deserve as human beings and as members of the community?
4 Do people believe that their motives are trustworthy and benevolent—that is, that the police are sincerely trying to do what is good for the people in the community?[132]

To some, this might seem like common sense political morality rather than an actual organizational strategy.[133] But the earlier chapters have suggested that a procedural justice mindset is not the norm in many places. And though procedural justice policing may sound lofty to others, its tactics may be implemented as a concrete model of policing—one that targets increased police legitimacy specifically and, ultimately, crime problems.[134]

Indeed, procedural justice has been presented as a distinct alternative to policing strategies that focus exclusively on crime reduction or the popular phrase "law and order," as commentators have noted:

> [There is] a fundamental tension between two models of policing: the currently dominant proactive risk management model, which focuses on policing to prevent crimes and makes promises of short-term security through the professional management of crime risks, and a model that focuses on building popular legitimacy by enhancing the relationship between the police and the public and thereby promoting the long-term goal of police community solidarity and, through that, public-police cooperation in addressing issues of crime and community order.[135]

An example would be Washington's King County Sheriff's Office, which implemented procedural justice policing in conjunction with its community policing program. The procedural justice component focused on how officers engage the community, emphasizing the LEED framework: Listen and Explain with Equity and Dignity. Officers were taught best practices that focused on interacting with the community in accordance with procedural justice principles, with the goal of changing the department's culture and increasing legitimacy.[136]

This may sound unrealistic to those focused exclusively on crime reduction. But if procedural justice policing reduces conflict with the police via increased citizen compliance, then the result might be an overall environment that is less likely to lead to the issues of escalation of force and brutality discussed earlier.[137] Still, we should be clear that—as with community policing—the research consensus seems to be that "there are an insufficient number of rigorous empirical studies on procedural justice policing to draw a firm conclusion about its effectiveness in reducing crime and disorder."[138] We should likewise be clear that the primary justification for procedural justice policing is not based upon empirical data that suggests a positive impact on crime or perceptions of legitimacy. Again, procedural justice policing's primary justification is that it is a manifestation of public reason and thus consistent with the basic tenets of a liberal society—including respect for the dignity of all persons.

On the other hand, some have argued that an emphasis on procedural justice is not without its problems. Legal scholar Eric Miller raises the following worry:

> [W]hile procedural justice has confronted the issue of police violence, it has turned its back on the ways in which the Constitution requires the public to contest policing or forgo their rights. ... [S]ome of the techniques endorsed by procedural justice are the very techniques used

by the police to procure waivers of rights and to reveal private information in ways that, when force is not at issue, we normally reject as end-runs around the Constitution.[139]

Ironically, then, the worry is that procedural justice (because of its psychological underpinnings) actually undermines one's constitutional right to resist certain police actions (for example, declining police encounters, police requests to search, and police demands to answer questions) by bolstering one's inclination to comply with the police (for example, talking to the police, not walking away, and so on).[140] Miller says that procedural justice's "strategies cause the subjects of regulation to internalize a sense of obligation and also feelings of trust toward the authorities with which they interact."[141] One might wonder: Given the predominant alternative (warriors demanding compliance through force inside a prediction box), what's wrong with strategies that generate feelings of trust? Miller says the problem is the "potential gap between a civilian's psychological feelings of obligation ... toward the officer or the law, and the actual lawfulness of police directives or the actual normative or democratic validity of the law."[142] In other words, the police may get away with unlawful and undemocratic behavior by generating feelings of goodwill. Fair enough, but note that this is a "potential gap." It certainly is not clear that police who emphasize procedural justice always (or even most of the time) are seeking to generate psychological feelings of obligation *in order* to engage in *unlawful* behavior. They no doubt do this sometimes (and some departments more than others), but it is plausible to think that many police pursue procedural justice because generating feelings of trust and legitimacy are intrinsically (not *just* instrumentally) valuable in liberal societies.

In short, it is of course true that procedural justice strategies should not be used to pursue cooperation in a way that denigrates the law generally and one's legal rights specifically. But the fact that procedural justice tends to generate feelings of trust and legitimacy—which in turn generates cooperation—is not a bad thing in all cases (again, especially considering the alternative strategies). When the police listen to the community, explaining their actions and goals with equity and dignity, it is a step in the right direction (if we reasonably assume the police's underlying motivation is not *illegal*).

No one doubts that questions of determinism are relevant in almost every aspect of criminal justice. For example, in what sense are a person's actions free such that the person may be considered truly culpable? Irrespective of such questions, we must nevertheless address the pressing practical questions of society—such as how best to maintain security despite metaphysical worries about freewill. Likewise: Which policing strategies are most justified in liberal societies given a commitment to a conception of persons as free and responsible?[143] It is by no means perfect, but I submit that we could do a lot worse than the pursuit of procedural justice.

The upshot is that the police ought to pursue community and procedural justice policing (with the above caveats in mind) because it is the right thing to do given the basic legal and philosophical tenets of liberal societies. The 2018 *Proactive Policing* consensus study report noted this point aptly: "procedural justice reflects the behavior of police that is appropriate in a democratic society ....[it] may not change citizen attitudes, but it encourages democratic policing."[144] These tactics are appropriate because they bolster public reason by promoting legitimacy, autonomy, justice, respect, and human dignity. We have thus come full circle: It is not always safe to assume that a police tactic is justified given data that the tactic promotes the value of crime reduction. Data is neutral with respect to pursuing the value of crime reduction versus competing values. Law enforcement is a big part of policing, but it's not the only part. The conception of justice sought by the police must include much more than reducing crime.

Notes

1 See https://www.youtube.com/watch?v=EYPapE-3FRw, for the lecture in which Feynman's statement occurs.
2 See HENRY M. COWLES, THE SCIENTIFIC METHOD: AN EVOLUTION OF THINKING FROM DARWIN TO DEWEY (2020), for a history of what we call "the scientific method."
3 See CLIFFORD SHAW & HENRY D. MCKAY, JUVENILE DELINQUENCY IN URBAN AREAS (1942), for an early example of social disorganization theory.
4 NEIL POSTMAN, AMUSING OURSELVES TO DEATH 23 (2005) (1985).
5 DAVID HUME, A TREATISE OF HUMAN NATURE (Ernest C. Mossner ed., 1985) (1739).
6 *Id.* at 521 (book III, part I, section I).
7 *Id.*
8 David Wiggins, *Categorical Requirements: Kant and Hume on the Idea of Duty*, in VIRTUES AND REASONS: PHILIPPA FOOT AND MORAL THEORY 300 (Rosalind Hursthouse, Gavin Lawrence, & Warren Quinn eds., 1995).
9 Responses to the is–ought problem are voluminous. For a charmingly brief response, see Rick Lewis, *Can an 'Ought' be Derived from an 'Is'?*, PHILOSOPHY NOW, Issue 130 (February/March 2019) (describing a note from philosopher Philippa Foot addressing the is–ought problem through the idea of "natural goodness," which exists within the logical space of concepts such function, health, and flourishing; Foot claims, for example: "[W]e can say 'adult human beings ought to protect and cherish and instruct children.' This is a straightforward fact about what it is to be a good or bad human being, about what a person ought to do. And it is derived from other facts of a certain kind about what is necessary for flourishing in living things in a particular (i.e. here the human) species."). I am sympathetic to various critiques of the fact–value distinction, and my central point is simply that there are some (important) distinctions between the descriptive and the normative.
10 See LUKE WILLIAM HUNT, THE RETRIEVAL OF LIBERALISM IN POLICING, chapter 2 (2019), for an examination of liberalism through a methodology based upon the relationship between ideal and nonideal theory.
11 *See* TED MCCORMICK, WILLIAM PETTY: AND THE AMBITIONS OF POLITICAL ARITHMETIC (2009).

12 *Id.* at ix.
13 For discussions of the legal right to individualized treatment, see Andrew E. Taslitz, *Myself Alone: Individualizing Justice through Psychological Character Evidence*, 52.1 MARYLAND LAW REVIEW 1 (1993); David A. Harris, *Particularized Suspicion, Categorical Judgments: Supreme Court Rhetoric Versus Lower Court Reality Under Terry v. Ohio*, 72 ST. JOHN'S LAW REVIEW 975 (1998). For political and philosophical discussions of the right to be treated as an individual, see HUNT, *supra* note 10, at 93–103 (on the rule of law), 104–33 (on liberal personhood), and 176–86 (on entrapment and probabilistic offenders). In Rawls's terms, one might describe the underlying criticism as failing to "take seriously the distinction between persons." JOHN RAWLS, A THEORY OF JUSTICE 24 (rev. ed. 1999).
14 WALTER L. PERRY, BRIAN MCINNIS, CARTER C. PRICE, SUSAN SMITH, & JOHN S. HOLLYWOOD, PREDICTIVE POLICING: THE ROLE OF CRIME FORECASTING IN LAW ENFORCEMENT OPERATIONS xiii (2013).
15 For example, operation LASER ("Los Angeles Strategic Extraction and Restoration") "targets and surveils specific individuals within select neighborhoods based off their recent history with the criminal justice system." Maha Ahmed, *Aided by Palantir, the LAPD Uses Predictive Policing to Monitor Specific People and Neighborhoods*, THE INTERCEPT, May 11, 2018. Under operation LASER, officers are "tasked with maintaining an ongoing list of community residents to monitor, by creating 'Chronic Offender Bulletins' for so-called persons of interest." *Id.* The place-based technique on which this chapter focuses—"Prediction Box"—is one of the more common "predictive policing" tools.
16 SARAH BRAYNE, PREDICT AND SURVEIL—DATA, DISCRETION, AND THE FUTURE OF POLICING 3 (2021).
17 Rachel Boba Santos, *Predictive Policing: Where's the Evidence?*, in POLICE INNOVATION 366 (David Weisburd et al. eds., 2nd ed., Cambridge, 2019). I thank Professor Santos—my colleague at Radford University from 2016 to 2020—for providing me with an early copy of her excellent chapter on predictive policing.
18 See HUNT, *supra* note 10, at 83–88, discussing the general role that security and reciprocation play in social contract theory.
19 William J. Bratton & Sean W. Malinowski Bratton, *Police performance management in practice: Taking COMPSTAT to the next level*, 2.3 POLICING 259, 264 (2008). For a discussion of the development of predictive policing's analytical techniques, see Darwin Bond-Graham & Ali Winston, *All Tomorrow's Crimes: The Future of Policing Looks a Lot Like Good Branding*, SFWEEKLY (Oct. 13, 2013); Stephen Goldsmith, *Predictive tools for public safety* (part of an article series based on Goldsmith's paper, *Digital Transformations: Wiring the Responsive City*), DATA-SMART CITY SOLUTIONS (Aug. 18, 2014), https://datasmart.ash.harvard.edu/news/article/predictive-tools-for-public-safety-506
20 PREDPOL, https://www.predpol.com/about/
21 Emma Thomas, *Why Oakland Police Turned Down Predictive Policing*, MOTHERBOARD (Vice) (Dec. 28, 2016).
22 *Id.*
23 Leila Miller, *LAPD will end controversial program that aimed to predict where crimes would occur*, L.A. TIMES (April 21, 2020).
24 *Id.* Such guidelines are undoubtedly a step in the right direction and will be discussed in the Epilogue.
25 On this point, see Elizabeth E. Joh, *Feeding the Machine: Policing, Crime Data, & Algorithms*, 26.2 WILLIAM & MARY BILL OF RIGHTS JOURNAL 287 (2017), for a

discussion of how "police are not simply end users of big data ... they *generate the information* that big data programs rely upon." See also BRAYNE, *supra* note 16, at 107–10 for a discussion of biased training data (historical data) and hidden feedback loops.
26 See, e.g., JOHN A. ETERNO & ELI B. SILVERMAN, THE CRIME NUMBERS GAME (2012) (describing how CompStat led to discriminatory police practices in New York City—in part because police commanders recorded crime figures in a way that made it appear that minority communities were committing more crimes than they were in fact).
27 See, e.g., MALCOM SPARROW, HANDCUFFED: WHAT HOLDS POLICE BACK, AND THE KEYS TO REFORM (2016) (arguing that we should dispense with the numbers game and focus on social dynamics and local problems).
28 See generally ANDREW FERGUSON, THE RISE OF BIG DATA POLICING: SURVEILLANCE, RACE, AND THE FUTURE OF LAW ENFORCEMENT (2017); Grace Baek & Taylor Mooney, *LAPD not giving up on data-driven policing, even after scrapping controversial program*, CBS NEWS (Feb. 23, 2020).
29 Sandra G. Mayson, *Bias In, Bias Out*, 128 YALE LAW JOURNAL 2218 (2018).
30 Mayson argues that criminal law and policy should delineate the risks that matter and acknowledge that some kinds of risk may be beyond our ability to measure without racial distortion (and thus cannot justify state coercion). Finally, Mayson suggests that the criminal justice system should strive to respond to risk with support rather than restraint. *Id*.
31 See PERRY, MCINNIS, PRICE, SMITH, & HOLLYWOOD, *supra* note 14. Other objectives include predicting locations of offenders, perpetrators' identities, and victims of crime. *Id*.
32 *Id*.
33 The predictive methods rely upon complex analysis of large datasets that require computer software. These analytical methods include a variety of data mining techniques, including the use of algorithms, risk terrain analysis, near repeat analysis, regression and cluster modeling, and geographic profiling tools. *Id*.
34 Santos, *supra* note 17, at 371 (citing RACHEL BOBA SANTOS, CRIME ANALYSIS WITH CRIME MAPPING (4th ed., 2017).
35 *Id*. at 372.
36 *Id*. The original algorithm was created with data from Los Angeles based upon seismic aftershock theory (when crime increases in an area one can expect crime "aftershocks" to follow) using a self-exciting point process (clustered event sequences) to forecast crime in the future. G.O. Mohler, M.B. Short, P.J. Brantingham, F.P. Schoenberg, & G.E. Tita, *Self-Exciting Point Process Modeling of Crime*, 106 JOURNAL OF THE AMERICAN STATISTICAL ASSOCIATION 100–08 (2011); see also *The Aftershocks of Crime*, THE ECONOMIST (Oct. 21, 2010), https://www.economist.com/science-and-technology/2010/10/21/the-aftershocks-of-crime
37 RACHEL BOBA SANTOS, CRIME ANALYSIS WITH CRIME MAPPING (4th ed., 2017).
38 G.O. Mohler, M.B. Short, S. Malinowski, M. Johnson, G.E. Tita, A.L. Bertozzi, & P.J. Brantingham, *Randomized controlled field trials of predictive policing*, 110 JOURNAL OF THE AMERICAN STATISTICAL ASSOCIATION 1399–1411 (2015).
39 See *id*.; Bond-Graham & Winston, *supra* note 19.
40 Mohler, Short, Malinowski, Johnson, Tita, Bertozzi, & Brantingham, *supra* note 38 (2015). This is particularly unhelpful if there is no actionable intelligence beyond a vague prediction. See JERRY H. RATCLIFF, INTELLIGENCE-LED POLICING (2016).

41 Santos, *supra* note 17, at 374.
42 See, e.g., BRAYNE, *supra* note 16, at 83–86, for a discussion of how officers perceive big data policing as a devaluation of the police role and identity. Other scholars have argued that when agents (such as the police) rely upon technological systems (such as predictive policing) in their decision-making processes, they can obscure moral responsibility for the results of the decisions ("agency laundering"). Alan Rubel, Clinton Castro, & Adam Pham, *Agency Laundering and Information Technologies*, 22 ETHICAL THEORY AND MORAL PRACTICE 1017–1041 (2019).
43 Isaac Chotiner, *Jalen Rose Has a Problem with Basketball Analytics*, THE NEW YORKER (June 6, 2019).
44 Santos, *supra* note 17, at 376.
45 *See, e.g.*, PERRY, MCINNIS, PRICE, SMITH, & HOLLYWOOD, *supra* note 14; and SANTOS, CRIME ANALYSIS WITH CRIME MAPPING, *supra* note 39.
46 Santos, *supra* note 17, at 377. Moreover, unhelpful locations such as police departments sometimes appear on the predictive policing maps. *See* Alene Tchekmedyian, *Burbank police implement changes following survey indicating low morale in department*, L.A. TIMES (Sept. 28, 2016).
47 *See* SANTOS, CRIME ANALYSIS WITH CRIME MAPPING, *supra* note 39, at 92–95, regarding how this idea is relevant to the crime analysis process called the "data modification sub-cycle." Of course, value judgments regarding broader goals of justice would go beyond the crime analysis process.
48 Richard Berk describes the human impact of faulty results this way: "[If] [t]he outcome to be forecasted is whether an individual on parole or probation will commit a homicide.... A false positive can mean that an individual is incorrectly labeled as 'high risk.' A false negative can mean that a homicide that might have been prevented is not. There is no reason to assume that the costs of these two outcomes are even approximately the same. Qualitative outcomes can also play a role in predictive policing." Richard Berk, *Asymmetric loss functions for forecasting in criminal justice settings*, 27 JOURNAL OF QUANTITATIVE CRIMINOLOGY 107–23, 108 (2011).
49 Jerry H. Ratcliffe & Ralph B. Taylor, *The Philadelphia predictive policing experiment: Summary of the experimental design*, CENTER FOR CRIME SCIENCE (Temple University, Philadelphia, PA, December 2017). The study was funded by the National Institute of Justice. *Id.*
50 *Id.*
51 PERRY, MCINNIS, PRICE, SMITH, & HOLLYWOOD, *supra* note 14.
52 Jessica Saunders, Priscillia Hunt, & John S. Hollywood, *Predictions put into practice: A Quasi-Experimental Evaluation of Chicago's Predictive Policing Pilot*, 12.3 JOURNAL OF EXPERIMENTAL CRIMINOLOGY 347–71 (2016).
53 *Id.* at 355.
54 *See id.* at 362–64.
55 U.S. CONST. amend. IV.
56 *Id.*
57 Thomas Y. Davies, *Recovering the Original Fourth Amendment*, 98 MICH. L. REV. 547, 556 (1999).
58 *Id.* at 724.
59 United States v. Jones, 132 S.Ct. 945.
60 *Id.* at 956 (2012) (Sotomayor, J., concurring) (quoting United States v. Di Re, 332 U.S. 581, 595 (1948)).
61 *See, e.g.*, Utah v. Strieff, 579 U.S. ___, 136 S. Ct. 2056 (2016). Even though the officers lacked "reasonable suspicion" to detain Strieff (making the

detention unlawful), the Supreme Court ruled that the drug evidence seized during the detention was admissible because "the discovery of a valid arrest warrant was a sufficient intervening event to break the causal chain between the unlawful stop and the discovery of drug-related evidence on Strieff's person." *Id.*

62 Terry v. Ohio, 392 U.S. 1, 21–30 (1968).
63 NEW YORK CIVIL LIBERTIES UNION, 2012 STOP AND FRISK REPORT 2 (2012), https://www.nyclu.org/sites/default/files/publications/NYCLU_2011_Stop-and-Frisk_Report.pdf
64 *See, e.g.*, Andrew G. Ferguson, *Predictive Policing and Reasonable Suspicion*, 62 EMORY LAW JOURNAL 259–325 (2012); Andrew G. Ferguson, *Crime Mapping and the Fourth Amendment: Redrawing "High-Crime Areas,"* 63 HASTINGS LAW JOURNAL 179 (2011) (examining Fourth Amendment questions raised by crime-mapping technology).
65 Ferguson, *Predictive Policing, supra* note 64.
66 *Id.* at 314.
67 Federal funds have been allocated for predictive policing for over a decade. *See* U.S. Department of Justice, National Institute of Justice, *Predictive Policing Symposiums* (2010), https://www.ncjrs.gov/pdffiles1/nij/242222and248891.pdf
68 Of course, I do not mean to suggest that bureaucratic social organization necessarily results in social harm. We need only consider the modern social welfare state's goal of providing a universal safety net, among other things. Moreover, I certainly would not equate bureaucratic social organization to, say, sinister causes of social harm such as charismatic political leadership, fervent social movements, and extremist ideologies of all kinds.
69 Frederick F. Schauer, *Statistical (and Non-Statistical) Discrimination*, in THE ROUTLEDGE HANDBOOK OF THE ETHICS OF DISCRIMINATION 47 (Kasper Lippert-Rasmussen ed., 2018); FREDERICK F. SCHAUER, PROFILES, PROBABILITIES, AND STEREOTYPES (2003).
70 Recent work on the relationship between policing and human rights includes, Roxanna Altholz, *Living with Impunity: Unsolved Murders in Oakland and the Human Rights Impact on Victims' Family Members*, INTERNATIONAL HUMAN RIGHTS LAW CLINIC, UNIVERSITY OF CALIFORNIA, BERKELEY, SCHOOL OF LAW (Jan. 2020) (arguing that "[t]he systemic failure to prevent violence, investigate, and provide support and assistance to family members without discrimination in Oakland is arguably a violation of international human rights law").
71 Joseph Goldstein & Nate Schweber, *Man's Death After Chokehold Raises Old Issue for the Police*, N.Y. TIMES (July 18, 2014).
72 Clifford Krauss, *Clash Over a Football Ends With a Death in Police Custody*, N.Y. TIMES (December 30, 1994). The officer who killed Baez was acquitted of homicide charges, but subsequently convicted for violating Baez's civil rights.
73 Goldstein & Schweber, *supra* note 71.
74 *See* Jimmy Orr, *No free vacation this year? Your human rights may have been violated (at least in Europe)*, L.A. TIMES (April 21, 2010).
75 Graham v. Connor, 490 U.S. 386 (1989).
76 The FBI's policy on the use of deadly force by its special agents is available at: https://www.fbi.gov/about/faqs/what-is-the-fbis-policy-on-the-use-of-deadly-force-by-its-special-agents
77 *See supra* chapter 2 of this book.
78 Although it might be reasonable to describe "security of person" and "legitimacy" as *consequences* of human rights, I will make the case that it is plausible to think of them *as* human rights.

79 Wesley Newcomb Hohfeld, *Some Fundamental Legal Conceptions as Applied in Judicial Reasoning*, 23 YALE L.J. 16 (1913). The sequel is Wesley Newcomb Hohfeld, *Fundamental Legal Conceptions as Applied in Judicial Reasoning*, 26 YALE L.J. 710 (1917). I have invoked Hohfeld's work as a general way to think of rights, rather than endorse all of his propositions explicitly. See Peter Westen, *Poor Wesley Hohfeld*, 55.2 SAN DIEGO LAW REVIEW 450 (2018), for a discussion of how criminal law theorists often invoke Hohfeld in a way that is inconsistent with seven propositions espoused by Hohfeld.

80 See A. John Simmons, *Human Rights, Natural Rights, and Human Dignity*, in PHILOSOPHICAL FOUNDATIONS OF HUMAN RIGHTS (Rowan Cruft, S. Matthew Liao, & Massimo Renzo eds., 2015), for a comprehensive discussion of these three accounts.

81 JEREMY WALDRON, DIGNITY, RANK, AND RIGHTS (M. Dan-Cohen ed., 2012); Jeremy Waldron, *Is Dignity the Foundation of Human Rights?* in PHILOSOPHICAL FOUNDATIONS OF HUMAN RIGHTS (Rowan Cruft, S. Matthew Liao, & Massimo Renzo eds., 2015).

82 See Simmons, *Human Rights*, supra note 80.

83 *Id.*

84 *See* JOHN RAWLS, THE LAW OF PEOPLES (1999); CHARLES BEITZ, THE IDEA OF HUMAN RIGHTS (2009).

85 *See, e.g.*, BEITZ, supra note 84. Beitz defines human rights as universal, focusing on how such rights are enforced through institutions within states.

86 Human rights often focus upon a protection, status, or benefit for the right holder. *Id.*

87 *See* RAWLS, supra note 84. Rawls argues that human rights may be explained by describing the primary roles they play in a particular political domain, namely, international relations. *See also id.*

88 See HUNT, supra note 10, at 22–23 for a discussion of the history behind "color of law" violations. This book does not focus upon theories of state legitimacy, but rather upon the derivative idea of police legitimacy. Although state legitimacy is not a foregone conclusion, I assume that such legitimacy is possible—including cases in which a state has partial legitimacy. See *infra* note 91 for a brief overview of theories of state legitimacy.

89 Although there are of course other options, I embrace a form of Rawlsian transitional nonideal theory, as discussed in the introduction of this book and more fully in HUNT, *supra* note 10, at chapter 2.

90 Work on public reason is voluminous and my goal is only to note several basic tenets of public reason that might serve as a foundation for community policing. See JOHN RAWLS, POLITICAL LIBERALISM (1996), for a prominent account of public reason, and Jonathan Quong, *Public Reason*, THE STANFORD ENCYCLOPEDIA OF PHILOSOPHY (Spring 2018 Edition, Edward N. Zalta ed.), for a comprehensive overview of public reason. I first considered the idea of public reason as a philosophical foundation for community policing in HUNT, *supra*, note 10, at 52–53, FN 149, and then in Luke William Hunt, *Ice Cube and the philosophical foundations of community policing*, OXFORD UNIVERSITY PRESS BLOG (Feb. 17, 2019), https://blog.oup.com/2019/02/ice-cube-philosophical-foundations-community-policing/

91 Generally, one might categorize accounts of legitimacy (and their correlative duties to obey the law) as transactional, natural, or associative. See A. JOHN SIMMONS, MORAL PRINCIPLES AND POLITICAL OBLIGATIONS (1979); and CHRISTOPHER HEATH WELLMAN AND A. JOHN SIMMONS, IS THERE A DUTY TO OBEY THE LAW? Part II (2005), for accounts of the weaknesses of each of these theories. Roughly, natural

duty theories argue that just states are legitimate, and one has a moral duty to support just and good states because they are just and good. See PLATO, CRITO, in PLATO: COMPLETE WORKS (John M. Cooper ed., 1997), for a version of a natural duty theory in which Socrates suggests that it would be wrong to disobey the law and flee Athens because he has a duty not to harm the state and the moral value of its Law. Associative theories claim that states may subject persons to legitimate authority because states are the kinds of associations that generate obligations (analogous to a duty one might be said to owe to one's parent or sibling by virtue simply of occupying the duty-laden role of "son" or "brother"). See RONALD DWORKIN, LAW'S EMPIRE (1986), for an account of associative theories.

92 Jason Sunshine & Tom R. Tyler, *The Role of Procedural Justice and Legitimacy in Shaping Public Support for Policing*, 37.3 LAW & SOCIETY REVIEW 513–48 (2003).
93 See Quong, *supra* note 90, for a detailed discussion of these points.
94 *Id.*; ANDREW LISTER, PUBLIC REASON AND POLITICAL COMMUNITY (2013).
95 Kristin Lam, *What happens after a transgender woman is murdered? For family and friends, a long and agonizing search for closure*, USA TODAY (Nov. 20, 2019).
96 U.S. CONSTITUTION, PREAMBLE.
97 *See, e.g.*, RAWLS, *supra* note 90, at 219
98 *Man Linked to Killing at a Portland Protest Says He Acted in Self-Defense*, VICE NEWS (Sept. 3, 2020).
99 The tweet stated: "Why aren't the Portland Police ARRESTING the cold blooded killer of Aaron 'Jay' Danielson. Do your job, and do it fast. Everybody knows who this thug is. No wonder Portland is going to hell!" Twitter account of Donald J. Trump (@realDonaldTrump).
100 FOX NEWS, interview with Jeanine Pirro (Sept. 12, 2020).
101 The case perhaps raises philosophical questions about the nature and limits of the President's national security emergency powers, including the prerogative power to deviate from the rule of law in times of national emergency. See HUNT, *supra* note 10, at 190–200, for a discussion of how Locke's "prerogative power" serves as a foundation for the limits of executive discretion to deviate from rule of law principles.
102 Two witnesses stated that they saw Reinoehl fire an assault rifle at the unmarked law enforcement vehicles when they pulled up to him, though another witness reported that he never saw Reinoehl pull out a gun. Tim Elfrink, *Police shot Portland slaying suspect without warning or trying to arrest him first, witness says*, WASH. POST (Sept. 10, 2020).
103 See Charles Larmore, *The Moral Basis of Political Liberalism*, 96 THE JOURNAL OF PHILOSOPHY 607–08 (1999).
104 An exception would be ALEXANDRA NATAPOFF, SNITCHING: CRIMINAL INFORMANTS AND THE EROSION OF AMERICAN JUSTICE (2009). In HUNT, *supra* note 10, I devote an entire chapter (chapter 4) to the police's use of informants and an entire chapter (chapter 5) to deceptive undercover operations in which the police (or informants as police agents) engage in sanctioned law-breaking activity ("otherwise illegal activity").
105 Sarah Stilman, *The Throwaways*, THE NEW YORKER (Aug. 27, 2012).
106 *Id.*
107 *See* Alexander v. DeAngelo, 329 F.3D 912 (7th Cir. 2003).
108 *See* ALICE GOFFMAN, ON THE RUN (2014).
109 *Id.* at 37.
110 *Id.* at 90.
111 In HUNT, *supra* note 10, at chapter 4, I develop the argument that some examples of the police's power to use informants meet the underlying

normative requirements of the legal doctrine of unconscionability (both procedural and substantive), raising issues about both the adequacy of the informant's consent to the bargain and the justification of the police's use of this power. In the cases in question, the state leverages its bargaining power over a person in order to facilitate an agreement in which the person will act in a way that the state itself deems (otherwise) illegal, as well as in a way that subjects the person to the risk of substantial harm. I argue that if these sorts of institutionally recognized interactions are unconscionable in the sense that they constitute an affront to liberal principles that become manifest in legal doctrine, then such interactions cannot be construed as transitionally just even if they achieve a competing state end.

112 Quong, *supra* note 90; Jonathan Quong, *On The Idea of Public Reason, in* THE BLACKWELL COMPANION TO RAWLS 265–80 (Jon Mandle et al. eds., 2013). This section is based upon Quong's comprehensive overview of public reason.
113 JOHN RAWLS, COLLECTED PAPERS 575–77 (Samuel Freeman ed., 1999).
114 RADLEY BALKO, RISE OF THE WARRIOR COP 139 (2014).
115 *See, e.g.*, Charlotte Gill, David Weisburd, Cody W. Telep, Zoe Vitter, & Trevor Bennett, *Community-oriented policing to reduce crime, disorder and fear and increase satisfaction and legitimacy among citizens: a systematic review*, 10 JOURNAL OF EXPERIMENTAL CRIMINOLOGY (2014) (finding that community-oriented policing has limited impact on crime, but improves police legitimacy).
116 See JOHN KLEINIG, THE ETHICS OF POLICING (1996), for a comprehensive discussion of these roles.
117 *Id.*
118 *See* HUNT, *supra* note 10, at 19–26 (providing a brief history of police in the liberal polity).
119 *See* JAMES Q. WILSON, VARIETIES OF POLICE BEHAVIOR: THE MANAGEMENT OF LAW AND ORDER IN EIGHT COMMUNITIES (1968).
120 Carl B. Klockars, *The Rhetoric of Community Policing, in* COMMUNITY POLICING: RHETORIC OR REALITY 239–58 (Jack R. Greene et al. eds, 1988); JEROME H. SKOLNICK & DAVID H. BAYLEY, THE NEW BLUE LINE: POLICE INNOVATION IN SIX AMERICAN CITIES (1986).
121 *See* Robert J. Sampson, *The Community, in* CRIME AND PUBLIC POLICY 210–36 (J.Q. Wilson et al. eds., 2d ed. 2011).
122 *See, e.g.*, Wesley Skogan, *Fear of Crime and Neighborhood Change, in* COMMUNITIES AND CRIME (Albert J. Reiss, Jr., et al. eds., 1986); WESLEY SKOGAN, DISORDER AND DECLINE: CRIME AND THE SPIRAL OF DECAY IN AMERICAN CITIES (1992).
123 PROACTIVE POLICING: EFFECTS ON CRIME AND COMMUNITIES (Consensus Study Report) 64 (Nat. Academies Press, 2018).
124 For the first case, see Daniel Shoer Roth, *A 7-year-old hit his teacher. Hours later he was taken from the school in handcuffs*, MIAMI HERALD (Jan. 27, 2018); and for the second case, see Charles Rabin, *Cop shoots caretaker of autistic man playing in the street with toy truck*, MIAMI HERALD (July 21, 2016).
125 *See, e.g.*, Lawrence W. Sherman & John E. Eck, *Policing for crime prevention, in* EVIDENCE BASED CRIME PREVENTION 295–329 (Lawrence W. Sherman et al. eds., 2002); FAIRNESS AND EFFECTIVENESS IN POLICING: THE EVIDENCE (National Academies Press, 2004).
126 *See, e.g.*, Gill, Weisburd, Telep, Vitter, & Bennett, *supra* note 115, at 415–16.
127 *See* PROACTIVE POLICING, *supra* note 123, at 325.
128 *Id.*
129 *Id.* at 312.

130 *See generally* Jon B. Gould & Stephen D. Mastrofski, *Suspect searches: Assessing police behavior under the U.S. Constitution*, 3.3 CRIMINOLOGY & PUBLIC POLICY 315–62 (2004).
131 *See* PROACTIVE POLICING, *supra* note 123.
132 *Id.*
133 Daniel S. Nagin & Cody W. Telep, *Procedural Justice and Legal Compliance*, 13 ANNUAL REVIEW OF LAW AND SOCIAL SCIENCE 5–28 (2017).
134 *See* Tom R. Tyler, Phillip Atiba Goff, & Robert J. MacCoun, *The Impact of Psychological Science on Policing in the United States: Procedural Justice, Legitimacy, and Effective Law Enforcement*, 16.3 PSYCHOLOGICAL SCIENCE IN THE PUBLIC INTEREST 75–109 (2015).
135 Tom R. Tyler, Jonathan Jackson, & Avital Mentovich, *The Consequences of Being an Object of Suspicion: Potential Pitfalls of Proactive Police Contact*, 12.4 JOURNAL OF EMPIRICAL LEGAL STUDIES 603 (2015).
136 Andrew McCurdy & Melissa Bradley, *Procedural Justice: High Expectations*, COPS OFFICE (6.9 Community Policing Dispatch, 2013), https://cops.usdoj.gov/dispatch/09-2013/procedural_justice_high_expectations.asp
137 *See* EMILY G. OWENS, DAVID WEISBURD, GEOFFREY ALPERT, & KAREN L. AMENDOLA, PROMOTING POLICE INTEGRITY THROUGH EARLY ENGAGEMENTS AND PROCEDURAL JUSTICE IN THE SEATTLE POLICE DEPARTMENT (2016). Data on procedural justice policing is limited, but survey-based studies have shown a positive association between procedurally just treatment and police legitimacy. *See, e.g.*, Tom R. Tyler, Stephen J. Schulhofer, & Aziz Z. Huq, *Legitimacy and Deterrence Effects in Counterterrorism Policing: A Study of Muslims in America*, 44.2 LAW & SOCIETY REVIEW 365–402 (2010); Kyle McLean & Scott E. Wolfe, *A Sense of Injustice Loosens the Moral Bind of Law: Specifying the Links between Procedural Injustice, Neutralizations and Offending*, 43.1 CRIMINAL JUSTICE AND BEHAVIOR 27–44 (2015); and Lyn Hinds, *Building Police-Youth Relationships: The Importance of Procedural Justice*, 7.3 NATIONAL ASSOCIATION OF YOUTH JUSTICE 195–209 (2007). But see Nagin & Telep, *supra* note 133, for a discussion of the shortcomings of such survey-based research.
138 PROACTIVE POLICING, *supra* note 123, at 312.
139 Eric Miller, *Encountering Resistance: Non-Compliance, Non-Cooperation, and Procedural Justice*, UNIVERSITY OF CHICAGO LEGAL FORUM 298 (Article 8, 2016).
140 For analysis of the psychological underpinnings of procedural justice, see, e.g., TOM R. TYLER, WHY PEOPLE OBEY THE LAW 20–26, 161–65 (1990); TOM R. TYLER & YUEN J. HUO, TRUST IN THE LAW: ENCOURAGING PUBLIC COOPERATION WITH THE POLICE AND COURTS 94, 20–24 (2002).
141 Miller, *supra* note 139, at 347.
142 *Id.* at 358. Miller focuses upon examples such as the "Christian Burial Speech" in *Brewer v. Williams*, 430 U.S. 387 (1977), as well as the popular police interrogation strategy known as the "Reid method." Although the psychological attributes of these examples might share broad attributes with procedural justice, they are much narrower in scope than procedural justice as a general policing strategy. It is not clear that the narrow goal of, say, a Reid method interrogation is comparable to a department that seeks to treat the community with dignity by emphasizing procedural justice. For discussion of the Reid method, see Luke William Hunt, *Legal Speech and Implicit Content in the Law*, 29.1 RATIO JURIS 3 (2016).
143 *See, e.g.*, RAWLS,*supra* note 13, at 212 (articulating a "principle of responsibility," which is closely connected to liberty and the rule of law).
144 PROACTIVE POLICING, *supra* note 123, at 312.

Epilogue
Reorienting the Police Identity

As is true of most FBI Agents, I kept a low profile and rarely had my name appear in the news. But during my first year on the job, a dramatic photo of me appeared in a local newspaper: I was speaking to a retirement and financial investment community about identity theft. As the new agent in the office, I was assigned this task because none of the senior agents wanted to do it. I don't recall much about the event (I like to think I made a reasonably good impression on those retirees), but what strikes me now is how most people (myself included) viewed the assignment as an onerous chore. Looking back, though, it is easy to see that this kind of community engagement is the sort of thing that law enforcement agencies must embrace. This is particularly true for the FBI given the criticism (some deserved, some not) the agency has received in recent years. The FBI is profoundly different from state and local law enforcement agencies, but a lot of the basics remain the same: All law enforcement agencies need to garner trust and legitimacy in the communities they serve. There is not only instrumental value in this goal (receiving community support, developing informants for intelligence collection, and so on), but also intrinsic value. Fostering legitimacy in our institutions is the right thing to do given the legal, political, and philosophical commitments of liberal societies. And fostering these commitments means fostering a police identity that is based upon a holistic, inclusive pursuit of justice. This is especially the case as we move deeper into the twenty-first century.

Since at least the early 2010s, it has become commonplace to record almost every facet of one's life through video, photo, and social media. On December 12, 2012, a large crowd gathered at the Vatican, where it was announced: "And now, the holy father will send his first tweet."[1] Snapchat—a multimedia messaging service—made its debut around this time, allowing users to create video-stories of their daily lives.[2] And then of course there was Facebook's introduction of its "Timeline" feature in late 2011—allowing users to show multimedia content based on year, month, and date.[3] I am grudgingly open to the idea that these technological advances might have some upside, even if I have yet to "tweet."[4] Such technology has the potential to connect family and friends in a positive way, and some commentators have argued that advances in social media promote democratic ideals through the rapid spread of information.[5] Almost a decade after the pope's first tweet, however, one might be forgiven for being less optimistic. It can be difficult to cut through the noise given the rise of information warfare, "fake news," and mass surveillance.[6]

Nevertheless, there has been something of a democratic revival when it comes to documenting and disseminating police abuses. Much of society had become almost numb to the steady stream of videos depicting the tragic uses of deadly force by the police. Perhaps George Floyd's death shook us awake. If that is the case, it took a video of an officer kneeling on a handcuffed man's neck—for eight minutes and forty-six seconds—all while the man begged for breath. Without smart phones, this sort of democratic revival was not possible during the preceding decades. One of the rare exceptions was the video camera recording of Rodney King's beating by Los Angeles Police Department (LAPD) officers in 1991.[7] Following King's beating—and the widespread riots in 1992—the LAPD engaged in a series of investigations and reform efforts. The "Christopher Commission" (headed by attorney Warren Christopher) sought "a full and fair examination of the structure and operation of the LAPD," including recruitment and training practices and citizen complaint systems.[8] In subsequent years, the LAPD entered into a settlement order with the U.S. Department of Justice, which helped formalize a Police Commission composed of citizens who review police policies and hold routine public meetings.[9]

There is much more work to be done, and one would hope that democratic revival can continue in other departments and cities without being prompted by highly visible incidents of police brutality. Legal scholar Eric Miller notes how increased public participation—social media or otherwise—has the potential to increase community social power: "[I]n cities like Baltimore, Maryland, and Ferguson, Missouri, protesters challenging police policies at the departmental and municipal levels have used direct action and social media to force law-enforcement officials to address their concerns."[10] These last pages summarize practical steps that might help reorient policing away from individual heroes, warriors, and guardians driven by algorithms, and toward a collective pursuit of justice. First, however, we should consider the loud calls to "defund" the police following Floyd's death, along with other political and legal issues that are external to the police.

Defunding the Police, Abolishing the Police, and Other Political Reforms

"Defunding the police" sounds radical (unfortunately), but it can in fact be a measured approach to addressing problems within policing and beyond.

The idea simply means "reallocating or redirecting funding away from the police department to other government agencies funded by the local municipality."[11] For example, many commentators have suggested that we should shift funding from the police to social services so that municipalities are better equipped to respond to mental health crises, addiction, and homelessness.[12] Given that mental health professionals are better equipped to handle these problems than the police, it is plausible to think that reallocating money away from the police (along with the responsibility of responding to such issues) would be a better use of taxpayer money. Perhaps more importantly, this sort of reallocation reduces the potential for unnecessary, violent encounters between the police and the community. Other commentators have suggested that—given the police's relatively poor track record of solving violent crimes—taxpayer money should better serve the needs in Black communities though higher quality education and healthcare, rather than increased police presence taking the form of "stop and frisk" and militarization programs.[13] The broader point of "defunding the police" is that funding more police is not the best way to reduce crime; rather, the idea is that we need to target the underlying structural problems in society relating to economic opportunity, education inequality, and so on, which will in turn reduce both crime and police violence.[14] Such common-sense suggestions to pursue a community's most pressing needs are promising, especially given that they are politically possible (some cities have in fact reallocated resources as described), effective (increased police does not necessarily reduce crime, while increased economic opportunity does), and morally permissible (consistent with a commitment to security, legitimacy, human dignity, and other political values).

On the other hand, some commentators have called to have the police literally abolished. In some ways, this is simply a dramatic step that goes well beyond "defunding the police." Here is how the idea was described in a *New York Times* opinion column following Floyd's death:

> We don't want to just close police departments. We want to make them obsolete. We should redirect the billions that now go to police departments toward providing health care, housing, education and good jobs. If we did this, there would be less need for the police in the first place. We can build other ways of responding to harms in our society. Trained "community care workers" could do mental-health checks if someone needs help. Towns could use restorative-justice models instead of throwing people in prison.[15]

When it comes to violent crime—such as rape and murder—it becomes less clear how society would function without a robust law enforcement apparatus such as the police. A typical response is that (with respect to, say, rape) "the current approach hasn't ended it." Moreover, police abolitionists claim, the police themselves sometimes engage in sexual misconduct.[16] Be that as it may, it is odd to think that abolishing the police would *improve* the way society addresses rape and murder (despite the fact that murder and sexual misconduct *by* police would end if the police were abolished). Nevertheless, this is how Alex Vitale puts it:

> We've all grown up on television shows in which the police are superheroes. They solve every problem; they catch the bad guys; they chase the bank robbers; they find the serial killers. But this is all a big myth. This is not what police actually do. They're not out chasing bank robbers or serial killers. The vast majority of police officers make one felony arrest a year. If they make two, they're cop of the month. Police are managing the symptoms of a system of exploitation.[17]

In many ways, this whole book has—in limited agreement with Vitale—pushed back on the conception of police as "superheroes." On the other hand, I submit that the point about the police's uselessness in apprehending bank robbers, serial killers, and rapists is being put too strongly. Anecdotally—and for what it's worth—as an FBI agent I worked with many local, state, and federal law enforcement officers who made regular, significant progress in these types of violent crime investigations. Although we need not conceive of them as heroes, warriors, or guardians, it is difficult to imagine how that progress would be maintained without an entity remarkably like the police (though perhaps smaller due to reallocation of resources). Hundreds of years of political thought—well beyond the work philosophers such as Thomas Hobbes and John Locke—have helped build a compelling case that life without some form of political authority and enforcer would be "solitary, poor, nasty, brutish, and short," or at a minimum highly inconvenient.[18] I get it: The point that police abolitionists are making is that life *with* the police is *already* like this for some people. My position is simply that we should think carefully about whether abolishing the police would actually improve those lives.

I noted in the introduction that I embrace *transitional nonideal theory*: the goal of addressing actual injustices in the world by pursuing policies that seek transition to a practicable ideal of justice. However, while transitional nonideal theory is constrained by tactics that are politically possible, calls to abolish the police tend to sound eerily utopian. For example, police abolitionists have stated that those "who want to abolish prisons and police … have a vision of a different society, built on cooperation instead of individualism, on mutual aid instead of self-preservation."[19] I am all for transitioning to an ideal steeped in cooperation and mutual aid, but abolishing the police seems to misconstrue the nature of ideal theory. True, ideal theory represents the best state of affairs based upon idealized assumptions about society. But for a variety of natural reasons—such as basic truths about societies and human psychology—it is inevitable that some people will act unjustly even in an operative ideally just society. This means that ideal theory must have something to say about cases of unjust actions, including those that create emergencies of security that might require just law enforcement.

It is for this reason that giving up on police reform (and instead focusing on abolishing all or most police) gives me pause. Many who call for the police to be defunded or abolished argue that it is simply impossible to "fix" the police through improved community policing, officer training, and so on.[20] As Vitale puts it: "The procedural reformers are caught in this mythic understanding of American society. They believe that the neutral professional enforcement of the law is automatically beneficial for everyone, that the rule of law sets us free."[21] To be sure, we should all be careful to avoid naivete. Any ideal for policing (or "mythic understanding of American society") is aspirational—a goal to which we seek to transition rather than a golden age to which we seek to return. But the same is true with respect to an ideal, utopian society that does not need police. I hope we can reach a broad consensus that crime and the need for police may be reduced by addressing the deep structural inequalities (social and economic) within society—notwithstanding questions about whether such a consensus is politically possible on a broad scale. But in the *meantime*, it seems reasonable to take steps toward police reforms that are politically possible, effective, and morally permissible in terms of the broad commitments (legitimacy, the rule of law, human dignity, and so on) of liberal societies. Police reform and structural reform are not mutually exclusive.

Beyond reforming the police institution itself, we should at least consider some of the broader legal and political issues that affect the police. For instance, holding police accountable for misconduct has been hampered by jurisprudence relating to two central areas of law: qualified immunity and public torts. Qualified immunity is a judicially created doctrine shielding government officials from being held personally liable for constitutional violations (such as brutal force) for money damages—given that the officials did not violate "clearly established" law.[22] More broadly, public tort law governs civil wrongs by officials resulting in harm or loss by a claimant. Legal scholars have argued that the best way to reform qualified immunity is legislatively because the doctrine is generally understood as "the product of statutory interpretation rather than constitutional elaboration."[23] However, reforming qualified immunity would not affect police misconduct that does rise to a constitutional violation. This has led others to emphasize the importance of reforming state tort law, which might include eliminating statutory privileges and indemnification regulations that hamper law enforcement accountability.[24] Accordingly, it is plausible to think that the most promising legal reform efforts will target qualified immunity specifically and tort law generally.

Of course, politics will always be a difficult, external obstacle for police reform. Consider the role and power of police unions, which often hold sway over legislators and other politicians. A variety of studies have linked the police's extensive collective-bargaining rights to toothless legislative reform, as well as increases in violent police misconduct. Police unions demand vast contractual protections relating to officers' exposure to discipline, which makes it difficult to hold officers accountable for misconduct (such as erasing disciplinary records after a short period of time). Although there is no single way to reform police unions, one idea—consistent with collective goals of justice—is to include community members in police contract negotiations.[25] Of course, this brief sketch of external political issues barely scratches the surface. I raise them simply to make the point that policing is intertwined with broader factors that make reform difficult. There is no doubt that these issues require more work, but I now turn to a summary of modest reform efforts we might pursue from within policing.

Recruitment, Training, and Values

It may sound obvious, but any reform of training and recruitment begins with the values that we want to see in policing and that we want to instill through training. There is no comprehensive list of police values that we can simply direct trainees to memorize, and I do not claim to have special access to anything approaching an exhaustive list of such values. Here, then, I simply review and highlight some of the values, concepts, and principles that have been discussed over the course of this book. While some are already common themes within police training and recruitment, others deserve a more prominent place in the curriculum, as it were. Indeed, the head of legal instruction at the Baltimore Police Academy put it this way in 2018: "Police recruits were being pushed through the academy despite lacking a basic understanding of the laws governing constitutional policing."[26] Let us then highlight a few themes from the preceding chapters.

The rule of law: Discretion is absolutely necessary in policing. Not only is it impossible for the police to enforce, say, every speeding violation—or every drug or jaywalking violation—it would not be in the best interests of justice for the police to do so. It is necessary for the police to have—as John Kleinig has described it—"a normative condition ... as a prerogative to use one's own judgment about how to make a practical determination."[27] However, the rule of law serves as a safeguard against unconstrained discretion of officials in political communities, bolstering the liberal conception of persons as free and equal agents with human dignity.[28] Legal philosopher Lon Fuller characterized the rule of law this way:

> To embark on the enterprise of subjecting human conduct to the governance of rules involves of necessity a commitment to the view

that man is, or can become, a responsible agent, capable of understanding and following rules, and answerable for his defaults.[29]

Fuller noted formal features that are important to the rule of law, including the precept that there should be congruence between declared rules and administration of those rules.

This is especially relevant to the police given that the police are often exempt from following the rules: Consider the many ways the police are permitted to break the law (or have others, such as informants, break the law on their behalf) as a means to enforcing the law. Although such "otherwise illegal activity" (as the FBI call it) may be justified in some cases, are we still be governed by law given the police's vast discretion to break the law? Joseph Raz's influential work on the rule of law is helpful here: "The discretion of the crime-preventing agencies should not be allowed to pervert the law."[30] In other words, the police's discretion must be constrained in order to protect the liberal conception of persons, or, as Raz puts it: "the rule of law is necessary if the law is to respect human dignity."[31] If the police are serious about respecting human dignity, then they must embrace an identity that is consistent with governing by law—not unchecked discretion.[32] Moreover, we should be careful not to assume that sophisticated tactics such as predictive policing will reduce (unjustified) police discretion. As sociologist Sarah Brayne puts it:

> [D]ata does not eliminate discretion, but rather displaces it to earlier, less visible (and therefore potentially less accountable) phases of the criminal justice process. Predictive policing and algorithmic control are at work well before any officer handcuffs a suspect and lawyers get involved.[33]

It is thus vital that we reorient the police identity to a collective pursuit of justice that reaches beyond the value of crime reduction.

Human dignity: The conception of dignity in liberal societies is based in large part upon the idea that all persons possess a high-ranking legal status that comprises a set of rights. In other words, a person's equal status establishes the content of certain legal rights (including human rights), irrespective of one's socio-economic, ethnic, or behavioral characteristics. Of course, the police may be justified in using force when someone, say, behaves badly by resisting arrest. However, such force must be conducted in a manner that does not denigrate the rights that constitute the person's high-ranking, equal, legal status. One can also construe dignity in a way that transcends social and legal status. Under this conception, dignity is based upon one's inherent human (rational) capacities: Persons are not valued merely by a contingent social status or rank, but rather their intrinsic value. As we have discussed, such conceptions of dignity might be relevant when the police use an informant as a mere means to a law enforcement end. Recall situations in which an informant has no real choice about whether to assist the police (calling into question the informant's "consent" to assist the police), as well as situations in which the informant is subjected to inherently dangerous situations that would otherwise be addressed by the police in their law enforcement role. In short, the police do not *minimize* affronts to human dignity in carrying out their law enforcement role; human dignity is rather something that the police may not violate under any circumstances given the liberal commitment to one's personhood.[34]

Security of person: In the United States, the Fourth Amendment to the Constitution protects the "right of the people to be secure in their persons ... against unreasonable ... seizures." A police officer's use of force (deadly, or otherwise) constitutes a seizure and must be reasonable. Courts have interpreted this in a way that permits police to rely upon broad deadly force polices. It is thus incumbent for police agencies to incorporate critical judgment training regarding tactics that might help to avoid use of force situations in the first place. This is justified inasmuch we are serious about the value of life, given one's human dignity and one's security of person. Belief structures are shaped in part through training and an officer's conception of the police role. Regarding questions about the necessity of force, what perspective would be taken by a reasonable officer? This will vary depending upon whether reasonable officers are conceived primarily as heroes, warriors, guardians—or rather as collective members in the societal pursuit of justice. As was discussed in chapter 4, a reasonable perspective for a warrior may very well be different from the perspective of others, in part because police warriors are often taught that it is reasonable for violent reflex to trump rationality. The larger point is that the Fourth Amendment embodies perhaps the most fundamental human right: security of person. And the extent to which that right is respected by the police is in part based upon the conception of the police role.

Legitimacy: Legitimacy may be viewed as a human right. It is intricately intertwined with policing given that legitimacy is based upon the idea of appropriate authority to wield power. This is especially true in light of the liberal commitment to a natural right to be free from the non-consensual coercion of political and legal institutions. Accordingly, one might say that liberal societies are based upon the ideal of legitimate institutions, meaning that we should at a minimum mitigate the illegitimacy of actual institutions (including the police institution). Police legitimacy is thus connected to a state's legitimacy: A police officer acts as an agent of the state; acts that lack requisite authority are illegitimate because they occur under a pretense of authority that is outside the rule of law. One way to enhance police legitimacy is to focus upon values beyond general security and crime reduction, such as policies that promote inclusivity and collectivity through public reason.

Public reason: Gaining serious traction in police reform can be difficult outside the narrow goal of crime reduction. It can thus be helpful to provide a moral foundation for strategies such as community policing. Chapter 4 examined how public reason stands for the idea that government principles should be justifiable to all those to whom the principles are meant to apply. Although public reason is often viewed as an idealized concept, we can expand and apply the tenets of public reason to actual deliberations within policing and beyond. More generally, public reason serves as a unifying rationale and moral foundation for a justified police role. Public reason promotes legitimacy and security of person by bolstering autonomy, justice, and respect regarding differences of ethnicity, gender, sexual orientation, and mental health—and, more generally, public reason promotes human dignity. The informal argument is straightforward: If human rights (such as security of person and legitimacy) should be pursued by the police, and if such rights have eroded in some communities, then we should embrace conceptions of policing that promote these rights through public reason. Accordingly, public reason can help bolster strategies beyond those focused upon crime reduction exclusively.

These are only a few of the prominent themes and values that were examined in this book. By incorporating these and other values—values that are core facets of liberal conceptions of justice—recruitment and training might move away from an unjustified emphasis on police archetypes such as heroes, warriors, and guardians, and toward a more holistic pursuit of justice. At the recruitment and hiring level specifically, evaluation of applicants may be tweaked to seek potential officers who display a commitment to these values (not just weed out bad apples). For example, scenario-based interview questions might be designed to evaluate whether applicants display a basic commitment to the rights of their fellow citizens—regardless of ethnicity, socioeconomic status, and other considerations. Such evaluations can help reveal whether an officer would be more likely to respond to community interactions rationally by respecting and weighing competing values, or whether the applicant would respond reflexively without critical judgment. At police academies and other training environments, a greater emphasis on the above themes and values can help balance the police's law enforcement role with other fundamental components of justice.

Ethical algorithms: The police have little control over the way that predictive policing algorithms are developed by designers. This is especially the case given the lack of transparency in predictive policing technology—technology that is private intellectual property. For example, designers—not the police—make decisions about tradeoffs between optimizing accuracy versus optimizing fairness (avoiding, say, discrimination based upon ethnicity) in predictions on test data.[35] However, to the extent possible, police departments should play an active role in the process of addressing ethical questions raised by various predictive policing technologies—including questions about the data collected and used in algorithms.[36] If the police are more integrated in the process, it is less likely that predictive policing tactics will be wielded in a way that results in a feedback loop perpetuating cycles of discrimination. This means that police departments must think strategically about how to integrate predictive policing (if at all) in a way that is consistent with a holistic conception of justice.

If—as this book has suggested—the police role is fundamentally about the pursuit of justice, then the police must consider values beyond the sort of crime reduction promised by predictive policing. The upshot is renewed emphasis on the human analysis of crime problems—human analysis that incorporates principles regarding the rule of law, human dignity, security of person, legitimacy, and public reason. Perhaps this sort of reorientation will take predictive policing in entirely new directions. Brayne puts it this way:

> We should think big. How can we use big data to predict not only offenders but also victims, to target not only punitive interventions but also services, to track not only civilians but also police? How can we use it to analyze the underlying factors that contribute to crime in the first place, and to evaluate which interventions are most effective in remedying them?[37]

We are in the early stages of answering these questions and it is possible that our answers will lead to even bigger problems. Regardless, predictive policing—in some shape or form—is here to stay. We must be open to both the different ways that algorithms may be wielded and the different ways to think about the people who wield them.

Seeking Justice Collectively

Police agency priorities should involve community oversight given the considerations that have been discussed. An example is the Columbia South Carolina Police Department's (CPD) Citizen Advisory Council (CAC), which includes civilian members from Columbia's diverse demographics and occupations.[38] The CAC is described as "foster[ing] proactive relationships with an open dialogue between CPD and citizens ... provid[ing] civilian oversight and review[ing] how CPD addresses complaints against officers, and other internal affairs matters."[39] These and similar programs serve as practical examples for increasing democratic policing and community engagement. Of course, police agencies vary widely—in terms of size, resources, and crime problems—and citizen councils are not one-size-fits-all solutions. But as Barry Friedman notes, it is no excuse to say that policing problems are difficult to solve:

In many of the smallest communities in America, we manage to have school boards and zoning boards and other government bodies. As well we should; these are the sorts of things that matter to residents. But surely the same is true of the security and privacy of all members of the community, which are implicated by policing policies.[40]

Police reform is not easy, but the examples that have been discussed show that reform is possible when pursued collectively. I thus close with a few practical considerations regarding the implementation of community policing specifically.

The importance—and challenge—of effectively implementing community policing continues to be a widespread concern in policing. This was made clear by a diverse range of members on the President's Commission on Law Enforcement and the Administration of Justice in a teleconference in 2020: A U.S. Attorney stressed the importance of "community partnerships convened at the federal level and focused on violent crime prevention."[41] A Chief of Police "highlighted the importance of devoting resources to high crime neighborhoods, not based on an enforcement model, but to develop *lasting relationships*, which will transform the lives of the people who live there."[42] And another police chief testified to the importance of repairing relationships in communities where high levels of mistrust of law enforcement exist, stating that "community policing has to be *meaningful* and it has to be based upon human contact ... [it's] not just a squad car sitting there with its windows rolled up and the officer reading a paper or ... texting on their phone."[43] What are the common themes regarding how the police might pursue lasting community relationships through meaningful community policing?

According to a recent Department of Justice guidebook by Roberto Santos—a criminal justice scholar and retired police commander—"the community policing philosophy is an effective means for a police organization to establish trust and a sense of legitimacy in the community to facilitate a collective responsibility for safety and quality-of-life issues by the community and the police."[44] We do not find words such as hero, warrior, guardian, valor, and righteous violence in this description. The priorities are rather *trust, legitimacy*, and *collective responsibility*. Santos emphasizes leadership at the supervisor level—not just line-level officers—to promote meaningful community policing.

Forging relationships: The process of forging relationships within a community can lead to more formal policing partnerships. There is no magic way to pursue this goal; it simply requires police supervisors to prioritize connections with other people and organizations. As with most any meaningful and lasting relationship, this includes investing time and committing to regular communication. It also includes the ability to see the relationship's intrinsic value—rather than merely viewing the relationship as a means to a law enforcement end. To be sure, a police–community relationship's instrumental value is vital, especially with respect to solving crime problems. But healthy, inclusive civic relationships are valuable in their own right given that such relationships are a fundamental component of just, liberal societies. Attending a neighborhood meeting—and sharing crime information—is a simple example of developing relationships:

> A neighborhood organization held monthly meetings and would occasionally call on the police to attend and speak to current crime concerns. A sergeant assigned to the neighborhood began attending every month even if there were no specific crime issues to discuss. This provided an opportunity to forge a long-standing relationship with those in the group, develop a better understanding of ongoing neighborhood concerns and needs, and resolve relatively minor issues before they became more serious.[45]

This sort of time and effort may not seem worth it given that it does not lead to quick, quantifiable results. But the decision to pursue meaningful and lasting relationships ultimately comes down to our basic conception of the police's role in society: Are the police at war with the community, or are they collectively seeking justice as members of the community?

Developing partnerships: Meaningful and lasting relationships lay the groundwork for community–police partnerships that address specific issues and problems. We often think of these partnerships as addressing common crime problems such as drug trafficking and property crime. However, as noted in the last chapter, the police role is far more extensive than traditional law enforcement. The police also address social problems such as domestic disputes, which sometimes do not require law enforcement. Consider this example:

> Police received repeat calls for service to a specific multifamily apartment building from women who were victims of domestic violence. After analysis of the repeat calls, in multiple cases, it was found that victims had called police three or more times. A police supervisor asked the organizations Women Helping Women and the YWCA to partner with the police department to aid repeat victims of domestic violence in this apartment complex. Both agreed to the partnership and offered services to the women, and expanded their assistance to other geographic areas in the jurisdiction. Repeat domestic violence victimization was reduced. Importantly, although they were instrumental in beginning this partnership, the police ended up playing a secondary role in the full program implementation.[46]

Such partnerships allow the police to establish a more comprehensive community presence, making clear that the police are more than an occupying law enforcement agency. Santos describes five distinct categories of partners: (1) Community members and groups; (2) other government agencies; (3) non-profit agencies and service providers; (4) private businesses; and (5) media.[47] In some cases, the relationships on which these partnerships are based may be enhanced through new communicative platforms such as social media. The police thus have the opportunity to come full circle with respect to their relationship with the media—leveraging the spotlight in positive and productive ways.[48] More broadly, it is important to note that these potential partnership categories will vary among different jurisdictions, including the ability to engage via social media. Police supervisors should thus identify the unique stakeholders and partners within their domain, as well as how best to engage with each partner. For organizational change to occur, it will be necessary for supervisors to lead line-level officers by making it clear that fostering community partnerships is an important facet of the police role. Supervisors can do this by making community policing training available to line-level officers, as well as identifying short-term and long-term problems that can be addressed through community policing.[49]

Dialogue, Decentralization, and Despecialization: From the perspective of line-level officers—such as patrol officers—community policing takes a variety of forms. Assistant Chief Adrian Diaz, Seattle Police Department, describes how dialogue establishes trust in communities:

> Patrol officers do it every day in our formal role of solving crime: we can build trust relationships even with suspects as we gather intelligence or information. But this principle applies not only to suspects and informants but to a patrol officer's communication with the larger community as well, because the community itself may have the essential information necessary to address crimes or other policing issues.[50]

Dialogues may evolve into more formal programs such as "Living Room Conversations" (programs in which community members invite beat officers and neighbors into their home to get to know each other and discuss the neighborhood), "Donut Dialogue" (programs in which officers and young people have conversation over donuts), and "Coffee with a Cop" (programs in which "police and community members [come] together in an informal, neutral space to discuss community issues, build relationships, and drink coffee").[51] Such programs may sound trivial given the profound problems that many communities face. Although these programs are small steps, they are concrete steps toward building meaningful, lasting relationships within the community—and such relationships go hand in hand with solving crime problems collectively.

For this to work, it is important that police agencies engage in some degree of decentralization. This means that agencies must do a better job of recruiting and training officers, who are then entrusted to collaborate with community members in a way that is not constrained by elaborate and complex hierarchies. In chapter 4, we saw how an agency's adoption of predictive policing programs can demean officers, advising them to simply "go to the box." On the other hand, police departments respect an officer's autonomy when the department commits to training officers in effective community policing. Again, it is a false dilemma to suggest that policing must *either* be subsumed by technocratic judgments encoded in obscure computer software, *or* be based upon a police ethic steeped in hero, warrior, and guardian policing. There is a third option that departs from both policing that is unduly technocratic and policing that is unduly individualistic. Consider this perspective on police reform from the 1990s—an aspiration that has aged well, but that has not been embraced or realized:

> [By] making it legitimate for rank-and-file officers to think and be creative in their daily work ... the potential benefits are of two kinds. The most important is the improvement that this could produce in the quality of the responses that the police make to oft-recurring community problems. In addition, such a change would be directly responsive to some critical needs in the police organization—the need to treat rank-and-file police officers as mature men and women; to demonstrate more trust and confidence in them; to give them more responsibility and a stake in the outcome of their efforts; and to give them a greater sense of fulfillment and job satisfaction.[52]

The idea, then, is not to reduce oversight or training, but rather to actually prepare officers to engage with the community. The goal is to put officers in a position to fulfill their potential and do the sort of police work that cannot be accomplished by an algorithm.

Similar to decentralization, the goal of fulfilling police potential requires some degree of despecialization. If police agencies are truly committed to community policing, then they must also be committed to comprehensive training that fosters the development of community policing generalists. To be sure, specialized policing units are necessary for specialized or technical problems that police agencies address. But retaining such units is not mutually exclusive with a comprehensive, generalist approach to community policing. Otherwise, as Officer Diaz notes,

> There can ... be continuing difficulties or miscommunications in how these specialized units interact with community policing initiatives. As one example, patrol officers may assume a newly created unit will handle a particular problem, yet the specialized unit might believe patrol officers are handling it.[53]

A holistic approach to community policing can head off these difficulties.

Of course, no amount of training and community policing will solve every problem. Crime and bad behavior (by both the police and the community) cannot be eradicated and—even as progress is made—setbacks will occur. How, then, should the police respond to this inevitability? If a community policing model is embraced, then setbacks should be addressed transparently and collaboratively. Examples include community mediation programs such as Los Angeles County's *Leveraging Innovative Solutions to Enhance Neighborhoods* ("LISTEN"), which focuses upon procedural justice in addressing complaints of police bias.[54] Mediators, community members, and police officers come together to discuss troubling incidents with the goal of enhancing trust and communication between the community and the police.[55] LISTEN and other community policing programs can work in tandem with more traditional problem-oriented strategies such as the SARA Model—a common problem-solving model standing for (1) scan, (2) analyze, (3) respond, (4) assess.[56] Taking this approach requires police officers and supervisors to view their role in terms of collectivity, not individuality. Inclusive organizational change is not easy, but it is important inasmuch as police agencies seek to promote the philosophical values underpinning a liberal conception of justice.

There is reason to be hopeful moving forward, despite the ongoing police–community tragedies in the U.S. and beyond. Community policing strategies have been known for decades, but police agencies often fail to take those strategies seriously. When they are taken seriously, we see positive developments—such as in Los Angeles, where a predictive policing program was recently discontinued and a handbook on data-informed community policing was introduced.[57] The foreword to that handbook emphasizes police legitimacy and trust: "Policing strategies that focus solely on proactive suppression may reduce crime, but often leave neighborhoods feeling over-policed, singled out, and unnerved."[58] The guidebook incorporates the community in the SARA problem-solving model: Scanning includes identifying issues that affect *quality of life in a neighborhood*; analysis includes determining the causes of problems by *engaging the community*; response includes resolving problems by *working with community organizations*; and assessment includes determining success by *walking, talking, and gauging public perception.*[59] Time will tell whether such policies will be pursued wholeheartedly, but the policies themselves are based upon principles that could result in meaningful change.

Peel's Principles at a Crossroads: Sir Robert Peel's policing principles are—if not widely known in society broadly—widely familiar within police culture. They encapsulate many of the values that have been discussed in the pages of this book, and are thus a good way to gain traction within police agencies to the extent that they "were conceived as a conscious democratic limitation on police power … [and] they still offer guidance for modern American police to follow today."[60] Several of these principles have tracked the central themes in this book, including what some have described as the "legitimacy principle" (policing needs public approval), the "trust principle" (policing needs public cooperation and respect), the "equality and community principles" (policing needs impartiality and inclusivity), and the "restraint and sanctity of life principle" (policing needs physical force only as a last resort).[61]

The problems of policing cannot be solved solely from within policing. The basic tenets of justice in liberal societies—tenets that underpin the arguments in this book—are much more inclusive, egalitarian, and interconnected. Police–community strife will not be resolved by simply focusing upon legal standards and reasonableness inquiries regarding the conduct of individual police officers. As Eric Miller aptly puts it, "[t]he basic idea is a republican one: that dialogue, rather than brute power, is the best way to promote responsive public policies, and that the inclusion of new voices in the policing dialogue can have a democracy-enhancing effect."[62] The identity crisis metaphor seems particularly appropriate here. There is an ongoing debate within police culture about the very nature of the police role and how police should conceive of themselves. The police are thus at a crossroads, struggling to move forward from their role confusion and find a cohesive sense of self. By reorienting the police toward the collective pursuit of justice—and away from conceptions of individual heroes, warriors, and guardians driven by algorithms—perhaps the police identity crisis may be abated.

Notes

1 Esther Addley, *The Pope's first tweet: no jokes, no kittens*, THE GUARDIAN (Dec. 13, 2012). The pope's first tweet read: "Dear friends, I am pleased to get in touch with you through Twitter. Thank you for your generous response. I bless all of you from my heart." *Id.*
2 Felix Gillette, *Snapchat Reaches Settlement With Its Disappearing Co-Founder*, BLOOMBERG (Sept. 10 2014).
3 Hayley Tsukayama, *Facebook releases the Timeline for everyone*, WASH. POST. (Dec. 15, 2011).
4 I lasted three months (in 2012) on Facebook. More to the point, see ANDREW MARANTZ, ANTISOCIAL: ONLINE EXTREMISTS, TECHNO-UTOPIANS, AND THE HIJACKING OF THE AMERICAN CONVERSATION (2019) (discussing how "the awful stuff" won).
5 *See, e.g.*, Paul Mason, *From Paris to Cairo, these protests are expanding the power of the individual*, THE GUARDIAN (Feb. 7, 2011) ("With Facebook, Twitter, and Yfrog truth travels faster than lies, and propaganda becomes flammable."). Overall, this sentiment has not aged well.
6 Rebecca Morin & David Cohen, *Giuliani: 'Truth isn't truth'*, POLITICO (Aug. 19, 2018). See LUKE WILLIAM HUNT, THE RETRIEVAL OF LIBERALISM IN POLICING, chapter 6 (2019), for a discussion of how big data surveillance threatens basic liberal tenets such as the rule of law.
7 A civilian recorded a videotape of the King beating on his camcorder from his apartment.

8 THE CHRISTOPHER COMMISSION REPORT, HUMAN RIGHTS WATCH, https://www.hrw.org/legacy/reports98/police/uspo73.htm
9 CONSENT DECREE, UNITED STATES V. CITY OF LOS ANGELES, No. 00-CV-11769 (C.D. Cal. June 15, 2001).
10 Eric Miller, *Challenging Police Discretion*, 58.2 HOWARD L. REV. 521, 525 (2015).
11 Rashawn Ray, *What does 'defund the police' mean and does it have merit?*, BROOKINGS (June 19, 2020).
12 Philip V. McHarris & Thenjiwe McHarris, *No More Money for the Police*, N.Y. TIMES (May 30, 2020).
13 Andre M. Perry, David Harshbarger, Carl Romer, & Kristian Thymianos, *To add value to Black communities, we must defund the police and prison systems*, BROOKINGS (June 11, 2020). See also Roxanna Altholz, *Living with Impunity: Unsolved Murders in Oakland and the Human Rights Impact on Victims' Family Members*, INTERNATIONAL HUMAN RIGHTS LAW CLINIC, UNIVERSITY OF CALIFORNIA, BERKELEY, SCHOOL OF LAW (Jan. 2020) (arguing that "[t]he systemic failure to prevent violence, investigate, and provide support and assistance to family members without discrimination in Oakland is arguably a violation of international human rights law").
14 Philip Bump, *Over the past 60 years, more spending on police hasn't necessarily meant less crime*, WASH. POST (June 7, 2020).
15 Mariame Kaba, *Yes, We Mean Literally Abolish the Police*, N.Y. TIMES (June 12, 2020).
16 *Id.*
17 An Interview with Alex S. Vitale, *Policing Is Fundamentally a Tool of Social Control to Facilitate Our Exploitation*, JACOBIN (June 8, 2020).
18 THOMAS HOBBES, LEVIATHAN (Cambridge, 1991) (1668). Hobbes was referring to life in the state of nature, outside political society, but the general point seems apt.
19 Kabe, *supra* note 15.
20 *See* Derecka Purnell, *How I Became a Police Abolitionist*, THE ATLANTIC (July 6, 2020).
21 An Interview with Alex S. Vitale, *The Best Way to "Reform" the Police Is to Defund the Police*, JACOBIN (June 3, 2020).
22 *See* Bivens v. Six Unknown Named Agents, 403 U.S. 388 (1971); United States Code, 42 U.S.C. § 1983.
23 Scott Michelman, *The Branch Best Qualified to Abolish Immunity*, 93.5 NOTRE DAME LAW REVIEW 1999–2020 (2018).
24 Paul Stern, *Tort Justice Reform*, 52 UNIV. OF MICHIGAN JOURNAL OF LAW REFORM 649–730 (2019).
25 Steven Greenhouse, *How Police Unions Enable and Conceal Abuses of Power*, THE NEW YORKER (June 18, 2020).
26 Kevin Rector, *Baltimore City Council schedules oversight hearing on police academy training*, THE BALTIMORE SUN (Feb. 6, 2018).
27 JOHN KLEINIG, THE ETHICS OF POLICING 83 (1996).
28 See HUNT, *supra* note 6, at 89–103, for a discussion of the rule of law in liberal societies.
29 LON L. FULLER, THE MORALITY OF LAW 162 (1969).
30 JOSEPH RAZ, THE AUTHORITY OF LAW 218 (1979).
31 *Id.* at 221.
32 *See* HUNT, *supra* note 6, at 196–200 (discussing a Lockean test for the rare deviation from rule of law principles).
33 SARAH BRAYNE, PREDICT AND SURVEIL – DATA, DISCRETION, AND THE FUTURE OF POLICING 119 (2021).

34 See HUNT, *supra* note 6, at chapter 3 (providing an account of liberal personhood, including human dignity) and chapter 4 (discussing how the police's use of informants can be an affront to liberal personhood).
35 Faisal Kamiran & Toon Calders, *Data Preprocessing Techniques for Classification without Discrimination*, 33 KNOWLEDGE & INFORMATION SYSTEMS 1–33 (2012).
36 See Andrew D. Selbst, *Disparate Impact in Big Data Policing*, 52.1 GEORGIA LAW REVIEW 101 (2017) (examining how "algorithmic impact statements would require police departments to evaluate efficacy and potential discriminatory effects of all available choices for predictive policing technologies").
37 BRAYNE, *supra* note 33, at 117.
38 CITY OF COLUMBIA POLICE DEPARTMENT, CITIZENRY ADVISORY COUNCIL, https://columbiapd.net/citizen-advisory-council/
39 *Id.*
40 BARRY FRIEDMAN, UNWARRANTED: POLICING WITHOUT PERMISSION 316 (2017).
41 United States Department of Justice, Office of Public Affairs, *President's Commission on Law Enforcement and the Administration of Justice Holds Teleconferences on Crime Reduction* (April 10, 2020), https://www.justice.gov/opa/pr/president-s-commission-law-enforcement-and-administration-justice-holds-teleconferences-crime
42 *Id.* (emphasis added).
43 *Id.* (emphasis added).
44 ROBERTO SANTOS, COMMUNITY POLICING: A FIRST-LINE SUPERVISOR'S PERSPECTIVE 2 (U.S. Department of Justice, Office of Community Oriented Policing Services, 2019). It was a pleasure working with Professor Santos when I was a member of the faculty at Radford University from 2016 to 2020.
45 *Id.* at 3.
46 *Id.* at 5.
47 *Id.*
48 See Chandlier Anne-Reneé Diven, *Using Social Media to Connect with the Public: An Exploratory Case Study of a Police Department Use of Facebook*, RADFORD UNIVERSITY, DEPARTMENT OF CRIMINAL JUSTICE (Master of Arts Thesis, 2017).
49 SANTOS, *supra* note 44, at 12–17.
50 ADRIAN DIAZ, COMMUNITY POLICING: A PATROL OFFICER'S PERSPECTIVE 6 (U.S. Department of Justice, Office of Community Oriented Policing Services, 2019).
51 *Id.* at 6–7.
52 Edwin Meese III, *Community Policing and the Police Officer*, 15 PERSPECTIVES ON POLICING 1–2 (1993), https://www.ncjrs.gov/pdffiles1/nij/139164.pdf
53 DIAZ, *supra* note 50, at 14.
54 VIVIAN Y. ELLIOTT & TAMMY FELIX, LESSONS TO ADVANCE COMMUNITY POLICING: FINAL REPORT FOR 2014 MICROGRANT SITES (U.S. Department of Justice, Office of Community Oriented Policing Services, 2018).
55 *Id.* at 9–10.
56 COMMUNITY POLICING DEFINED 10–12 (U.S. Department of Justice, Office of Community Oriented Policing Services, 2014).
57 Leila Miller, *LAPD will end controversial program that aimed to predict where crimes would occur*, L.A. TIMES (April 21, 2020).
58 CHIEF MICHAEL R. MOORE, DATA-INFORMED COMMUNITY-FOCUSED POLICING IN THE LOS ANGELES POLICE DEPARTMENT, available at http://assets.lapdonline.org/assets/pdf/Data-Informed-Policing.pdf
59 *Id.* at 9.

60 Debo P. Adegbile, *Policing Through an American Prism*, 126 YALE LAW JOURNAL 2230 (2017).
61 *Id.* at 2232 (citing *The Roots of Policing: Sir Robert Peel's 9 Principles*, CLEVELAND. COM (June 8, 2016)).
62 Miller, *supra* note 10, at 525–26.

Index

abolishing the police 150–54
algorithms 111–12, 157–58; see also policing (predictive policing)
analytic-synthetic distinction 2
archetype 5, 82, 94–97
Aristotle 29, 36–37, 88–89
authority 34–35; specific and general authority 70; see also legitimacy; public reason

Baez, Anthony 122–23
Balko, Radley 54–55, 132
Becker, Ernest 16, 28–30
Bederman, Gail 26
Beitz, Charles 125
Benforado, Adam 78
Berman, Jay Stuart 23–24
Blake, Jacob 8–9, 65
Boyarin, Daniel 37–38
Brayne, Sarah 3, 141n16, 142n25, 155, 158
Brown, Michael 56
brutality 8–9, 21, 47, 125–26, 138, 150; see also human dignity; human rights; personhood

capitalism 10–11, 150–54
Castile, Philando 9, 19, 65
collectivity 5, 17, 31–32, 34, 158–64
CompStat 113
consequentialism see utilitarianism
crime analysis 112–13

Darwin, Charles 27
Davies, Thomas 119
Davis, Angela 4
defunding the police 150–54
Dworkin, Ronald 58, 146n91

Erikson, Erik 13n1

FBI Academy 1, 17–18, 23, 30, 41, 64, 70, 72, 123
Ferguson, Andrew 120
First Step Act 50
Floyd, George 8–9, 128–29, 150–51
Freud, Sigmund 14n11, 37–38
Friedman, Barry 56, 98–101, 158
Friedrich, Nietzsche 27
Fuller, Lon 105n91, 154–55

Gallie, W.B. 57
Garner, Eric 122–23
Garrett, Brandon 100–101
general moral requirements 50, 59–61, 66, 68–72; see also human dignity; human rights; personhood
Goffman, Alice 130–31
Graham v. Connor 57, 72, 100
guardian: contemporary police conception of 89–94; see also policing (democratic); Plato

Harcourt, Bernard 13n5
hero: epistemic entitlement 39–42; existential fear 27–32; gallantry 22–23; manly heroism 32–39
Hobbes, Thomas 74n19, 152
Hohfeld, Wesley Newcomb 124
human dignity 59, 67, 88, 92–93, 124, 155–56
human rights 4, 121–27, 144n70, 155–57
Hume, David 109, 140n9
Hunt, Luke William 13n3, 104n39, 145n90, 148n142

ideal theory 6–8, 127, 152
identity crisis metaphor 2, 17, 97, 164; see also Erikson, Erik
individuation 5, 11, 31–32, 88–91, 94–97
is-ought problem see Hume, David

James, William 27, 29
Jung, Carl 94–97
justice see collectivity; human dignity; human rights; ideal theory; legitimacy; nonideal theory; personhood; public reason; social contract theory
justification 66–67, 85–86

Kant, Immanuel 53, 92–93, 124
Kierkegaard, Søren 28
King, Rodney 150
Kleinig, John 13n2, 133, 147n116, 154
Knox, Jean 97

Lebron, Christopher 10
legitimacy 6–7, 13n5, 34–35, 52–53, 66–67, 85–86, 124–28, 132, 145n91, 156; see also human rights
Locke, John 53, 74n19, 76n84, 95, 124–25, 127, 152

Manne, Kate 40–41
Mansfield, Harvey 33–40
Mayson, Sandra 115
Miller, Eric 9, 80, 138–39, 150, 164
Miller, Seumas 13n2
Monaghan, Jake 76n77

Nagy, Marilyn 94
nonideal theory 6–8, 127, 152
Nussbaum, Martha 36–38

Peel, Sir Robert 19–22, 24, 81, 92, 101, 163
personhood 6–7, 59, 67–69, 93, 141n13; see also human dignity; human rights
Petty, William 110–11
Pietikainen, Petteri 95–96
Plato: on archetypes 94–95; on democracy 82–84; on guardians 86–89; on philosopher-kings 84–86

policing: community policing 6, 17, 99, 132–36, 158–64; comparative analysis of 3–4, 80; democratic policing 97–102; discretion in 21–22, 24–25, 43n22, 61, 67–70, 76n84, 105n91, 119, 136, 154–55; Fourth Amendment (U.S. Constitution) constraints on 9, 57, 100–101, 119, 123, 156; history of 19–25, 49–50, 54–55; militarization of 54–57; predictive policing 110–21, 157–58; procedural justice policing 137–40; racism in 8–11, 49, 65, 79; training, recruitment, and values 154–58; see also heroes; guardians; warriors
Popper, Karl 85
positional moral requirements see special moral requirements
Postman, Neil 108
public reason 6, 126–32, 135–38, 145n90, 157

qualified immunity 101, 153
Quantico see FBI Academy

Rank, Otto 29–31
Rawls, John 6–7, 53, 68, 125, 141n13
Raz, Joseph 105n91, 155
reasonable suspicion 57, 119–20
reciprocation see social contract theory
Reed, Adolph 15n31
rights see Hohfeld, Wesley Newcomb
right to individualized treatment 50–54, 110–11, 121, 141n13
Ristroph, Alice 9
Rogers, Mister (Fred) 38–39
Roosevelt, Franklin D. 37
Roosevelt, Theodore 20–32, 37, 48–49
Rose, Jalen 117
rule of law 24–25, 61, 67–69, 98, 126, 128–29, 154–55

Santos, Rachel Boba 115–17, 141n17
Santos, Roberto 159–61, 166n44
Schauer, Frederick 121
Schopenhauer, Arthur 29
Scott, Dominic 83, 103n26
security of person see human rights
September 11, 2001 terrorist attacks 33, 47, 49

sheepdog metaphor 1, 17, 31–33, 64
Shelby, Tommie 10
Sherman, Nancy 71
Simmons, A. John 76n78, 145n80, 145n91
Sklansky, David 13n4
social contract theory 3, 34, 53, 112, 127
special moral requirements 50, 59–62, 65–70
Spielberg, Steven 1, 111
Storr, Anthony 96
Stoughton, Seth 58–64, 70, 74n37 100–101

Taylor, Breonna 8
Terry v. Ohio 70
tort law 153
Tyler, Tom 13n5, 146n92, 148n134–35, 148n137, 148n140

unions 154
United States v. Jones 119
unpopular laws 66–69;
    see also justification;
    legitimacy
Utah v. Strieff 57
utilitarianism 50–54, 136
utopian 152–53

Vitale, Alex 152–53

Waldron, Jeremey 75n41, 124
Walzer, Michael 71
warrior: domestic use of soldiers 47–48, 59–60; ideal (honor, duty, resolve, righteous violence) 57–64; *see also* policing (militarization); utilitarianism
Wiggins, David 109

Yankah, Ekow 9, 80

Printed in the United States
by Baker & Taylor Publisher Services